MARGARET MERRY'S CORNISH GARDEN SKETCHBOOK

Written and Illustrated by

MARGARET MERRY

Published by Margaret Merry
24 Chirgwin Road, Truro, Cornwall. TR1 1TT

ISBN 0 948752 01 7
© Margaret Merry 1994

All rights reserved. No part of this publication may be reproduced, stored in a retrieval system, or transmitted in any form or by any means, electronic, mechanical, photocopying, recording or otherwise, without the prior permission of the publisher.

Lanhydrock

Peacock Butterfly

One bright spring afternoon, when I was six years old, my mother, my great-aunt and her next-door neighbour, my baby sister and I boarded a 'bus at Falmouth, where we lived, and rode into the countryside. I was told that we were going to a garden called Penjerrick. As we were disembarking, I asked if this was the place but they said it wasn't and that we had to walk a little way yet before we got there. So we set off down narrow, high-banked lanes which were massed with the great clumps of primroses growing in such profusion on the outskirts of towns in those days. I eyed them with interest; I knew that I only had to put my hand into one of those clumps of soft, crinkled leaves, grasp a handful of the rosy stalks and instantly I would have a posy of flowers. But I was not allowed to stop to pick them because, my mother said, people would think I had stolen them from Penjerrick. So I trailed along, sulking, until at length we came to a lodge by a gate which opened onto a drive. We had arrived, it seemed.

My spirits rose as we walked up the drive. The grass verges were radiant with multitudes of celandines and daisies open to the sun and the air was fragrant with wetness and earthy, spring scents. In the distance, wheeling and homing above groups of tall trees, the rooks made a great clamour. High, puffed clouds raced across the sky and flecked the grass with dancing light and shadows. We reached a little iron gate and I wondered, vaguely, why it had not shared the same fate as the wrought iron gate of my great-aunt which, as she had so often told me, had been taken away in the war to be made into battleships. Perhaps, I reflected, the owners had kept quiet about it. We pushed it open and I found myself in a wonderful, unknown world.

Until that moment, gardens had never interested me. Most of those in which I had been allowed to play had been dull, uninspiring places with clipped lawns which you were not permitted to run about on and soldierly rows of flowers which you were forbidden to touch. As for the hedges and shrubs, they were generally so neatly pruned that they were useless for hiding under or making dens. Now, suddenly, I was confronted with a vision of fairyland. Gleefully, I ran backwards and forwards exclaiming with delight at the almost bewildering display of colour, for every tree and bush seemed to drip with blossom. I marvelled at the huge, trumpet-flowers of rhododendrons and the thick, creamy petals of magnolias and breathed in the sweet scent of azaleas which seemed to saturate the air with fragrance. The

camellias, which were now past their flowering peak, had showered the grass with blooms. Every time a blossom fell to the ground with a gentle thud I ran to it, picked it up and tried to put it back onto the bush; it seemed to me a very great tragedy that something so beautiful should have to turn brown and perish.

I explored intriguing paths which seemed to wind and loose themselves in hidden places made even more secret by tangled shrubberies and the overhanging branches of weeping beeches. At length, we came to a glade carpeted with bluebells and starred with frail wood-anemones (these died, I knew, almost as soon as you picked them) and from there we crossed the road by an ornamental wooden bridge (thrilling it was to peer through the gaps in the planks at the tarmac below) and found ourselves in a wilderness of lush vegetation. Primroses and dainty wood-sorrel grew in profusion amongst the mossed tree roots as we wound our way down to a water garden around whose margin was some very satisfyingly squelchy mud. Varnished yellow king-cups rose out of the oozing blackness and gunneras, like crouching, menacing figures, were beginning to unfold their huge leaves. Here was the garden of all my childhood fantasies; there were low-hanging, horizontal branches from which to hang swings, bamboo thickets where you could play hide-and-seek and endless secret places for making camps. I was very sorry when the time came to leave in order to catch the 'bus home to Falmouth. And no, they told me: there was no time to stop to pick primroses on the way back.

Certain things, seen with the clarity of a child's vision, remain in the memory for a lifetime and I have never forgotten that first visit to Penjerrick. When I returned, years later, on an afternoon in April, I was delighted and surprised to discover that the garden had hardly changed at all. Exotic vegetation grew with the same haphazard luxuriance: towering tree ferns with feathery fronds,

Penjerrick

riotously rampant rhododendrons, blazing pieris and showy azaleas, all dominated by huge copper beeches. Flowering in the glade which stretches away from the house, amongst the bluebells and wood-anemones, were snakeshead fritillaries. The air was redolent of all the elusive fragrances of spring, just as it had been on that first visit. The ornamental wooden bridge crossing the road to the water garden was still there and even the little iron gate at the entrance to the garden remained.

Looking through the family photograph album, it is interesting to see how frequently gardens in and around Falmouth are featured, particularly the Queen Mary Gardens which seem to have provided a backdrop for family photographs from as far back as 1912, when they were opened. For example, in one photograph dated 1959 I am kneeling on the grass in these gardens with a school friend, both of us self-conscious in our new summer frocks, and the lavish formal displays and sumptuous borders were as stunning then as they are today. Also in the album is a photograph of my sister as a pig-tailed schoolgirl peeping behind the banana tree in Kimberley Park (I remember one particularly heavy summer cloudburst when the pond in the park overflowed and the fish were carried down the hill and past what was then the Police Station, where I happened to be standing. I have always wondered what became of those poor fish.) There is another of my sister and me posing by the grotto in Gyllingdune Gardens and again under the trees in Fox and Rosehill Gardens. Looking at these photographs of us as children reminds me of the many occasions when, in order to escape the early morning wrath of our mother (which at times was truly terrible) during weekends and school holidays, we would creep out of the house as soon as we heard her getting up and walk around until she had had time to breakfast when it would be safe to return. Our route would take us past the Fox and Rosehill gardens and often we would wander in and stroll around the leafy paths. We went there one spring morning just as the glossy buds of the first crocuses were bursting open to the sun and they grew naturalised under the trees in such careless profusion that, for some reason, we thought they were wild flowers and gleefully set about picking them. We had only gathered a few, however, before a gardener, who seemed to have materialised out of nowhere, suddenly appeared and gave us a thorough telling off.

Leaving the Fox and Rosehill Gardens and making our way to The Princess Pavilion, we would not infrequently encounter a very distinguished-looking gentleman taking his regular morning constitutional. Whenever he passed us, he would take off his hat and wish us a good-morning. We felt very flattered, for he was obviously someone important.(It was not until years later that we found out that he was Howard Spring, the famous novelist.) We would walk past the Princess Pavilion to Gyllingdune Gardens, pausing en route to inspect what had been scribbled on the shells which decorated the walls and ceilings of two alcoves which had always been a source of fascination for us. From there, we would make our way down some steps to the grotto, an eerie place of damp gloom and shadowy recesses, which we were always afraid to enter. Emerging onto the road opposite Gyllingvase beach we would then make our way home, stopping sometimes to walk around Queen Mary gardens, particularly if the Guinness Clock or some other seasonal attraction was on display.

Years later, when I was a student at Falmouth Art School, I spent many happy hours drawing or painting the plants in the adjacent Fox and Rosehill Gardens and indeed, by that

Fox and Rosehill Gardens, Falmouth

Falmouth

time I had come to appreciate how fortunate the people of Falmouth were to have all-year-round, free access to such lovely gardens.

It is hardly surprising that Falmouth, with its equable climate, has within its vicinity some of Cornwall's finest gardens. Penjerrick, Glendurgan and Trebah are examples of these. Penjerrick, which was established in the early part of the last century, is the source of some famous hybrid rhododendrons. These gardens, as well as several others, were made by members of the prosperous Quaker Fox family who, as shipping agents, had access to exotic plants from all over the world. Despite the mild winter temperatures and high humidity in which tender woody plants thrive, it was necessary to make a framework of trees (the Mediterranean maritime pine, *Pinus pinaster*, and later the Monterey, *Pinus radiata*, and *Cupressus macrocarpa*) to provide shelter from the relentless, salt-laden gales and searing easterly winds which have the same parching effect on tender young leaves as severe drought. These windbreaks are a feature of Cornish gardens and though, by themselves, groups of pines seem to create a sinister atmosphere with their solid shapes and the inky darkness of the shadows they cast, their black plumes do, however, when mingled with other trees, lend form and texture and help to break up the bare trees on the winter skyline.

Trebah in winter

Trebah in summer

Trebah in spring

Of these three gardens, which are within a few miles of each other, TREBAH has the most dramatic and spectacular setting. It is situated on a slope above a valley which falls down a steeply wooded ravine to the Helford River and the panorama, which you come upon shortly after entering the gardens is truly astonishing. There is an abundance of exotic foliage - palms, yuccas, tree ferns- in which every variation of green in the spectrum, every shape and texture of leaf, is to be found. The lush vegetation produces an effect of light and shade and mass which is stunning. Indeed, the garden has something of the appearance of a prehistoric jungle so that, instead of the buzzards wheeling and mewing overhead, you might not be surprised to see pterodactyls swooping down from the sky. The steep sides of the valley have paths which lead you to unexpected vistas and sudden glimpses of water between the trees. Moisture-loving plants thrive alongside the stream which flows through the valley and cascades over boulders in a series of waterfalls and rock pools. Under the trees are silent, ferny glades and flowery slopes. In late summer, a sea of hydrangeas, in extravagant, full-flowering splendour, covers the lower part of the valley floor and sweeps down to the actual sea in a drift of blue.

Trebah in January

Whatever the season, Trebah is a place of infinite enchantment and is, in fact, the inspiration for this book. I visited it one day in early January when the low winter sun, slanting through the trees, glowed on the bare branches, glinted on the distant water and illuminated the towering banks of blossoming rhododendrons and camellias. I returned the following day to paint the scene and so completed the first garden picture I had ever painted.

Glendurgan

GLENDURGAN, (National Trust) like Trebah, is a sheltered valley garden with its own micro-climate and an example of how certain conifers, such as the Winter's Bark, with its fragrant flowers and aromatic bark, may flourish in the moist, damp conditions which these locations provide. Some conifers have trunks and boughs which have grown horizontally into twisted, serpentine shapes, while others give off a warm, resinous fragrance. Below the trees, on the valley slopes, are glades radiant with flowers in the spring and in the damp and sheltered places are bamboos and the tree ferns which are so much a feature of this type of Cornish garden. Un-typical of Cornish gardens, however, is the maze of clipped laurel which was planted in 1933 and has recently undergone restoration. Below the maze is a pond spanned by an ornamental wooden bridge; arum lilies flower in the spring and later, in summer, the giant leaves of *Gunnera manticata* spread over the water.

At the end of the valley a gate leads to a cluster of cottages around a quayside and a small beach; this is Durgan, and a visit to Glendurgan is not complete without a stroll around this pleasantly peaceful and attractive hamlet .

Magnolia

Durgan

Carclew

If I had to choose a favourite from all the Cornish gardens I have seen, then I think it would be CARCLEW. This is the secret garden of my childhood fantasies and the romantic garden of my adult daydreams. I fell in love with it at once when I visited it in early summer. Situated between Truro and Falmouth, near Perran-ar-Worthal, the gardens comprise a series of terraced lawns divided by low walls of weathered brick and stone; a beautiful wisteria smothers the entire length of one wall and at the end of another terrace is a round lily pond. Little, secret paths, overhung with low, horizontal branches, lead to dark bowers and tangled shrubberies. The terraces run down to a very large, rectangular lily pond dominated by two impressive fountains playing on the water. Nestling amongst the rhododendrons, which were flowering in masses of gorgeous colour when I saw them, is a small temple. The shafts of sunlight breaking through the huge trees which encircle the gardens made dapples of light on the pond in which the reflections were broken by clusters of floating lily leaves. The effect was heart-achingly romantic.

Carclew

If you drive through the village of Feock in spring, you cannot fail to notice a particularly lovely magnolia; its flower-laden branches rise above a high wall and its petals are shed on to the road below. Beyond this wall, in a most beautiful setting, is the garden of POLGWYNNE which contains many fine trees and shrubs and boasts what is possibly the largest British specimen of a female ginkgo biloba (maidenhair tree). However, for me the most unusual feature is a narrow leat, similar to those made by the Moors to irrigate their gardens, filled with fast-flowing water which feeds a series of small, froggy ponds. A velvety lawn falls away from the house from which are wonderful views of the Fal and the Carrick Roads. There is also a woodland walk down to the shore canopied by by enormous oaks. Woodpeckers call from the uppermost branches while further down, treecreepers and nuthatches scurry about searching for insects.

The immaculately kept herbaceous borders are filled with a miscellany of interesting flowers but, for me, the most impressive plant was the exquisite rose (Complicata) growing against a sheltered wall in the large vegetable garden. Its huge petals, in varying shades of sweetest pink, give it the appearance, from a distance, of some gorgeous clematis.

Complicata

Polgwynne

The Fal estuary has been a source of inspiration and, with its secluded creeks, bird-haunted mudflats at low tide, glassy reflections at high tide on still mornings or evenings and thickly wooded banks, has provided me with endless subject matter throughout my painting life. In its magnificent setting overlooking the Fal and the Carrick Roads, TRELISSICK (National Trust) with its extensive parkland and woodland walks, gives access to many creekside beauty spots. It is a favourite haunt for me, being only a short drive from Truro, where I live, and even though the garden is closed in winter, the woodland walk may be enjoyed all year round and is always beautiful, regardless of the season.

Autumn, Trelissick

The gardens themselves, famed for their collections of rhododendrons and camellias, are extremely fine and are of interest in spring and summer alike. Formal planting merges imperceptibly into the woodland setting; groups of blue wood anemones cluster under the trees in spring while crocuses are naturalised in grassy glades and hellebores, green or crimson-tinted, thrive in the moist shade. Hybrid foxgloves are grouped under the trees and in early summer their pastel colours gleam palely against the dark foliage. The fine herbaceous borders are carefully planned to give a succession of flowers throughout the year and I particularly admire the display in late summer of feathery, lilac-coloured thalictrum mingling with pale pink Japanese anemones. As if all this were not enough, some of Cornwall's finest displays of hydrangeas are to be found at Trelissick with colours ranging from vivid pinks to the most intense shade of indigo.

The gardens are divided by the steep, narrow road, spanned by a wooden bridge, which leads down to the King Harry Ferry. Wild maidenhair fern- a great rarity- still grows in the high, sheltered wall near the attractive water-tower.

The gardens are separated from the park, which is grazed by sheep and cattle, by a ha-ha. Below the great sweep of grass in front of the six-columned portico of the south front of the mansion, in a sheltered grove overlooking the little beach, daffodils appear as early as December. In the wooded walks, with their towering beeches, they are plentifully naturalised and carpet the forest floor, mingling with primroses and celandines in early spring.

The Water Tower, Trelissick

Woodland Walk, Trelissick

Trelissick from Turnaware Bar

Perhaps the sheer magnificence of Trelissick's natural setting can best be appreciated from the water, either from a boat or from the popular fishing and picnic spot at Turnaware Bar which you reach by crossing the river at King Harry Passage and turning off on the right shortly after leaving the ferry.

BOSVIGO, situated a few minutes drive from the centre of Truro, is a pleasant Georgian house surrounded by a three-acre site comprising a series of walled or enclosed gardens which have been developed by the present owners.

Bosvigo

The skilfully planned herbaceous borders are the result of what happens when you have a plantsperson with an artist's eye: all the plants and shrubs have been carefully associated for colour harmony. Indeed, the meticulously defined colour schemes, as well as the layout of the garden, are reminiscent of the beautiful and famous Kiftsgate Garden in Gloucestershire.

Bosvigo

It is a particularly satisfying garden to paint since, because of its good design, there are many compositions; vistas have been contrived in such a way that the eye is led to a specific feature - a seat, for example, or a stone urn. There is also a host of unusual plants, many of them for sale, and the garden retains interest from spring right through to autumn.

Bosvigo

Chyverton

Mr. Holman, of CHYVERTON, remembers well the original house at Carclew, which was described as the finest Palladium mansion in Cornwall, because he was there days before it was destroyed by fire in 1934. Like Carclew, the garden at Chyverton has obviously been contrived for romantic effect; a wide sweep of grass rolls down to a lake spanned by a graceful stone bridge in the manner of those great landscape gardens of the eighteenth century, such as Stourhead, in Wiltshire. Behind the trees and splendid rhododendrons grouped around the lake is more romance: a wooden footbridge identical to that which the Impressionist painter Monet, inspired by Japanese prints, erected at his garden at Giverny. Beneath the bridge is a stream filled with naturalised candelabra primulas - a clamour of mauve, orange, pink and yellow, and other moisture-loving plants.

Chyverton

    The garden boasts a magnificent collection of plants, including some fine magnolias and rhododendrons as well as rarities such as the *Dacrydium*, a small tree from Tasmania with drooping branches; an unusual feature is the tall hedge of myrtle with striking, cinnamon-coloured, peeling bark.

Trerice

Situated between St. Newlyn East and Newquay is the rather fine and distinguished Elizabethan manor house of TRERICE (National Trust). The warm, golden colour of the Growan stone with which it is built is complemented by the gold, crimson and purple shrubs which line the walled courtyard in front of the house. The terraced gardens are small but attractively laid out and there is an interesting collection of summer perrenials as well as a pretty orchard beside the house.

Trerice

TREHANE, situated between Tresillian and St. Erme, is a garden of which those who have visited it speak enthusiastically: it is not difficult to see why. I first went there on a day in midsummer when the wonderful collections of old roses, rose species and cranesbill geraniums were at their best. But as well as botanical interest, it is a garden of romance and nostalgia. In 1946 the Queen Anne mansion - its imposing ruins still stand, lending an air of mystery- was burnt down and the garden fell into a state of dereliction and it was not until 1963 that restoration began when it was discovered that many of the original plants had survived. The plant fancier must browse slowly around this garden for there are many treasures which might easily be overlooked.

R. moyesii

Comma Butterfly

Trehane

The herb garden, Trehane

Trehane is a garden is full of fragrances: you are literally beseiged with scent wherever you walk, not only in the herb garden with its fennel, coriander, lavender and marjoram but also along the paths which are carpeted with aromatic plants. It was a delight, too, to see so many unusual and often exquisitely scented roses. I particularly admired the *R moyesii*, a lovely rose which gives double pleasure; when I first saw it in June the bush, with its delicate, pale green flowers, was covered in blood-red blooms. Later, when I returned to the garden in August, the flowers had been replaced by beautiful, elongated, bottle-shaped hips which had the appearance of strange, exotic flowers.

A path runs through a five acre woodland area which, when I walked along it, was engulfed by a sea of pale mauve montia (claytonia) a variety of which grows wild in damp places in Cornwall and is commonly known as Water Blinks.

Trehane is a sanctuary for wildlife and is home, in summer, to one of the country's largest colonies of Greater Horseshoe Bats. Birds, especially flycatchers, must love the cover provided by the dense growth of ivy which covers the ruined building, in the midst of which may be found tawny owls' feathers. In late summer the air is full of flitting butterflies and the drone of a million insects.

If you are passing through the village of Grampound, THE HOLLIES is an unusual and informal garden which is well worth a visit. It is an intimate garden with lovely herbaceous borders which, when I went there on a June day, were crammed with a colourful medley of interesting and unusual plants. There are lots of intriguing paths leading you to secluded recesses and at the end of the garden a gate opens on to a footpath which disappears into distant trees and fields.

The Hollies

If you leave the main road at Grampound and take the turning to Creed, you very soon find yourself in countryside which, with its spreading, broad-leafed trees and gentle wooded hills, is more typical of Sussex than Cornwall. After a while, you come upon a pretty, granite-towered church and opposite is the lane leading to CREED House (once the rectory).

Like Trehane, the garden was neglected for many years and has been in the process of restoration since 1974. There are some rather fine trees and old rhododendrons and features include walled gardens, an orchard, ponds and a woodland walk as well as some unusual plants.

Papaver orientale

Red Admiral Butterfly

Creed

Meconopsis

For anyone coming to Cornwall with a view to looking at its outstanding gardens and plant collections then a visit to TREWITHEN is imperative for it is here that many hybrid plants, such as the famous ceanothus 'Trewithen Blue' or rhododendron 'Trewithen Orange' were raised by George Johnstone, a former owner and eminent horticulturalist, and there is a magnificent collection of trees and shrubs, many of them rare, to fascinate and enthral the plant enthusiast. Mr. Johnstone was an expert on Asiatic magnolias and those at Trewithen, having reached the full beauty of maturity, are particularly lovely when in flower.

The great, sweeping lawn which rolls away from the impressive south front of the very fine eighteenth century house merges into the surrounding trees and shrubs and shady paths lead off to glades and ferny dells. In May, stately groups of foxgloves in shades of magenta and white grow under the trees in the dappled light. There is a fine show of candelabra primulas and clumps of aptly named skunk cabbage; what a pity that this handsome plant, with its big, shiny, spinach-like leaves has such an unpleasantly pungent odour. In the damp shade, too, are clusters of *Meconopsis*, most beautiful of all the poppies, in blue and purest white.

Trewithen has a truly delightful walled garden. It is of formal design with an ornamental pond at one end and a little Hansel and Gretel summer house at the other and a pergola hung with wisteria. The borders which line the attractive,

Trewithen

The Italian Garden, Heligan

narrow paths made from granite railway setts are filled with perennials traditionally associated with English gardens. I sat by the pond one June day listening to the fountain playing on the water and the birdsong in the surrounding trees, enjoying the sense of calm and enclosure and the feeling of being cut off from the outside world. There could be no better place to be on a perfect summer's day.

Driving from Truro to Mevagissey, I often used to wonder what lay beyond the dense line of trees on the right shortly before you begin the approach down to the village. Two years ago, I heard about the attempt to restore what was once one of Cornwall's most outstanding gardens and which had, for more than seventy years, been buried under an entanglement of rampant weeds and fallen timber. It was early spring when I visited HELIGAN for the first time.

Already, a good deal of work had been carried out to restore the gardens to their former state and it was evident that they must, indeed, have been rather splendid; astonishingly, many of the original plants had survived and grown, moreover, to enormous size: the huge rhododendron which grows by the lawn known as 'Flora's Green' is possibly the largest in the country.

The gardens comprise a number of fascinating features of nineteenth century horticulture: walled kitchen gardens; cool, ferny rockeries of mossed stones reflecting a strange, green light; an Italian garden with formal pool and statuary and a summerhouse; a romantic crystal grotto; a wishing-well.

I was particularly taken with the set of bee-boles, a row of vaulted structures in which were housed straw skeps; looking at them, it was not difficult to imagine the gentle roar of hundreds of bees on a summer's day.

The Bee Holes, Heligan

Heligan

From the formal gardens, a wooded walk takes you down to the 'jungle' which is, in fact, a sub-tropical valley garden containing a remarkable collection of tree ferns. Here, there are lakes overhung with lush foliage; the sun shining through the trees and the transitory play of light on the water intensifies the atmosphere of romance with which Heligan is associated.

The Jungle Garden, Heligan

Heligan in Spring

Abutilon vitifolium

I could not have chosen a more perfect day for my first visit to LANHYDROCK (National Trust). It was May Day and an exquisite morning of clear, cobalt skies and the first, really warm sunshine of the year. The beeches which line the magnificent drive leading to the house had burst into leaf in delicate, coppery tints or pale, yellow-green and were of that transparency which is peculiar to the young foliage of the beech.

After passing through the grand, Gothic-style gatehouse, I came upon the formal gardens, the dominant feature of which is the beautifully sculpted, cone-shaped yews, cut flat at the top; these are, apparently, very old. A low, castellated wall encloses grass parterres on which are arranged geometrically patterned flowerbeds. At the time of my visit they were planted with tulips grouped in blocks of yellow, white, magenta and garnet, together with contrasting masses of yellow and mauve pansies and huge drifts of forget-me-nots, so that the overall effect was of sheets of intense, brilliant colour, setting of to perfection the splendid bronze urns.

The formal gardens are a pleasing contrast to the upper woodland gardens which are explored by winding paths on the slopes behind the house. The air was full of insect hum and birdsong that morning: woodpeckers laughed high up in the branches of great beeches while higher still, buzzards wheeled and swallows soared in the cloudless sky. Bluebells covered the grassy slopes and wafts of their delicious scent drifted on the moist, warm air. The steep slopes leading to the upper woodland gardens were well worth the climb: from here there was a panoramic view, framed with glowing crimson rhododendrons, of the house and its extensive parkland in all its splendour.

Lanhydrock

Wandering around the gardens of TRENGWAINTON (National Trust) for the first time, I found myself recalling the famed gardens of the Alhambra Palace in Granada, Spain. This was strange, since they in no way resemble each other. Indeed, I experienced a sense of deep disappointment on first seeing the latter, not because of the design of the gardens, which is exquisite, but with the crass choice of plants: beds of leggy pansies, for example, or bedraggled marigolds in pots, quite unlike the varied and fascinating plant collection at Trengwainton. Then, of course, I realised: it was the sound of running water from which, like the Alhambra, you are never far away at Trengwainton. Indeed, the long drive leading to the house runs parallel with a fast flowing stream and this stream garden, with its masses of yellow and magenta candelabra primulas and skunk lilies, with their distinctive yellow spathes, as well as other moisture-loving plants, is very much a feature of this garden. The other main feature is the series of inter-connecting, walled gardens which provide a congenial environment for the tenderest plants. In early spring, the magnolias dominate for, when they flower, they have a glamour which is unmatched even by the showy splendour of the rhododendrons and azaleas in full-flowering glory.

Abutilon (*A. vitifolium*) thrives in the walled gardens. Its abundant flowers are either pure white or delicate mauve and its pale, green-grey leaves are like those of a vine. There is Solomon's seal, too, growing in big clumps. I love those graceful sprays of mysterious, ghostly-white flowers. Fascinating, too, are the shiny red flowers of the aptly named 'Lobster Claw' (*Clianthus puniceus*) scrambling up the walls. On another visit, in April, the air was filled with warm waves of fragrance, not unlike the heady scent of lime blossom, which came from an abundance of white, rose-flushed rhododendrons and which I seemed to smell long after I had left the gardens.

Trengwainton

Trengwainton

47

St. Just in Roseland

Situated at the end of a wooded creek, peacefully sequestered, is the church of ST. JUST IN ROSELAND. There cannot be another church in England with so lovely a natural setting and you could be forgiven for thinking that, with such an idyllic and beautiful location, a garden would be unnecessary and out of place. However, the sub-tropical trees and shrubs in the churchyard and adjoining Memorial Gardens have been planted in such a skilful manner that they blend in, and have the appearance of being part of, the natural vegetation. A luxuriant growth of tree ferns, gunneras and Chinese fan-palms thrives in the shelter of the wooded slope, made accessible by little paths and steps with vantage points from which to admire the tidal estuary which is ever-changing with the ebb and flow of the water.

There is a fine collection of camellias and, in early spring, they are the dominant feature; they are followed by the rhododendrons, azaleas and magnolias and then, in summer, there are fuchsias and banks of hydrangeas.

In the winter of 1990, a terrible storm struck Cornwall and many of the mature pines which for so long had been a part of the landscape were destroyed. Replanting has begun and although it will be a long time before the setting of the church will be restored to its former beauty, it is still, nevertheless, a lovely place, whatever the season.

Contrary to the impression it gives, the name 'Roseland' has nothing to do with the roses. It is derived from the Cornish word 'ros' or 'roos', meaning promontory

As well as the great gardens of Cornwall and those smaller ones made accessible to the public by the kindness of their owners, the plant connoisseur or garden lover may get a good deal of satisfaction simply by strolling around some of the numerous pretty villages with which the county abounds. On the following pages I have illustrated just a few of them.

Coal Tit

The two mile coastal walk from St. Just in Roseland Church to ST. MAWES is well worth the effort: the sheltered harbourside village provides a congenial environment for a host of tender species. Giant echiums rear up from unexpected places, startling and confounding visitors from those parts of the country with a less favourable climate who have never seen them before. Palms flourish along the water's edge and gardens, window boxes and hanging baskets are crammed with colourful flowers in an exuberance of unrestrained planting. In summer, mesembryanthemums smother the tops of sunny walls with a blaze of colour.

FLUSHING, like St. Mawes, is another harbourside village which enjoys a particularly mild winter climate. Colourful window boxes and hanging baskets adorn every house and cottage and there are always particularly splendid displays of pansies in the summer.

Also in the Roseland area VERYAN, guarded by its four famous Round Houses at either entrance, is an example of a village with a thriving cottage garden tradition and gardens are filled with a colourful miscellany of flowers. Even the stone and granite walls are smothered with flowers, such as aubretia and valerian, depending on the season, and the little white, crimson-tinted daisy, *Erigeron mucronatus*, which seems to find a foothold in every nook and cranny in dry walls here as it does throughout the county. Beside the church are lovely, shady water gardens, an oasis of tranquility.

Small Tortoiseshell Butterfly

Veryan

Stippy-Stappy, St. Agnes

When you live on Cornwall's rugged North coast, at the mercy of unrelenting Atlantic winds, it must be difficult to garden successfully. Below the high ground of St. Agnes Beacon, with its industrial relics of mining days, the village of ST. AGNES enjoys a more sheltered situation and so is able boast a good number of attractive gardens. Stippy-Stappy, a row of cottages built on a steep hillside below the church, has some particularly charming gardens and always looks pretty, whatever the season.

Penberth

    There are certain places in Cornwall which winter never seems to touch: one of these is PENBERTH, a fishing cove owned by the National Trust, near Lamorna. It comprises a few cottages dating back to the seventeenth century and the cove which is also a natural harbour. It is truly the land that time forgot and if you visit it in January, you will find yourself not only in another time but also in another season, for here spring will already be well underway and the valley slopes will be carpeted with daffodils. In fact, when the pilchard shoals which provided the local population with their livelihood disappeared at the beginning of this century, the people made use of the congenial climate to grow daffodils and other flowers to supplement their incomes. If you take the coastal path from Mousehole to Lamorna, you will see evidence of this industry in the dug-out, terraced plots where arum lilies, scented violets and other flowers still grow.

Victoria Gardens, Truro

    Truro, too, is proud of its floral displays and although Boscawen Park with its colourful, formal beds always looks picturesque, my favourite garden is the beautiful, leafy VICTORIA GARDENS situated by The Leats, one of the few remaining parts of the city which has not been ravaged by development.

I could not resist saying a word or two about cats. While visiting gardens, I have discovered that, although cats are hated for the havoc they wreak upon the ordered rows of begonias or alternating clumps of alyssum and blue-and-white lobelia in suburban gardens, in those gardens of prestige they definitely seem to have a place. On several occasions I have been escorted around a garden by a friendly cat, each of which has obviously taken its position as official guide very seriously. Interestingly, many of the most famous gardeners were cat lovers - Gertrude Jekyll, for example- while others, including the National Trust, have realised their importance in controlling pests such as moles and rabbits in the garden or mice in greenhouses.

In this book, I have illustrated only a few of the many Cornish gardens open to the public; there are many more I have yet to visit. There are also gardens which I have not had room to include, such as LANTERNS, a small but interesting garden, situated off the steep hill which leads to the Pandora Inn at Restroguet. As well as the major gardens, including those run by the National Trust, there are a number of smaller, private gardens open to the public, often for the benefit of charities and frequently for the National Gardens Scheme which was started in 1927 to raise funds for district nursing. Because opening days and times vary from year to year,

I have not mentioned these. Information, produced by the Cornwall Garden Society and the Cornwall Tourist Board, is readily available from places such as public libraries, tourist information bureaux and the gardens themselves.

It has been said that Cornish gardens lack those elementary notions of design which have made gardens in other parts of the country outstanding; I feel bound to agree with this. Too often, trees and shrubs have been planted in such desultory fashion that they are not shown off to their best advantage and in some cases have been allowed to grow to such breadth or height that vistas which should have been features are obliterated. Nevertheless, the plant collections are second to none and I have yet to see a garden which can compare with a Cornish one in spring; without a doubt, the visitor who comes to the county at this glorious time of year without seeing at least one of its gardens has not seen the best of Cornwall.

The illustrations in this book were painted on Whatman (not) watercolour paper using a basic palette of: lemon yellow; cadmium yellow (pale); raw sienna; cadmium red; alizarin crimson; burnt sienna; burnt umber; ultramarine blue. Extra colours include: cadmium orange; monestial blue (phthalo); permanent rose; permanent magenta.

MARGARET MERRY

Margaret Merry grew up in Falmouth where, after leaving Falmouth High School, she spent a year at Falmouth School of Art. Then followed three years at Hornsey College of Art in London where she obtained a Diploma in Art and Design. She then spent a post-graduate year at the West of England College of Art in Bristol where she gained an Art Teacher's Diploma and a Certificate in Education of the University of Bristol. She has lived and worked in Truro since 1969 and has become one of Cornwall's most popular artists. Her paintings have been exhibited in New York, Tokyo, Paris and London and been bought by collectors from all over the world. Her first book "The Natural History of a Westcountry City", an illustrated guide to the flaura and fauna in and around Truro, was a local best-seller.

Published by Margaret Merry
24 Chirgwin Road, Truro
Cornwall, TR1 1TT
Tel & Fax: 0872 75652

£7.50

ISBN 0-948752-01-7

Printed by Troutbeck Press, Antron Hill, Mabe, Penryn, Cornwall. Telephone (01326) 373226

CW01338606

Newcastle under Lyme
1173-1973

hardback
ISBN: 0 9502745 1 8

paperback
ISBN: 0 9502745 0 X

Newcastle under Lyme 1173-1973

'The town useth to come to a chapel of St Sunday by the castle. All the castle is down save one great tower. There was a house of Black Friars in the south side of the town.' John Leland, 1535–43.

'The appearance of the town at the present time is such as to indicate its prosperity. During the last quarter of a century numerous handsome villas have been erected and many improvements have been effected. Signs of the antiquity of the town remain, but architectural display is not a characteristic of Newcastle.' J Ingamells, 1871.

'Ask the much-tried traveller on the A34 his impressions of Newcastle under Lyme and he was likely to say 'Bakeries as you go from the south, a traffic jam in the town centre, and collieries as you go out'. This is now no longer true – the bakeries and collieries are still there, albeit improved in appearance but the traffic jams have disappeared . . . This thriving growing town on the edge of the Potteries and on the threshold of a lovely countryside to the west and south, is emerging in our own time, from small and humble beginnings, into an important unit in the nation's economy, supporting a population "of upwards of 76,000".' *The Borough of Newcastle under Lyme : Official Guide*, Thirteenth Edition 1970.

Acknowledgements

The editor and contributors to this volume wish to thank the Council for affording this opportunity of collecting together and interpreting the history of the borough: what they have written however remains in each case a personal statement. Special debts of gratitude are due to the Borough Librarian, Mr G Bradley and his reference librarian Mr D W Adams for help with locating sources, to the Curator of the Museum, Mr P Bemrose and his staff for providing illustrative material, to the officers of the Council for supplying information, to Mrs C Busfield, of the History Department, University of Keele for typing most of the manuscript, and to Dr D M Palliser and Miss D M Rosman for helping with the proofs. Radio Stoke, the Staffordshire Record Office, the Editor of the Victoria County History and Mr B Oldacre have all made helpful contributions. Mr J Lagden, Mr D Stuart and Mr A Wood all helped to get the project off the ground. Finally thanks are due to Mr Peter Bragg and Mr Tom Hill of the North Staffordshire Polytechnic whose splendid work in design, makes the book so much more attractive and effective.

This book was prepared and designed as part of a project in the Department of Graphic Design and Printing, North Staffordshire Polytechnic.

© Copyright John Briggs, 1973

design and co-ordination	**Tom Hill**
illustration	**Pete Coombs**
contemporary photography	**John Rainford**
photographic printing	**Douglas Moore**
design tutor	**Peter Bragg**

Illustrations

The Borough Museum and Library both have handsome collections of photographs which testify to the excellent work done by Newcastle photographers, principally H Corfield, E Harrison and Sons, A Hollins, T Pape, J Parton and E J D Warrillow, together with the press photographers of earlier years. The use of these collections is gratefully acknowledged as is the work of the North Staffordshire Polytechnic and the Borough Museum in photocopying many old photographs loaned by members of the public including among others Mr J Copeland, Mr J Davies, Mr G Edwards, Mr E W Hoon, Mr A Hulse, Miss F Leese, Mr J McDermott, Miss N Mould, Mr F Shufflebothan, and Mr A Wardle.

Every endeavour has been made to trace the source of the old photographs used, but many have been copied and now lack provenance. If unwittingly any offence has been incurred through lack of acknowledgment, the editor offers his apologies.

Thanks are also due to the following owners for permission to reprint prints or photographs:

Aerofilms Ltd. p7–8

The Trustees of the British Museum p6, p55, p115, p116

University of Keele p51–2, p53, p55

University of London (Victoria County Histories) p177

Miss E Beard p155–6

The Planning and Development Department, Staffordshire County Council p106

N Brightmore p119

G Cavenagh-Mainwaring p55

Introduction

When the borough commissioned an octocentenary history in April of 1972, there were less than twelve months to see the project through the press. In some measure this determined the kind of book this would be. There was no time for much consistent historical research over the whole period, though clearly there are parts of Newcastle's history here published for the first time. Time also dictated that the work be the result of several pens rather than one. From the beginning it was also hoped that it would be possible to communicate as much through picture and illustration as through words alone, especially since only 3,000 words would be allowed for each century. In fact there is much unevenness: some parts of the story are indebted to work that has been done over many years, in particular the work of Thomas Pape in his three volumes which tell the history of Newcastle up to the Restoration, and to the work of those who contributed to the ever valuable Volume Eight of the *Victoria County History of Staffordshire*.

In the later period much of the initial research has still to be undertaken so that what is here presented, though fuller than the account of the early years of the borough, is in no way a finished story. It is rather a progress report which it is hoped will encourage others to delve into the records and write up parts of the story themselves. Indeed it is my hope that as a result of this presentation of Newcastle's history over eight hundred years someone will be encouraged to tell in detail the history of Newcastle in the last three centuries. In this sense the last chapter is a crucial one for there the reader will find out how he can continue the story.

John Briggs

Contents

title	author	page
Introduction	J H Y Briggs	
A Town is Born	D M Palliser	1-12
Stalls and Shops	D M Palliser	13-24
Church, Castle and Borough	D M Palliser	25-36
From Pauper's Badge to Social Security	D Stuart	37-48
Reformers, Royalists and Roundheads	D Stuart	49-60
Hassocks and Harmoniums	J H Y Briggs	61-72
North, South, East and West	B J Turton	73-84
Hats, Pots and Clocks	P J Bemrose	85-96
Mines and Mills	P J Bemrose	97-108
From Bribery to Ballot Box	J H Y Briggs	109-120
Law and Order	J H Y Briggs	121-132
Clean and Decent	J H Y Briggs	133-144
Spare the Rod	M J Cruikshank	145-156
All Work and No Play	G J Lagden & J H Y Briggs	157-168
The Old Order Changeth	J H Y Briggs	169-176
Finding Out More	J H Y Briggs	177-180

- Eardley
- Redstreet
- Chell
- Norton i'th Moor
- Audley
- Bignall hill
- Chaterley
- Badi
- ollene
- Hammerenc
- Tunstall
- R
- Millton
- P
- Y
- Ford green
- Chesterton
- Burslem
- Sneydgreen
- Hilt
- Apedale
- Bradwall
- Hanley green
- Dimsdale
- Bucknall
- Heyley
- Grubbers Ash
- Wulftanton
- Shelton
- L. Madeley
- Knuton
- Botlow
- Newcastle under lyme
- N. Ho
- Keel
- Stoke sup Trent
- L. Fenton
- O. Holm
- Keelhall
- Penkhull
- Park hall
- Madeley
- Sheabridge
- Boothen
- Mear lane end
- Weston coyn
- Shutland head
- Madeley Manor
- Clayton
- G. Fenton
- Longton
- Meare
- Butterton
- Acton
- Hanford
- Whitmore
- Hanchurch
- Blurton
- Normacot
- Camp hills
- H
- I
- L
- L
- Meare
- Chawton on y hill
- Shelton under Harley
- Trentham
- Cockuage
- Gaflilea
- Chorlton
- Barleston
- Weston
- Beech
- Knenha
- odmer ards
- Simushead
- Hatton
- Tittensor
- Modersall
- Bowers
- Swinnerton
- Darlaston
- Oulton
- Woodhouses
- Standon
- Mayfore
- Cotwalto

A Town is Born

Charles Masefield's *Little Guide to Staffordshire* (1910) describes Newcastle as 'comparatively a modern town, not being in existence at the time of the Domesday Survey'. 'Modern' may seem an odd description to the burgesses who may well prefer to reserve the term for newer creations like the City of Stoke on Trent or even Telford. Yet Masefield was right if we take a long perspective: apart from the towns born of the Industrial Revolution, and the post-war New Towns, the larger English towns usually go back at least to *Domesday Book* (1086), and often a good deal further. But there is no mention of Newcastle in the Conqueror's great survey, and although some places were missed out through haste, the likelihood is that Newcastle simply did not exist then, even as a small village.

At that period north west Staffordshire was thinly peopled and largely covered with woodland, the great Lyme forest. The site of the future town was simply an area between the villages of Trentham, Penkhull and Wolstanton where two main roads forked. The London – Carlisle road ran through the area roughly on the line of the A34, following the present ring road rather than the High Street; and where St Giles' now is, the Chester road turned off through Nantwich. The area formed part of the vast estates which made William the Conqueror the greatest landowner in England, for he had inherited the manor of Trentham from the Saxon kings, and had seized Wolstanton and Penkhull after the battle of Hastings. What now is Newcastle, it seems, then formed part of the manor and parish of Trentham.

After the Conqueror had put down initial opposition, there was a long period of peace: but in the 1140s troubled times returned. Matilda and Stephen, daughter and nephew of the last Norman King, fought a civil war for the throne, and Staffordshire was in the thick of it because of the rival ambitions of neighbouring barons, especially the powerful Earl Ranulf of Chester. The strategic road junction near Trentham became too important to be neglected, and a castle was thrown up to command it. The first evidence for this is in a generous charter by which King Stephen bought Earl Ranulf's support. Among many other possessions, he gave him 'the New Castle of Staffordshire with all the lands belonging to the same'. Whether the king had first built the castle, or whether the earl had done so without permission and was now acquiring a valid title deed, we do not know: he did not however enjoy it for long, as he died in 1153. In the following year, when the war was over, Matilda's son became king as Henry II, and began a firm policy of curbing the barons' power to make another war more difficult. As part of this policy, the New Castle was seized from the young earl and became a royal possession again.

Another unexplained point about those distant origins is the name of the castle. Many others were built during the civil war: why should this one be singled out and called the New Castle? One idea is that it was called 'new' in relation to the older castle at Stafford, which the Conqueror had built in 1070 but which was now decayed. A more likely suggestion is that it was named in relation to an older fortification at Chesterton, either the Roman fort, or an unrecorded medieval castle. Certainly William Camden, who described Staffordshire in his *Britannia* in 1586, firmly explained Newcastle's name as 'upon the account of an older Castle which formerly stood not far from it at Chesterton under Lime, where', he adds, 'I saw the ruinous and shattered walls of an old Castle.'

The term 'castle' still summons up ideas of stone walls, turretted and battlemented; but the castle of the 1140s, like most others thrown up hastily during the civil war, was built only of earth and timber, on the usual Norman 'motte and bailey' plan. The garrison's living quarters would have been wooden buildings set in a large flat enclosure surrounded by a bank and ditch, and on one side, connected with it by a drawbridge, was a motte or mound of soil crowned by a wall of sharpened stakes, and probably supporting a wooden tower. This was the strongpoint to which the garrison would retreat if the bailey was captured. Usually a moat surrounded the castle, but the designers of Newcastle, a low-lying site needing strong defences, did better than that. They dammed the Lyme Brook at Pool Dam, and at Rotterdam

Joseph Browne's Map of Staffordshire (1682) puts Newcastle in its geographical context. Lying on the south side of the great Lyme (or Elm) Forest, traces of whose existence can be detected in names like Audlem and Burslem, it stretched from the upper Trent into South Cheshire and provides the name not only for Newcastle but also for the Lyme Brook.

2

The Bayeux Tapestry provides contemporary comment in embroidery on the way in which the Normans built their castles with English forced labour. The New Castle would have been similarly constructed.

further north, and so created an artificial lake round the site just as their contemporaries did at Kenilworth. The motte still survives at one end of the Queen Elizabeth Gardens, and the flat land of the Gardens represents part of the silted pool. This may seem a curious position, but it must be remembered that the main road then was on the line Upper Green, Lower Street, Stubbs Gate, roughly the present by-pass, rather than along the High Street as it was later. In the early thirteenth century the castle walls were rebuilt in stone. Considerable stretches of the stone bailey walls have been discovered by excavation, and the foundations of a stone gate are still visible in John o' Gaunt's Road. The main road, with its traffic of kings and notables, made the castle an important halting place. In 1157 Henry II passed by and stayed at Chesterton, probably because the castle was not in a state to receive him, but in 1206 his son John stayed in the castle, as did John's son, Henry III, on several occasions. In 1215, the year of Magna Carta, John had to surrender the castle to the Earl of Chester as one of his concessions to the baronage, but Henry III recovered it in 1234. At this time North Wales was still independent and a constant source of danger to the English borders, and Henry's excuse for retaking possession of the castle was that it was an important strategic link between Cheshire and the rest of England. In 1267, however, Henry felt secure enough to let the castle out of his hands again, granting it to his younger son, Edmund Earl of Lancaster; and so the castle, instead of being royal, became one of the many possessions of the earls and dukes of Lancaster.

Excavations on the castle site in 1935 led to the uncovering of old masonry. The foundations of a gatehouse remain uncovered in John of Gaunt's Road and some of the old timbers can be seen at the Borough Museum.

Henry III's fee-farm charter of 1251 granted the town its first rights of self-government. The original has been lost, but here is a medieval copy of the same charter from Preston.

The genuineness of a royal charter was established by attaching the great seal to it. Newcastle's first charter would have borne this great seal of Henry II.

Borough ceremonial preserves Newcastle's ancient customs: this seal, used from at least the fifteenth century with only minor changes, symbolizes in stylised form the castle and its pool.

The castle was the origin of Newcastle and the reason for its name, but it did not remain an isolated fortress for long. In 1162 the possessions of Trentham Priory included 'a certain small township of Newcastle', and in the year 1166–67 the men of 'New Town under Lyme with its soke' (i.e the borough with its surrounding rural dependency) were fined by the king for breaking forest laws. By 1168–69 the 'men of New Castle' were among the royal tenants contributing to royal taxes, and in 1172–73 the 'borough of New Castle' paid more in tax than any other royal estate, even more than Stafford. Clearly a settlement, by the castle, had grown very rapidly from a small village to a borough, and had also somehow escaped from the control of the priory at Trentham, the lords of the manor, to become a royal town. How had this happened?

It was quite usual for a small town to spring up at the gate of a medieval castle, to benefit from its protection, and to supply food, drink and hospitality for the garrison and for visitors. But Newcastle's growth was so rapid that this is not an adequate explanation. The king seems to have taken over the site next to his castle when it was still a small village, removed it from the control of Trentham Priory, and sponsored the growth of a 'New Town'. This was not an unusual development in the middle ages: between the Norman Conquest and 1368, at least 175 new towns were created in England in this way. During the same period, the bishop laid out a new town at Lichfield, and the earl of Derby created another at Newborough. But of these three, Newcastle was the nearest to our idea of a New Town, for it was laid out on an almost virgin site by the castle, whereas at Lichfield and Newborough there were already old-established villages in existence before the towns were created.

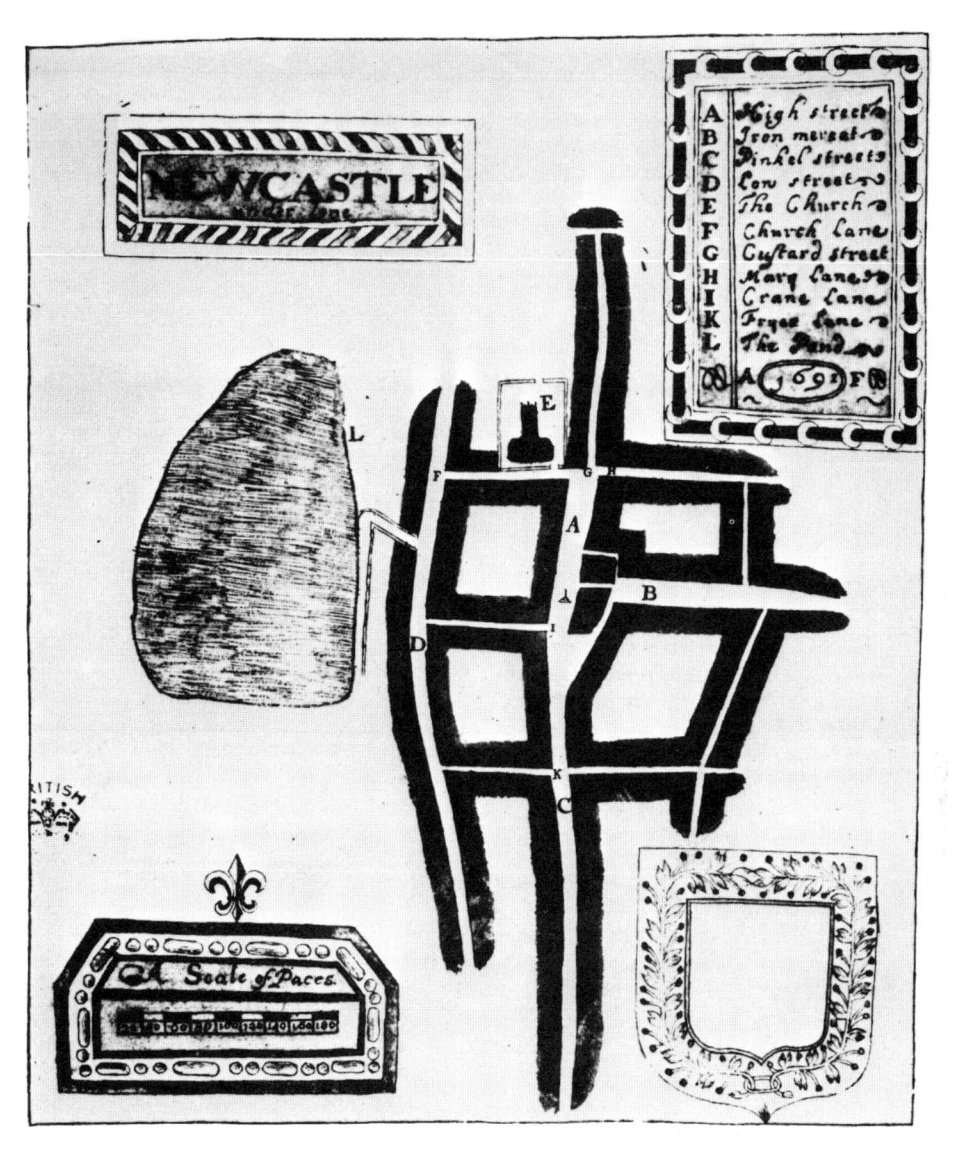

This, the earliest plan of Newcastle (1691), is crude and simple. However, it shows well the regular street plan of the medieval borough and the central position of the town's two markets.

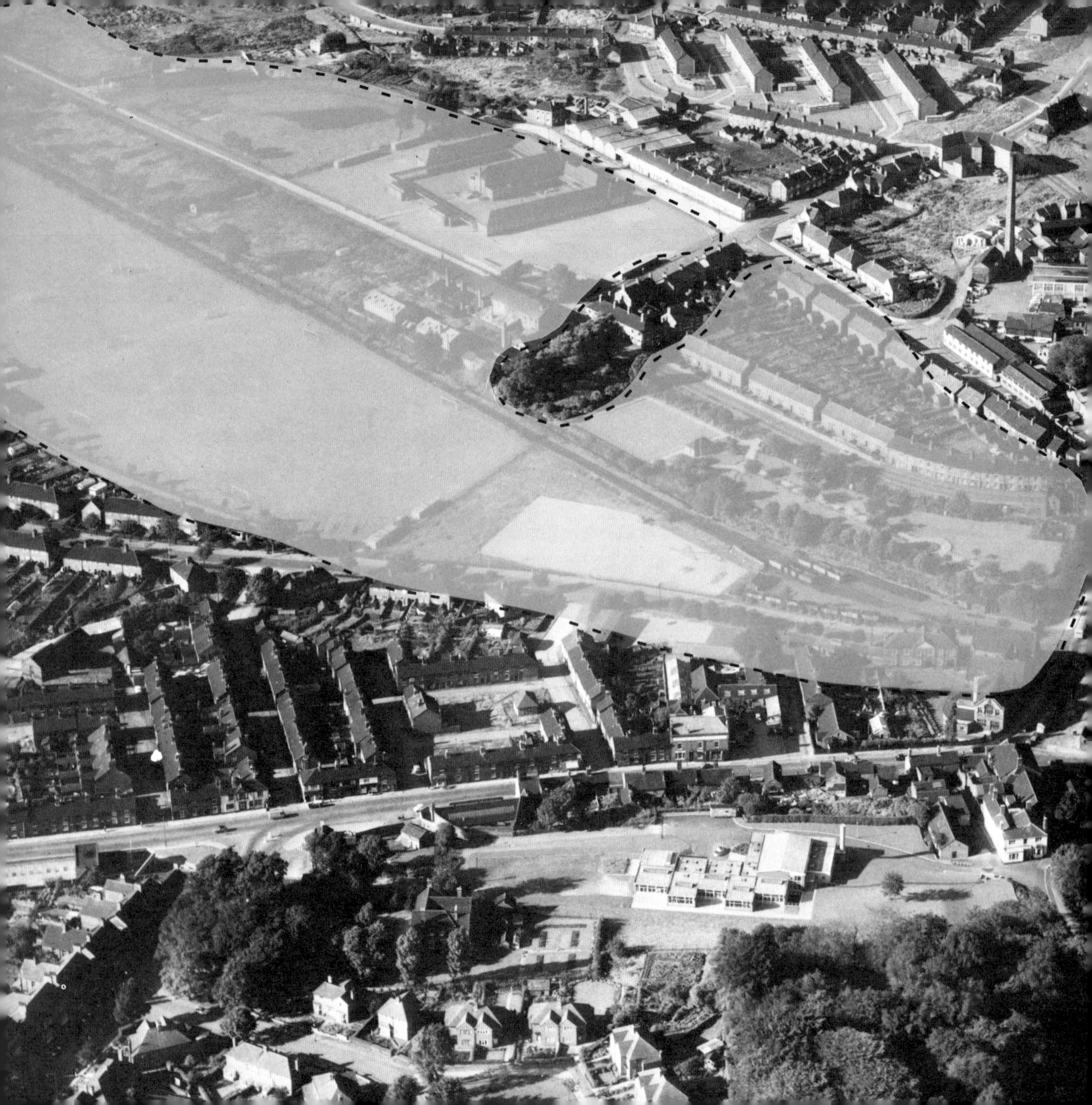

The castle and its defensive pool can still be easily traced from the air. It needs little imagination to reconstruct Pool Dam, and to visualise a great expanse of water from Poolfields to Rotterdam, with the castle motte and its associated works located on the eastern side between Queen Elizabeth Gardens and the top of Castle Hill Road.

The loss of the early borough archives leaves us ignorant of early stages of the town's history and growth; but we can infer a certain amount from the history of other medieval New Towns. When a lord founded one on his own land, he would be hoping for profits from the general growth of commerce and trade that took place in the twelfth and thirteenth centuries. A market, for instance, could be very valuable to a lord, who would receive tolls on the sale of goods there, especially when the market was sited at a major road junction, like Newcastle's. In 1172 the king received 10 shillings extra revenue for rent for a new market at Trentham. This almost certainly meant the market at Newcastle, and the 10 shillings will have been a sum paid by the townsmen for the right to collect the tolls themselves. In 1173 the rent was doubled to 20 shillings, and in 1174 it was doubled again to 40 shillings, a sure sign of growing prosperity. The market, like many others at that time, was held on Sunday, the best day to attract busy countryfolk working a six day week.

With such rapidly growing prosperity, the town also won the right of borough status. The tax return of 1172–73 is the first record that calls the town a borough, but just when the status was won is not clear. There is a traditional belief in histories of Newcastle that Henry II granted a charter, now lost, making the town a borough, and Thomas Pape thought that the charter would have been granted in the year of the 1173 Pipe Roll (i.e the royal financial returns for the year beginning on 29 September 1172). But there is no certain evidence for a charter at all; many places in those early days received privileges without formal charters. All that is recorded definitely is that in 1179 the king granted to his burgesses of Preston (Lancs), 'all the same liberties and free customs which I have given and granted to my burgesses of New Castle under Lyme'. However, Pape showed that the townsmen of Newcastle paid off the large sum of over £20 to the king in instalments, starting in 1173, and this is the kind of large sum often paid for the right to special privileges. So perhaps there was a charter, issued some time between Michaelmas (29 September) 1172 and Michaelmas 1173. If there was, the townsmen were paying handsomely for it. The value of £20 is made clearer if we consider that the sergeants who guarded the castle, a well paid body of picked men, were given wages of sixpence a day.

What did this creation of a borough mean to its inhabitants? How did it affect their lives? In the twelfth century much more than today, borough status involved a radical change in the lives of the townsmen, and was worth substantial expenditure. The normal form of local government in the countryside and in many towns was manorial and each manor had a lord wielding extensive rights over its inhabitants. He was owed labour services by most of his tenants, and could extract fees and fines from them through his manor courts. Newcastle until the 1160s was part of Trentham manor, which meant that the inhabitants owed services and suit of court to the prior of Trentham and his monks.

The Castle Mound and adjacent Colour Works as they are today at the north west end of Queen Elizabeth Gardens in Silverdale Road. The motte was reduced in size when the surrounding buildings were erected.

The first castle consisted simply of raised earthworks around which defensive staking formed a palisade. From the beginnings it was defended by its surrounding pool.

The creation of a borough, on land taken over by the king from the monks, meant that the townsmen were freed from this manorial control, in return for payments to the king. When a lord created a borough, he laid out building plots or burgages along the new streets: those renting these plots were called burgesses. At Newcastle the burgess paid a standard rent of a shilling a year for his burgage, together with holdings in the open fields of about two acres, and he escaped from all manorial services. The lord was pleased to encourage a trading community which would increase his wealth through taxes and market dues and the burgesses were pleased to escape from manorial control and from the time-consuming labour services.

The town, then, was separated altogether from the manor of Trentham. At the same time the king set up a new manor of Newcastle, administered from the castle, but this was a rural manor which did not include the new town. It originally covered Knutton, Fenton, Longton and Hanley, and was later extended to include Penkhull, Wolstanton, Shelton, Clayton and Seabridge. It was a typical manor based on a rural area with labourers providing rents and service in the fields. Its only special feature was that a group of 'sergeants' held certain lands in it with no labour services, but with an obligation to guard the castle instead. It is not clear whether the borough officially formed a small manor on its own, or whether it was outside the manorial pattern altogether.

So, with royal encouragement, the new borough had a flying start. Within ten or twenty years of the first small settlement's appearance at the castle gates, it was built up into a town with borough privileges and a large body of traders. A royal survey made in 1212 revealed that there were 160 burgages in the town, not far short of the 179 burgages at Stafford or the 180 at Tutbury. As the town grew more prosperous, the burgesses were able to buy charters from the crown granting them rights of self-government. Little wonder then that the more old-fashioned barons and clergy of the time were suspicious of boroughs; they were outside the traditional framework of a rural and manorial society, and depended largely on commerce and industry (in spite of their town fields). To the conservatives of about 1200, brought up in an England of lords and manors, sheep and corn, it was disquieting to see so many boroughs springing up, although to the burgesses themselves, and to the lords sponsoring them, it was an exciting commercial challenge. On the eve of the 1974 local government reorganization, when boroughs 800 years old have an immemorial aura, it is salutary to remember that the changes of the 1170s brought about a much more radical change in and around Newcastle, Preston and the other new boroughs than those we face today.

The thirteenth century arms' race, produced an expensive rebuilding in stone. In its turn this fortress, with the pacification of the Welsh Marches, was changed into a fortified residence. By the late fifteenth century even this stately home was in decay.

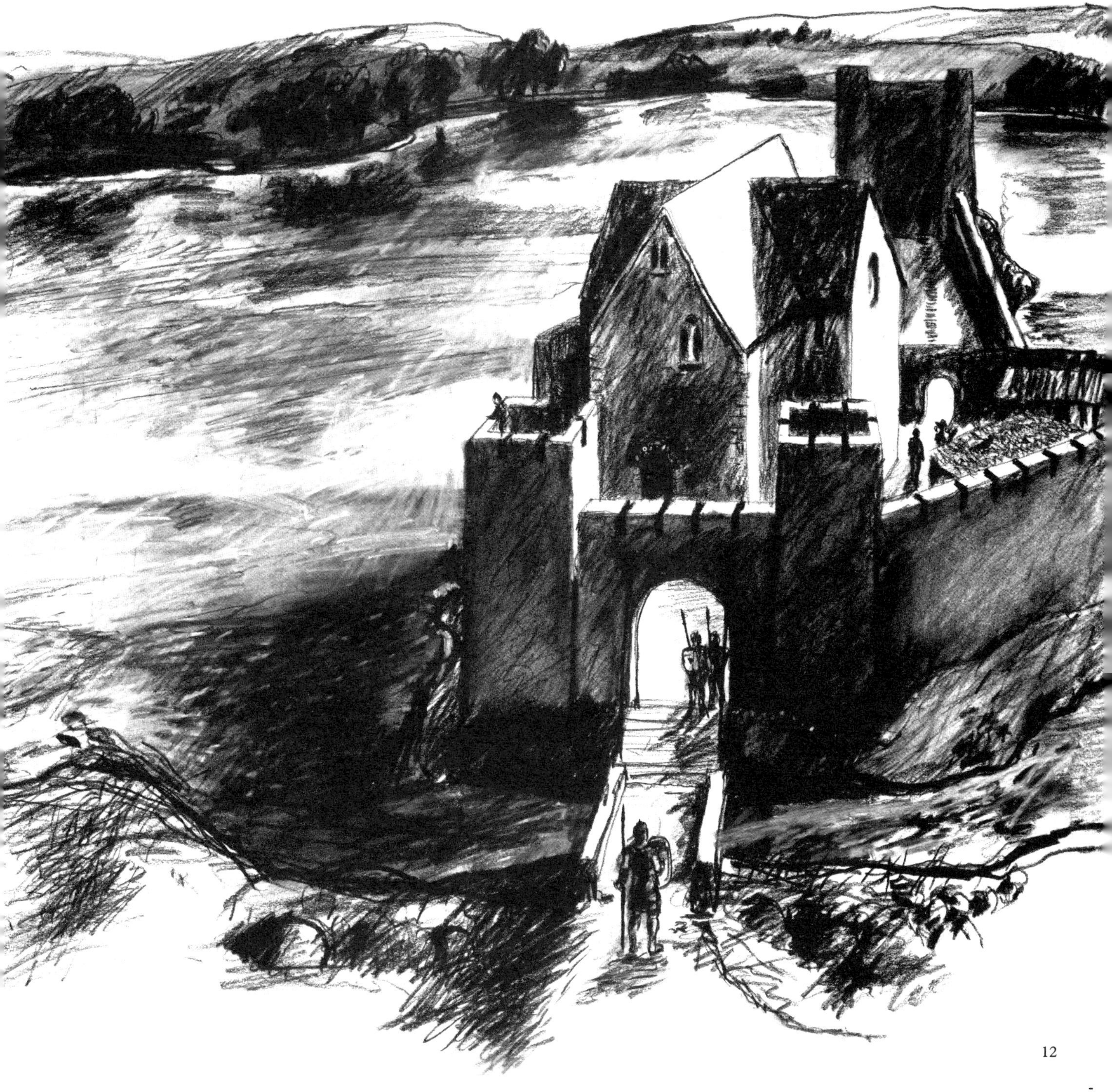

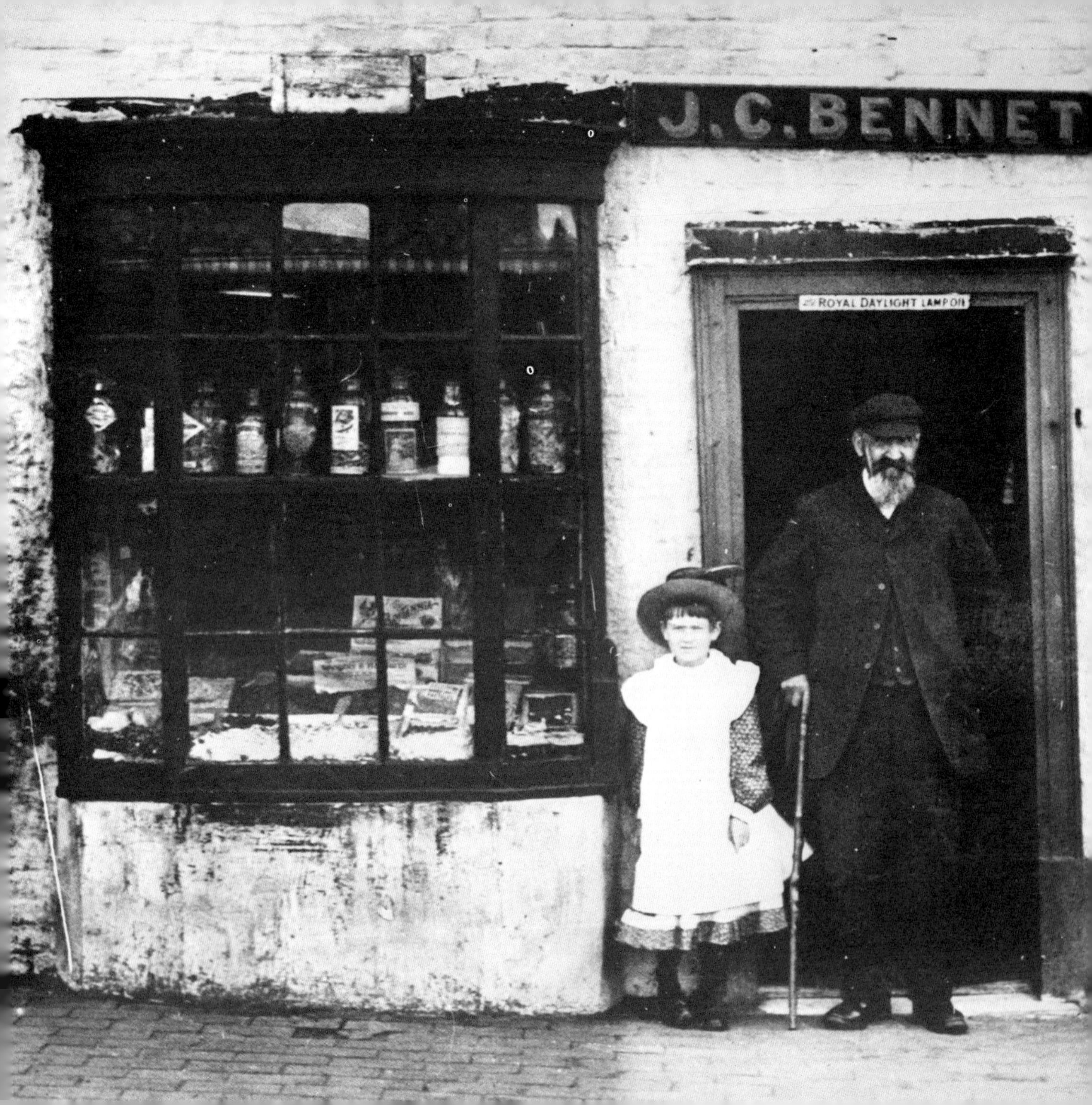
J. C. BENNET
ROYAL DAYLIGHT LAMP OIL

Stalls and Shops

Very little is known about the early growth of the town. It started as a small settlement by the castle, perhaps sited along Lower Green and Upper Green, and there is some evidence that Upper Green was the first market place. The settlement may even have been within an outer bailey of the castle, which might explain why no town walls were built. At some later date a planned extension was built on the higher ground to the north east. The Ironmarket, High Street and surrounding area are built on a grid plan, with streets intersecting roughly at right angles, and with regular burgage plots running back from the streets, and lanes between them giving access to the backs of the properties. The High Street and the Ironmarket would have been intended from the start as market places for livestock as well as goods – hence their unusual width. It is not known when this planned extension was laid out, but perhaps it was in the early thirteenth century, when we know that Newcastle was growing, and when other towns like Salisbury and Stratford were also being laid out with regular plans.

By 1280 there is a hint that the main market had moved from its original site, probably to the High Street. The whole of the present High Street would have been a large market place starting as a narrow road at the south east end, and gradually widening until it ended by the churchyard. Movable stalls would be set up on market days from the very beginning, and the stalls which are still used in part of the street are the direct heirs of seven or eight centuries of marketing there. Later, however, some blocks of stalls were replaced by permanent structures (wooden booths, probably, and a market hall) and so 'islands' of building started to appear in the middle of the street. So today, with the Guildhall and the blocks of building either side of the Ironmarket running back to the line of Lad Lane as the successors of these early islands, it takes an effort to imagine how vast was the original street.

In 1203 the original Sunday market was moved to Saturday, and in 1590 it was moved again to Monday, which it has been ever since. In the early nineteenth century Saturday was added again as a second market day, and later Friday became a third. From the first the market prospered. By the late thirteenth century Stafford merchants came regularly to sell wool and cloth there, and meat, fish and leather are also mentioned among the goods sold; while by the Tudor period at least, Uttoxeter men were also using the market regularly, probably selling butter. It would have been possible even in the thirteenth century for an enterprising stallholder to make a circuit of the markets, as he can today. All the surrounding markets were held on different days from Newcastle: Talke for instance on Tuesday, Leek on Wednesday and Betley on Thursday.

Another sign of prosperity was the granting of several fairs, held yearly rather than weekly, which drew buyers from a wider area than did the markets. The town's first fair was obtained for it by the Earl of Lancaster in 1281, to be held on Trinity Sunday and on the Saturday before and the Monday following. Others were added by charter in 1336 and 1590, and at their peak in Victoria's reign the town had no less than seven fairs a year. But they have proved more vulnerable to change than the open market, and none of them is held today.

Markets and fairs were the normal places for buying and selling before the rise of permanent shops, and nearly fifty places in the county shared with Newcastle the privilege of having a market. But in 1235 the King recognized that Newcastle was more than an ordinary market town. He granted to the townsmen the right to form a Gild Merchant (a kind of general employers association for all merchants and traders) and the right to buy and sell toll-free throughout the whole country except London. The Gild quickly became the real power in the town, and not only regulated its economic life but probably its political life as well. Later on, it became less important, as a town council emerged to administer the town and separate craft gilds were formed for different trades. But a continuing memorial of those early days is that the town council's meeting place continued to be called a Guildhall rather than a Town Hall: and the Guildhall today, a little to the south of the original site, still perpetuates the name.

Mr Bennett's shop, here pictured about 1902, stood on the corner of West Street and Hassell Street. Specially licensed to sell Lamp Oil it was typical of the many street corner shops that provided for the unexpected needs of the family.

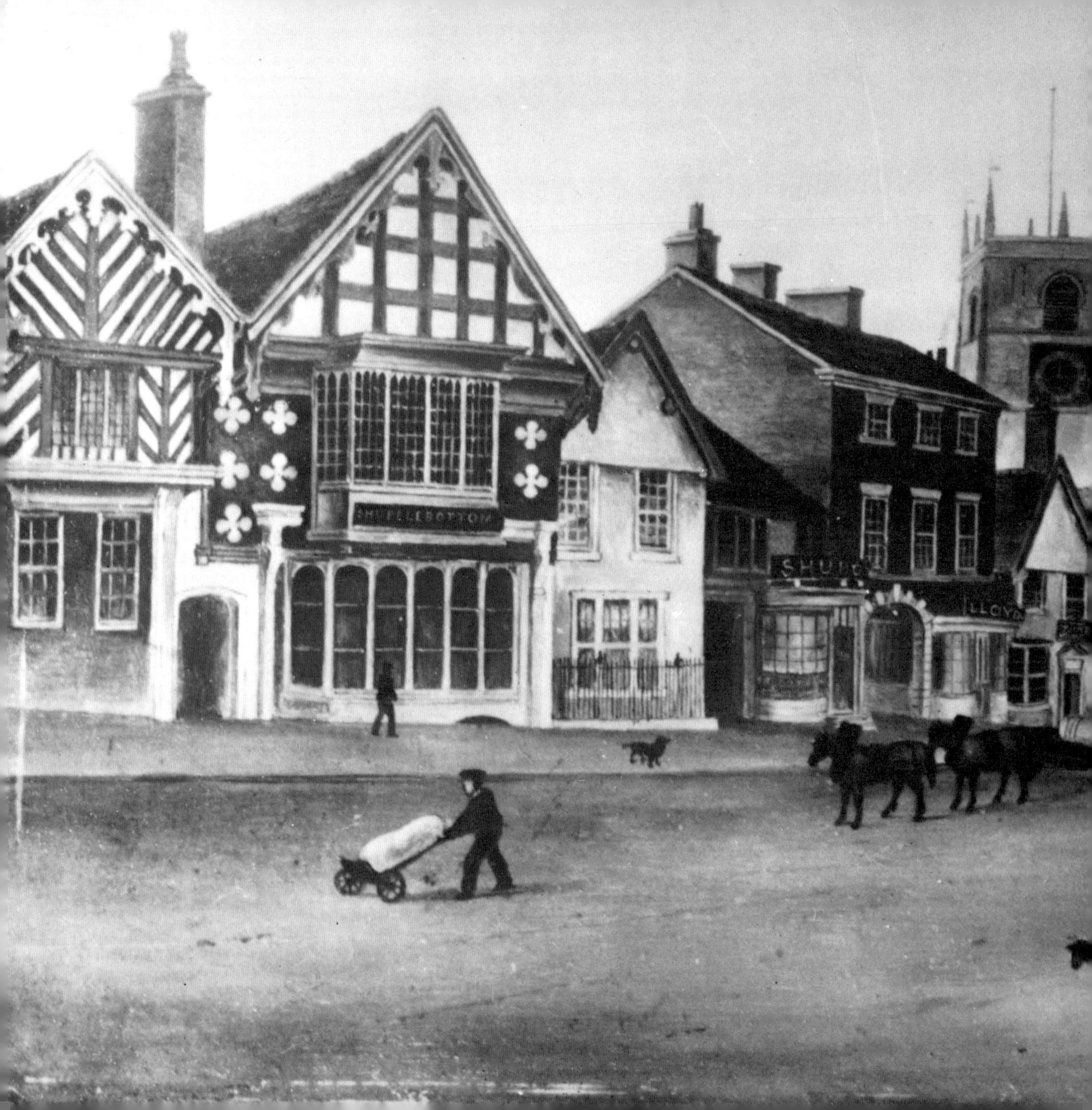

Sheep being driven through Red Lion Square in H L Pratt's painting of 1854 indicates the close relationship between town and country in a market town, a tradition still maintained in the weekly Monday cattle markets.

As the town developed in the later middle ages, economic life became more complex. The Gild Merchant became less and less important as the craftsmen and traders formed separate 'gilds' or associations of their own. By the reign of Henry VIII there were gilds of butchers and smiths, and possibly there were others not recorded. A fair number of different trades was practised. Among the townsmen of the late fourteenth century, when a surname still often described the trade of its holder, were Adam the Smith, William the Locksmith, Thomas and Benedict the Goldsmiths, Henry Quarrier, Richard Saddler, John the Fletcher (arrow maker) and Geoffrey the Stringer (bowstring maker). Hickman Street was originally called Salters Lane, which may be an indication of a route taken by salt carriers coming from the Cheshire salt towns. The most important small industry in the town was iron working, especially nail making, which was carried on from the fourteenth to the nineteenth centuries, hence the name of the Ironmarket and the 'Iron Hall' which stood there in Tudor times. Later, industry became more diversified, with hat making and pipe making in the Stuart and Georgian periods, and silk throwing, paper making and the manufacture of uniforms added in the nineteenth century.

Alongside the growth of different trades went the growing importance of permanent shops instead of fairs and markets. Most of the shops in the middle ages were more what we would call workshops, since before the age of the factory goods were usually made up or treated and then sold at the same place. A small house of a craftsman would have a single downstairs room, the 'shop', where he and his family worked. During working hours, the wooden window shutter (for there would be no glass) was lowered to form a counter facing the road, and over the counter goods were sold to passers-by. So when in 1510–11 the council wanted to stop butchers from selling meat during the time of church services, it ordered them 'to set open no windows' at those times. Quite a number of the early shops were rented out by the corporation, at four shillings a year in the 1370s. Perhaps they were shops built in the middle of the High Street, where the ground would belong to the town.

Before the monopoly of the Mint and the Bank of England was established national coinage and banknotes competed with local currencies. Here are illustrated Newcastle Bank Notes and tokens of the last century.

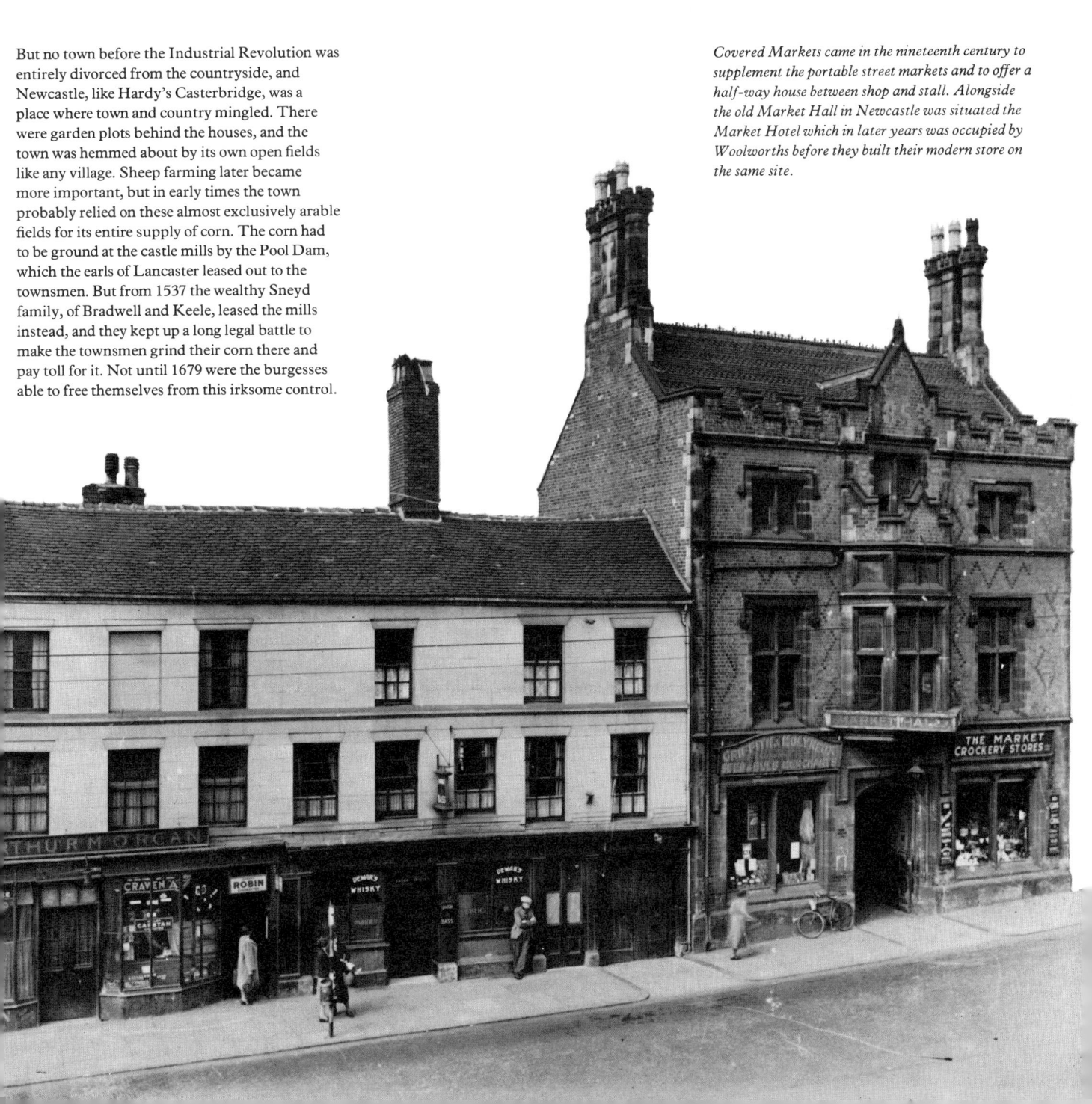

But no town before the Industrial Revolution was entirely divorced from the countryside, and Newcastle, like Hardy's Casterbridge, was a place where town and country mingled. There were garden plots behind the houses, and the town was hemmed about by its own open fields like any village. Sheep farming later became more important, but in early times the town probably relied on these almost exclusively arable fields for its entire supply of corn. The corn had to be ground at the castle mills by the Pool Dam, which the earls of Lancaster leased out to the townsmen. But from 1537 the wealthy Sneyd family, of Bradwell and Keele, leased the mills instead, and they kept up a long legal battle to make the townsmen grind their corn there and pay toll for it. Not until 1679 were the burgesses able to free themselves from this irksome control.

Covered Markets came in the nineteenth century to supplement the portable street markets and to offer a half-way house between shop and stall. Alongside the old Market Hall in Newcastle was situated the Market Hotel which in later years was occupied by Woolworths before they built their modern store on the same site.

What was medieval Newcastle really like? Although one of the largest towns in the county, it would seem very small to us today, with just half a dozen streets huddled round the church and Guildhall on the hill. In 1377 the total population was perhaps 750 or 800. By 1563, perhaps because of the numerous plagues of the period, it had fallen to around 400, and by 1665 it had risen again to 1300 or 1400. To put these figures in perspective, however, we must realise that the whole population of England and Wales was only about three million in 1377, and about five million in 1665. At that time towns were usually so unhealthy that the death rate exceeded the birth rate, and towns could only continue because of a perpetual supply of countryfolk coming in to try to make a living. Even as early as the late fourteenth century this was happening in Newcastle. The surnames of the townsmen at that time show that among them were not only men from the surrounding area but also from as far away as York, Wigan, Manchester and Coventry.

Nothing is left of the appearance of the medieval town except the castle remains, the church tower and the street plan; all the other buildings have long since been replaced. It must have appeared very much as a huddle of low buildings (the more prosperous ones built with timber and the poorer ones of hardened mud) grouped along streets which were mostly unpaved, and which would be seas of mud in wet weather. This medieval shanty town appearance was what struck the Earl of Huntingdon on a visit as late as 1636. Coming along 'foul lanes' from Uttoxeter, he found Newcastle 'a long town, the street very broad, ill paved and poor houses thatched and very few either tiled or slated'. By contrast, he praised Nantwich, flourishing through its salt industry, for its 'fair wooden houses', obviously rather grander than those at Newcastle. It was, in fact, only just at this time, in the Tudor and Stuart periods, that the richer English townsmen could start to build comfortable houses with some of the conveniences that we all take for granted, like chimneys and glass windows. In 1510–11 the Prior of Trentham paid fourpence rent for the right to have a chimney at his house in Newcastle, then a rare luxury. He was probably paying the town rent because the stack would be built into the street against the front or side of his house.

In the High Street, here depicted as it was in 1839, pubs and shops and banks presided over by the dignity of the Guildhall comprised the commercial world of Newcastle at the accession of Queen Victoria.

Let it not be thought that advertisements are contemporary novelties—seventy years ago the shopkeepers of Newcastle certainly believed that it paid to advertise.

The smash and grab gangs of our grandparents' generation may, with justification, have claimed that shops like Hales, the jewellers, were provocation indeed.

Pearson's hat shop recalls what was once Newcastle's staple trade.

'Read late Tilsley'—the traditions of commercial succession in a market town reflect upon the importance of reputation and goodwill. Note the shutters on the adjacent premises: before the advent of plate glass, the shutter was a crucial adjunct of Elizabethan and earlier shops.

What else did the Earl find worth commenting on in 1636? 'There is a reasonable fair town house', the Guildhall or council house, next to which stood a market cross. 'The church is a tower steeple, but neither fair nor handsome'. This was the thirteenth century tower which still stands. Then he noted the decayed state of the castle; and finally he took note of that family of aspiring gentry that succeeded the lords of the castle. 'A mile off (a long mile!) is an ancient gentleman's house, built of stone, called Keele Hall, one Mr. Sneyd's.' The Sneyds were certainly an old family, but they had only recently become wealthy through the law. They were setting themselves to become the dominant family in the Newcastle area in succession to the Dukes of Lancaster, for the Duke was now the King and was no longer very concerned with local politics. Not only did the Sneyds buy up Keele and build a new house there, but they also leased the castle mills from 1537, and the castle site itself in 1610, finally buying it outright from the Duchy in 1828.

The life of the borough continued in the sixteenth century to revolve around its markets which from about 1590 to about 1700 came under the supervision of the 'bellman' or town crier, who remained an important officer of the borough to the end of the nineteenth century. He rented from the borough the rights to levy a corn toll, though Newcastle's own burgesses, who until 1889 had the right to set up stalls in the market free of toll, gained exemption from payment in some years. In the eighteenth century the collection of the corn toll passed by purchase into private control, but after 1757 the corporation kept it in its own hands.

The increasing scale of market activities called for more plant and between 1622 and 1626 a Market House was erected close by the Guildhall, perhaps replacing an older building which had similarly served as a place where tolls and taxes were collected. In 1835 an octagonal Weights and Measures Office was built to the South of the Guildhall, and between 1853 and 1854 still more formal provision was made with the erection of the first covered market in Tudor style of red bricks decorated with courses of blue bricks and with stone dressings on a site to the west of the

Shops sell not only goods but services—here Mr Wardle at his Bridge Street establishment waits ready to administer the customary 'short back and sides'.

Markets attract people, people who can at a moment's notice become an audience, not only for the sales-talk of the stall-holder but for the native comic, the wandering musicians, the travelling menagerie. This secondary function of markets over the years became formalised into Wakes. The fun of the fairground here jostles with the business of the market in the Wakes of 1908.

High Street and below Friars Street. This was demolished in 1961 to make way for a more up-to-date covered market (1963) approached by two arcades of small shops which are repeated at basement level. Though perhaps desirable from a planner's point of view, the clinical functionalism of the new building lacks the vital liveliness of the open market, where, wet and wind notwithstanding, purchases happily continue to be made three days a week. In addition to its markets, Newcastle is well supplied with both small shops and large supermarkets. With all its commercial facilities, Newcastle remains a major centre for the north of the county well able to face the challenge of larger competitors. There is also a weekly cattle market, a successor to 'the great beast markets' held every fortnight at the end of the eighteenth century. Since 1871 it has been housed in the Smithfield Cattle Market, purposely laid out for it in Blackfriars Road. The bustle of life that fills the town centre each Monday indicates very clearly the close community of interests that exists between the borough and its farming hinterland. Newcastle is far more than a commuter suburb, remaining still a genuine market town, able to service the needs of modern technological farming.

Salesmanship anywhere, but especially in a market, is an art : the customer has to be humoured, wooed, persuaded. For her part the customer has to pit her wits against the small talk to be sure she really is getting a bargain.

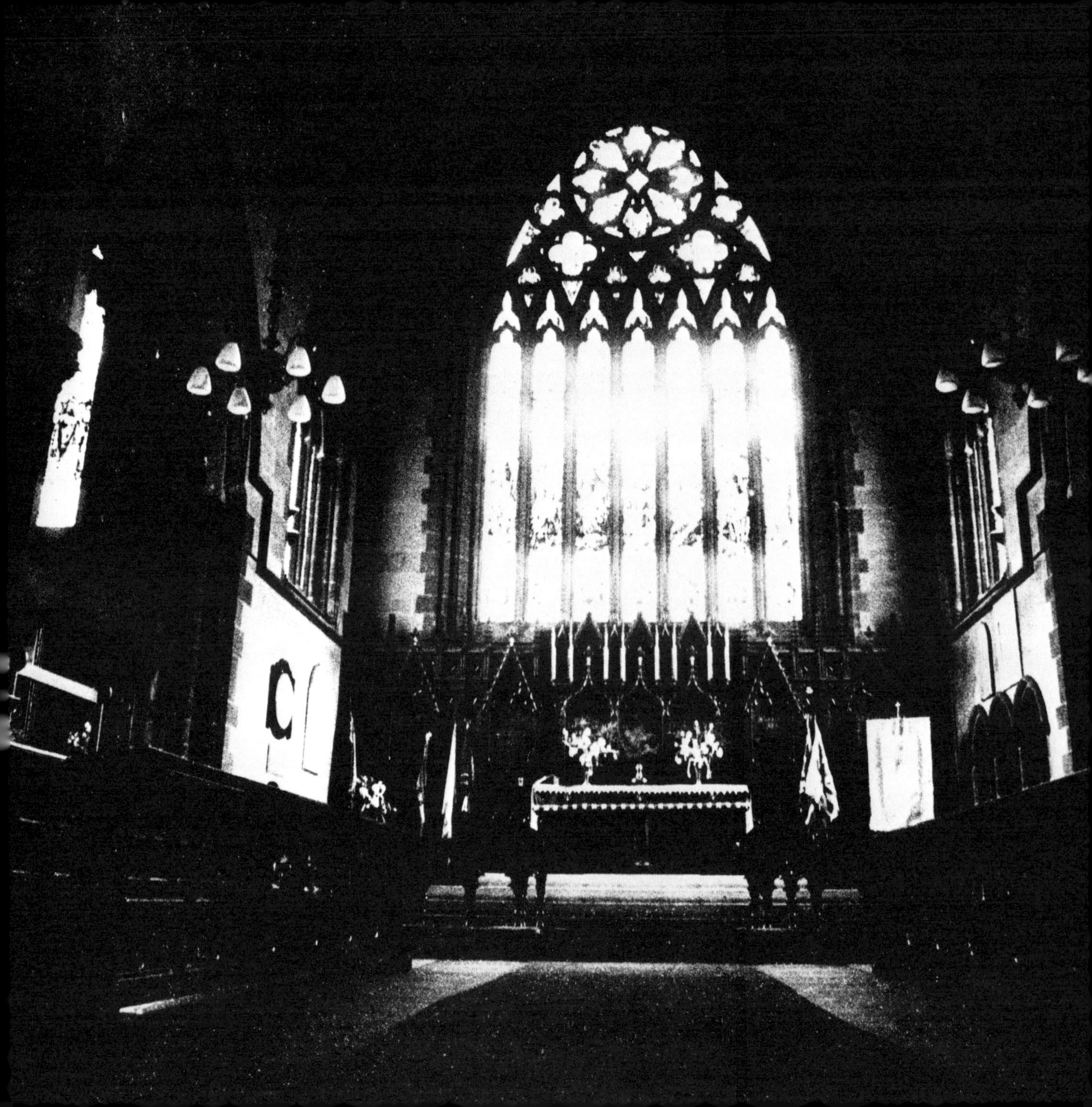

Church, Castle and Borough

Medieval England was divided into manors, and we have seen that Newcastle originally formed part of Trentham Manor. But for church purposes the country was divided into parishes, and here again Newcastle originally came under Trentham. A church was first mentioned at Newcastle about 1180, when it was a chapel dependent on Trentham Priory, but before 1297 it was transferred to Stoke, and remained a chapel of Stoke until 1807. Why did it take so long to become a parish church? By the twelfth century the parish system was well established, and a rector stood to lose valuable fees (for baptisms, marriages, burials etc) if a daughter chapel became a parish church. Thus St Giles' at Newcastle (like the churches of Congleton and other new towns) long remained only a chapel.

The church must have been a large building almost from the start, judging from the size of the thirteenth century tower which still survives. But we know very little about the rest of the church, as it was entirely rebuilt in 1720–21 and again in 1876. All that is left of it is a stone effigy from a medieval tomb, and a medieval oak lectern, which originally did duty as a roof carving. The church was not just used for prayers and services, but was in early times a kind of meeting hall and community centre as well. It is said to have been the townsmen's meeting place before the first Guild Hall was built, and the place where the borough court was held and the common lands allotted: against its walls were erected the earliest stalls for the sale of bread and meat, and nobody was shocked by this because religion was then more integrated with daily life.

Concern for the doctrine of Purgatory in the late middle ages introduced new practices in devotion: three or four chantries were founded at altars in the church, at which masses were sung for the founders and their benefactors, in an attempt to shorten their time in Purgatory. In addition, the crafts in the town probably held regular services there with masses for their deceased members; certainly the butchers did so. In 1510 they agreed to make a banner and to keep a 10 pound wax candle burning before an image of the Virgin. But all of these observances were abolished at the Reformation, and the endowments of the chantries were confiscated by the king in 1548, when prayers for the dead were forbidden. Although there is no definite record, there is a possibility that one of the chantry priests had run a school for the town as a sparetime occupation, and so education as well as religious observance may have been put at risk. The borough is not known to have paid for a schoolmaster until 1565, perhaps because until then it had been a church responsibility.

There was also a Dominican Priory (Blackfriars) in the town, founded before 1277 on a site at the southern end of what is now Friars Street. A record of a royal gift to them in that year shows that the Friars numbered at least 20. In contrast to the monks and nuns of the older orders, nearly all of whom continued to live in enclosed orders, the Dominicans who came to England in 1221, like other early groups of Friars undertook a popular religious mission, setting up priories in nearly all towns of any size, involving themselves in preaching and work among lay folk. The Newcastle friars were popular with the kings and the Dukes of Lancaster, and received many gifts and privileges. On one occasion, in 1471, the Friary was the location for a Provincial Chapter, when Blackfriars from all over southern and midland England met there. But it was never a very important friary, and little is recorded of it except for its end. It was suppressed by the government in 1538, along with all other English friaries. At Newcastle the royal agent was the Bishop of Dover, a former friar himself, and a specialist in the farce of persuading the unhappy friars to make a 'voluntary surrender' to the crown. He described the priory as 'all in ruin, and a poor house, the choir leaded and the cloister lead ready to fall down, the rest slate and shingle.'

Besides the church and priory, there was St Mary's Chapel, which probably served the castle garrison, and which was also closed during the Reformation. It was once called St Mary's beyond the Water, and seems to have stood near the Higherland. There was also a Hospital of St John or St Eloy on the edge of the town (in fact, in Newcastle Lane inside the present Stoke boundary). Like most other medieval 'hospitals',

From at least the mid-thirteenth century, a substantial church has existed on the present St Giles' site. The eastern end of the church here shown is entirely the work of Sir George Gilbert Scott who started work exactly a hundred years ago. Worship on the site however has taken place for at least 700 years.

it was probably built as an almshouse to shelter the sick or the poor, for there were then no hospitals in our modern sense of the word. It appears in records spasmodically between 1409 and 1590, but seems even by 1409 no longer to have sheltered any poor.

The main secular building in Newcastle, corresponding to the church and priory was of course the castle. It was not part of the borough but formed a 'tongue' of Newcastle manor projecting into the town. Even when the manor disintegrated, this area remained under separate jurisdiction and was not incorporated into the borough until 1875. It passed out of royal hands in 1267, when King Henry III gave it to his younger son Edmund. This made a considerable difference to the townspeople, for their new lords, the Earls (later Dukes) of Lancaster, though of royal blood, were not always on good terms with their kingly relations. The earls were, however, more powerful in the rural manor of Newcastle than in the town which was acquiring some rights of self government. In 1293 Earl Edmund claimed no rights in the borough except his lordship and an annual rent of 40 marks (£26 13s 4d) admittedly a very large sum. But in the manor of Newcastle he still enjoyed the extensive rights of frankpledge (holding court and supervising the popular militia), free warren (hunting), infangenthef (the right to hang thieves caught red handed), gallows, and wayf (the right to impound stray animals?).

Nothing definite is recorded about the earl's gallows, but Robert Plot later recorded a tradition that criminals were hanged at Gallows Field.

Only the tower is left of the medieval church of St Giles. Built of local red sandstone in the thirteenth century, it still dominates the oldest part of the town.

Edmund's son, Thomas Earl of Lancaster, was an oppressive landlord who increased rents to finance his opposition to the king, his cousin. At Newcastle he increased the borough rent by 50 per cent, to £40, a huge sum. Eventually he led a rebellion in 1322, in which he was captured and executed. Some of his supporters in arms came from Knutton; none were known to have come from Newcastle, but the town was certainly involved in the troubles before the rebellion. Several riots occurred there on market days in 1320, including the occasion when an armed band from Congleton raided the market stalls. It is significant that the town jury did not complain of these doings until 1323, when Thomas was dead. But although the Manor and Castle were forfeit to the king because of the earl's treason, he did not keep them, but granted them back to his widow. The most famous owner of the castle later in the century was John of Gaunt, Duke of Lancaster and King of Castile, and lord of Newcastle from 1362 to 1399. Like Earl Thomas he was a national figure with vast estates, and does not often seem to have visited the town. He did have the castle repaired and made more habitable, but probably for his local officials rather than himself.

When John of Gaunt died, his exiled son Henry of Bolingbroke invaded England and seized the crown. Thereafter the Duchy of Lancaster estates were united to the Crown, although they have always continued to be administered separately. Under the Lancastrian and Yorkist kings the castle continued to be maintained, but no repairs are recorded after 1480, probably because the king had many other castles and residences and no longer needed it. In any case, with the changing nature of warfare (artillery was gradually coming in) and the more peaceful state of the country, castles were less necessary. When John Leland visited the town in Henry VIII's reign, he reported that 'All the castle is down, save one great tower'. Some of the older houses in the town centre have red sandstone foundations, perhaps of stone pillaged from the castle.

It may be pleasanter to take leave of the castle, not with its destruction, but with a romantic and loving account written even later, after 1610, but based on old memories handed down of what it had been like in its heyday. The unknown Jacobean writer tells us that 'There be many that need be told what John of Gaunt's Newcastle was, and will sore lament it now is not, to give the needy sojourner largesse of bread, beef and beer. Our grandames do say that their grandames did delight to tell what it had been, and how well it was counted off before their day; although they say only of it what they had been told; as how that the New Castle was no more nor 150 paces from south to north, but well nigh two hundred from east to west; and had two transepts and four bays with dungeon tower of twenty paces square, which rose in three stories of the full height of seventy feet; that it did stand over all the knoll in the midst of the picturesque vale and gentle rising hills, very delightful and rich in pasture and woodlands, and to the west and north remnants of diverse parks belonging. A low portal, and not well lighted passage, did admit to the hall, very large and spacious, with roof lofty, and painted with devices, gallery for the minstrels and the walls clothed with gear of warfare, helmets, coats of mail armour, buff jerkins, like shirts, and such like doublets. Wending a gloomy staircase did lead to the state rooms and bed chamber of the Prince, and other on the upper for company. The Drawbridge to the north did approach into the Court, ninety paces in length, with thirty in the width, and south and west were two lesser. The walls outer had good buttresses to the height of thirty feet and the whole was more fit as a stately comfortable dwelling than as a fortress of defence, because of the rising lands south and east. It almost now is all carried away, and Master Sneyde doth hold the ground, and the moat and the mills.'

The surviving medieval lectern at St Giles' depicts a pelican pecking its breast to feed its young with its own blood. This legend about the bird was a popular symbol for Christ and His Crucifixion. Hence the lectern is inscribed in Latin, 'Thus Christ loved us'.

28

This medieval effigy, clothed in a long robe with the left hand clasping what may be a sword was recovered in 1848. It is so weathered that identification is impossible. Pape thought it was the figure of a priest—others that it represented an unknown medieval knight.

But while the castle gradually fell into decay, the town to which it had given rise continued to flourish. In 1235 Henry III had granted its traders a Gild Merchant, through which they could govern their own commercial affairs, and in 1251 he gave them their first rights of political self-government, the right to collect all the dues owing to the King, paying him instead a lump sum of 40 marks (£26 13s 4d), the sum that they later paid to the Earls of Lancaster and which Earl Thomas increased to £40.

The townsmen had already begun to elect a mayor by 1251, and about this period they began to use a common seal to authenticate official documents, for the seal still in use is probably thirteenth century in origin. The earliest borough archives begin in 1369, and they show that by then the mayor was assisted by two bailiffs (who collected the £40 for the Duke), a sergeant, and two wardens who supervised the sale of bread and ale. The mayor was advised by a council of 24 seniors or aldermen. But the system was not as stable or independent as a brief description makes it sound, for small town councils were easily overawed by nobles and gentry with their bands of armed retainers. In 1408 a gang of gentlemen led by Hugh Erdeswicke of Sandon were plundering the King's Lancastrian possessions, including property in Newcastle. The constable of the castle ordered an inquiry into the outrage, but the mayor refused, saying he was afraid for his life.

The Dominicans or Friars of the Order of Preachers are called 'Blackfriars' because of the black mantle worn over their white habits.

The cross in the parish churchyard is all that has been salvaged from the Friary site.

Very little remains of the Newcastle Blackfriars, although the name survives in the area.

A riot in the market in 1320, as it may have been. Armed men, probably supporting the Duke of Lancaster, pillaged the stalls and terrorized the townsmen.

Another way in which the domination of the town by outsiders can be seen is in its choice of MPs. Newcastle first acquired the right to send two MPs to each parliament in 1354, and at first townsmen were normally chosen. But gentry wanting to sit in parliament were often keen to take over borough seats, and in the fifteenth century it became the rule for the Duchy of Lancaster to fill one of the two Newcastle seats, often choosing outsiders. This may well have suited the burgesses, for, because of the heavy wages bills that boroughs had to pay, parliamentary representation was often resented rather than sought. Surrendering one's rights to a local patron was a popular means of economy for fifteenth century towns.

Another great difference between the medieval system and today's was that not all townsmen had equal political rights. Only the class called freemen or burgesses really enjoyed any power, either in running the business affairs of the town (through the gilds) or in choosing the council and having a say in political matters. Only a burgess could run a shop, have a share in the common fields, or sit on the council; and many men (and most women) were not burgesses. But this system, which is so undemocratic by present day standards, was there because it worked. The poor could not have afforded to take a share in town government, which involved responsibilities as well as privileges. Only the burgesses paid rates and taxes, and if they were councillors or town officers they might have to lend their own money to meet deficits, loans which might not be repaid them for several years.

When a man or woman was elected a burgess (of the first 221 recorded 7 were women), he or she paid a fee that might be anything up to £2, but the price was reduced for those who had served an apprenticeship. Those who were sons of freemen, or who had performed some special services for the town, were admitted free of charge. Most had to promise to live in the town, but a few were enfranchised without this condition. The burgesses took some part in electing the councillors and town officers, although a complicated system ensured that there were not too many direct elections: the 1590 charter abolished the system altogether, and made the council a self-electing body. A burgess wanting to rise to leadership usually had to work his way up a prescribed 'ladder' of office, becoming first a church warden, then a constable, then a junior bailiff, then senior bailiff, and finally mayor. The burgesses also farmed the town fields as a side line to their trading, guarding their common rights jealously. It seems that the town originally had three arable fields (later increased to six), large open areas without hedges, cultivated in strips which were re-allocated every year among the burgesses, just the same open field system which was once common in villages all over the midlands, and which can still be seen at Laxton in Nottinghamshire. One field would be sown with winter corn, one with spring corn, and one would lie fallow. There were also pastures held in common, and furthermore the beasts would be allowed to graze the stubble of the open fields after harvest. Gradually pasture farming became more important, and by Elizabeth's reign three of the six arable fields had been converted to pasture.

The first folio from the surviving borough council minutes (1369) records the elections of the borough officers for that year, and also the election of freemen. The date 1368 is wrongly superimposed.

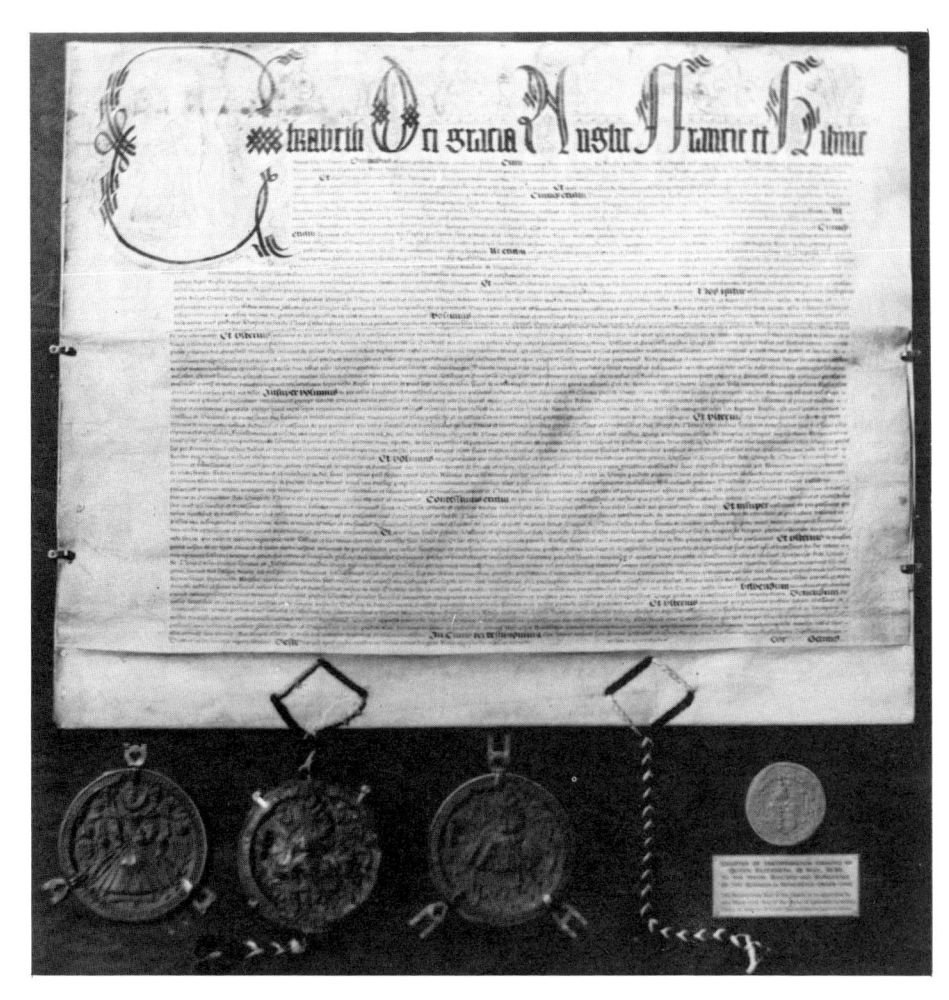

The 1590 Charter confirmed the privileges already possessed by Newcastle. It made the borough a 'close corporation', the Council becoming a self-perpetuating oligarchy.

Some of the richer burgesses acquired so many cattle and sheep that in 1590 a 'stint' or rationing system had to be introduced. A quota of beasts was allowed to each, ranging from six for an ordinary burgess to sixteen for the mayor. The six field names have all left traces to this day. Round the west of the town were grouped Ash, Pool and Clayton Fields, all names connected with modern districts. On the north east, Brampton Field has given its name to the Brampton; King's Field to the east is commemorated by King Street and Kingsfield Oval, and a small part of Stubbs Field still survives as Stubbs Walk.

Such was the Newcastle of the middle ages. It is never easy to say precisely when 'medieval' life came to end, for the pattern of life only gradually gave way to a different one. Of the medieval trio discussed in this chapter, the castle was the first to feel the forces of change, when it ceased to be kept up in the late fifteenth century. The church was drastically reordered during the Reformation. And finally the borough system of government was in 1590 given a form it retained, almost unaltered, until 1835.

The change was brought about by Elizabeth I's charter of 1590, and the man who helped to arrange it was her great favourite, the Earl of Essex. Spreading his influence throughout the county he had already secured Tamworth a new charter in return for the right to choose its two MPs; and now he persuaded the Queen to give Newcastle a charter. As a reward, the town let him nominate one of its MPs in 1593.

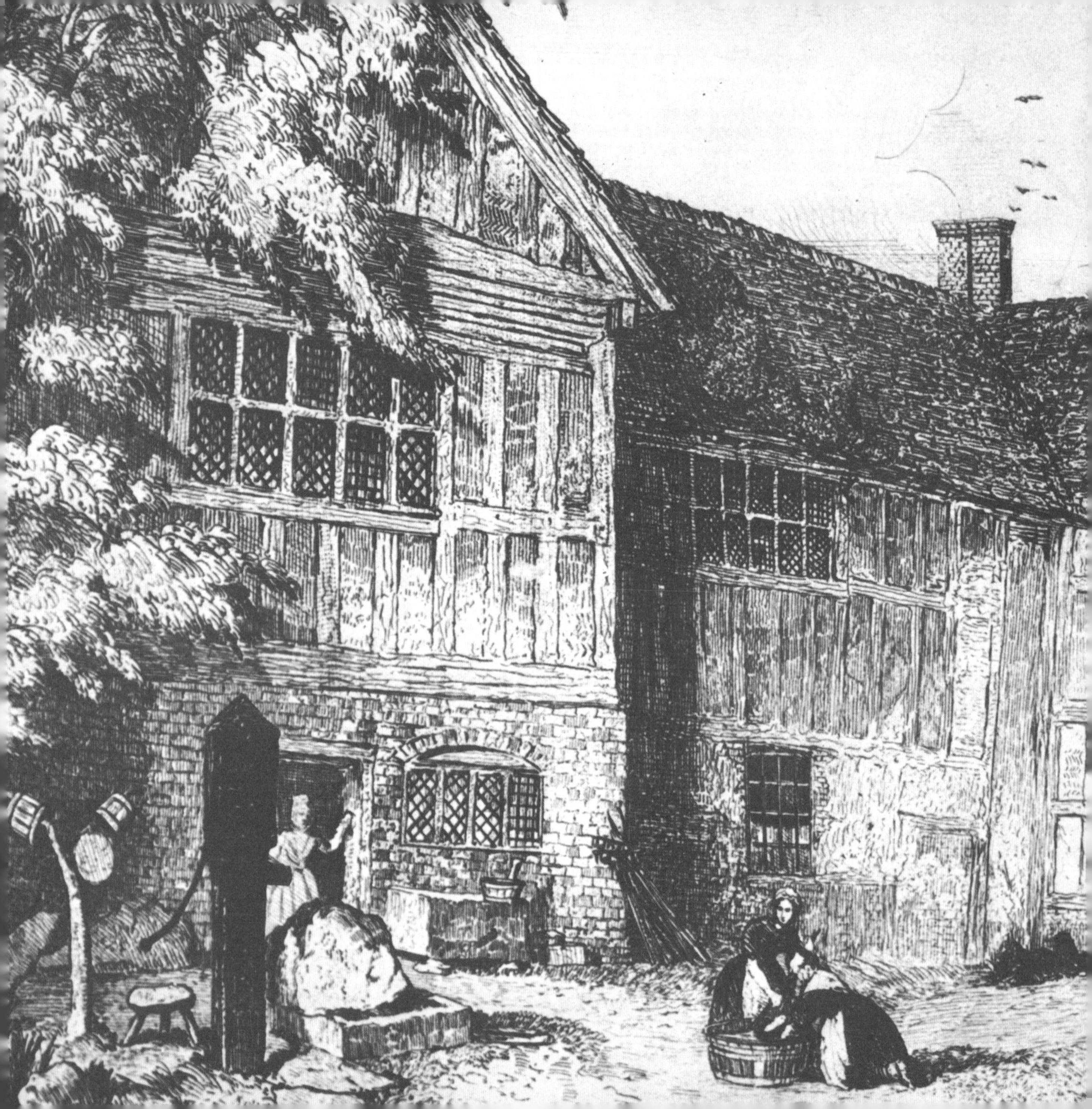

Much of the grandly worded charter really amounted to a recognition by the Queen of the powers that the town already held. Previous charters were confirmed; ancient customs were ratified; and the form of government by a mayor, two bailiffs and 24 assistants (now called Capital Burgesses) was recognised. But two features of the charter were new and important. The Mayor, Bailiffs and Burgesses were to 'be forever one body corporate and politic'. This meant that Newcastle was now 'incorporated', and could sue and be sued, or hold corporate possessions by law, just like a private individual. The other was that the form of electing the Councillors was left to the Council itself, so that from henceforth until 1835 the Mayor, Bailiffs and Burgesses became a 'close corporation', remaining in office for life, and co-opting new members to fill vacancies, henceforth without any obligation to consult the ordinary townsmen.

Housing high and low: a sixteenth century timber-framed house at Dimsdale, the home of the Brett family, wealthy townsmen who provided the borough with at least one mayor and one town clerk in the Stuart period. It contrasts well with the humble thatched cottage at Wolstanton.

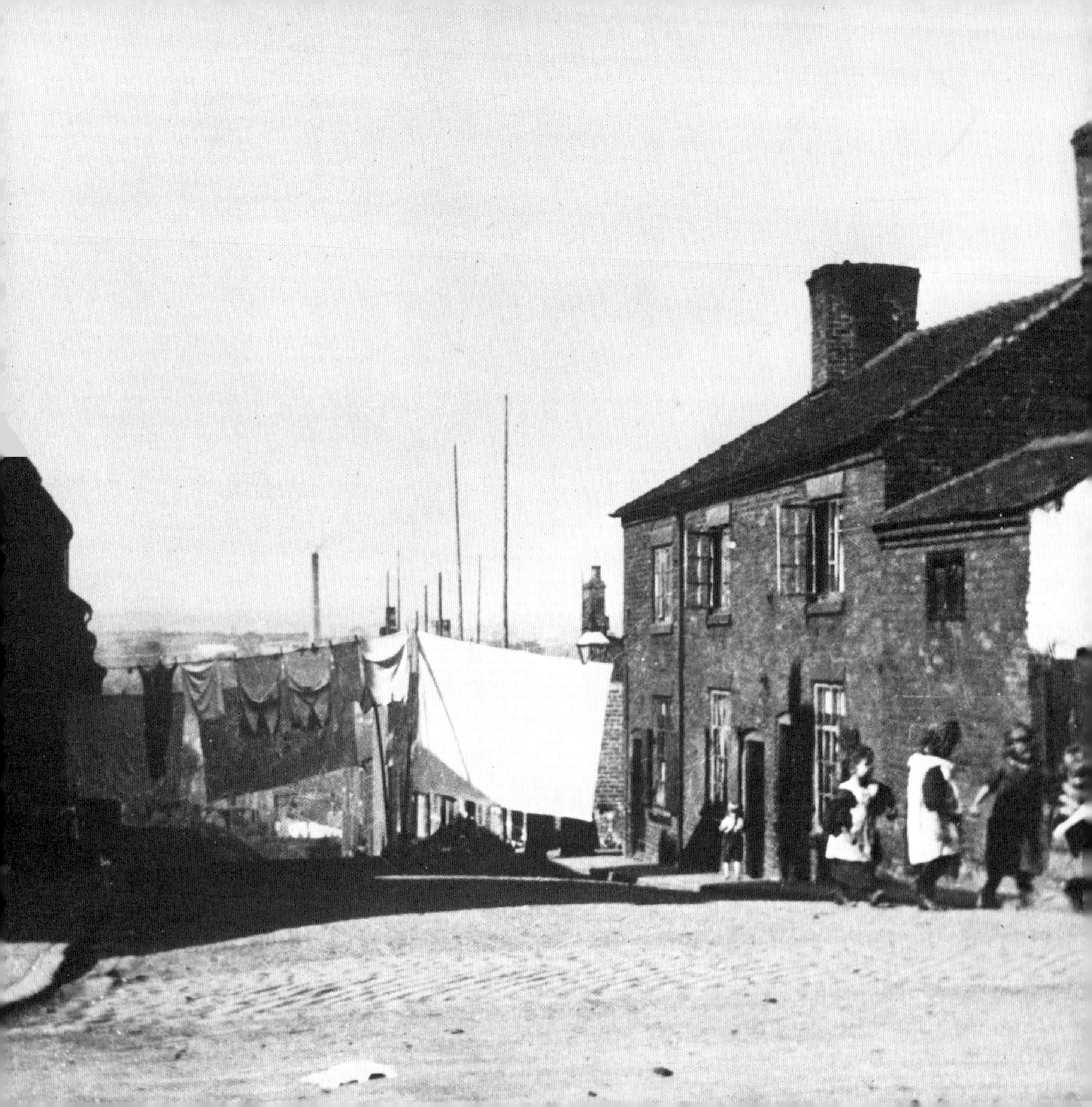

From Pauper's Badge to Social Security

During the early middle ages it was the duty of a Christian community to care for the needy and relieve the poor, even though legally the obligation remained with the lord of the manor. Theoretically part of the tithes paid to the church were for the upkeep of the poor. The parish clergy, if they could afford it, gave alms and encouraged pious laymen to do likewise. The monastic houses gave out doles of 'broken meats' at their gates. In Newcastle the church also provided the hospital of St John or St Eloy which served as a hostel for the aged and sick. Charitable bequests, which included endowments from the craft and merchant gilds, originating in this period, still had a part to play even after the introduction of statutory poor relief: in Newcastle up to 1933 there were 51 separate endowments for the poor.

The earliest acts of Parliament dealing with the poor had been merely repressive in their aim, like the statute of 1388, which forbade vagrancy and enjoined severe punishments for 'sturdy beggars'. Realizing such police measures were inadequate, Tudor governments slowly moved from Christian charity to compulsory secular provision. The Beggars' Act of 1531 authorised magistrates to license the aged and impotent poor to beg within a limited area; the act of 1536, which made explicit the assumption that each parish should look after its own poor, still relied on voluntary contributions for the upkeep of the poor but provided for moral and civil sanctions if necessary to prompt such voluntarism! At the end of the century the Elizabethan Poor Law made the parish legally responsible for the relief of the deserving poor and for providing employment and, if necessary, deterrents for the able-bodied poor. Overseers, appointed at Easter for one year, were authorised to levy a rate on all inhabitants and occupiers of land in the parish to raise the funds necessary to carry out their duties.

The records do not show how and exactly when Newcastle Corporation acquired legal responsibility for poor law administration. Until 1807 the borough was, in ecclesiastical terms, only a chapelry of Stoke upon Trent. In practice from quite early on Newcastle borough officials had controlled their own church affairs. In 1622 the first overseers' appointments appear in the corporation minute books. The office was unpaid, but persons chosen had to perform the duties, or alternatively find a substitute, or pay a fine. Most of the seventeenth century overseers were substantial tradesmen of the town, capital burgesses and even mayors. Thus Richard Heath, overseer in 1641, was a tanner; Bagnall's father owned the Angel Inn; whilst Sherwyn was a mercer and grocer, licensed to retail tobacco (which may explain why as mayor in 1637 he admitted a pipemaker on to the roll of burgesses).

The Poor Relief Act of 1662 laid the foundations of the law of settlement: any stranger coming to reside in a parish who could not rent a tenement of more than £10 annual value, or find someone to indemnify the parish if he became 'chargeable', could be sent back to the parish of his birth. Anyone settling temporarily in a parish had to bring a certificate signed by the officers of his own parish agreeing to his return there.

An act of 1697 revived the Tudor practice of 'badging the poor', that is making them wear some mark which showed they were receiving relief. The expectation was that the sense of humiliation experienced by the wearer would induce him or her to seek an independent means of livelihood and thus relieve the parish of its burden. Newcastle Corporation anticipated the Law. In 1685 they ordered that anyone receiving weekly payments as relief should wear a badge of red cloth in the shape of a castle. This was altered in 1717 to the letters N P (Newcastle Pauper). A refusal to wear the badge, or its defacement, deprived the pauper of all relief.

Inevitably a busy market town like Newcastle attracted many vagrants and beggars. In an effort to reduce their numbers the Corporation in 1707 ordered a fine of ten shillings to be imposed on anyone who relieved a beggar. In the following year a special official was appointed to arrest and punish vagrants.

Workhouses were not common in England until the eighteenth century, though some of the larger towns had had them for many years.

In 1845 the Mayor reported 'our population are only half employed and half starved having nearly lost the hat and shoe trade.' Half the poor relief went to 'that part of the population occupying Lower Street, Holborn, Green, and the Higherland'. A street from the Higherlands is here depicted about 1900.

38

The Workhouse Act of 1722 allowed parishes to buy or rent houses in which to lodge or employ the poor, and permitted the union of parishes where one was too small to maintain the cost of a workhouse alone. In Newcastle as elsewhere the cost of maintaining the poor was growing: by 1730 there were increasingly frequent references to poor relief. In that year a committee was set up to inquire into the state of the poor in the town and to consider how 'serviceable' it would be to erect a workhouse. The committee reported favourably, public approval was obtained, and on 1 June 1731 the Corporation resolved that. 'The houses in Ireland (Higherland) be immediately repaired and converted into a workhouse'. The standing overseer (a post created in 1720), a Mr Raisbeck, was ordered to remove all the poor into the workhouse and to employ them in a proper manner, acting as master of the workhouse for a salary of four shillings a week. The health of the inmates was provided for:

'1731 August 3rd. Peter Spendelow has engaged to care for the poor in future in surgery and physic and to receive two bags of malt yearly for such service'.

The first Annual Report of the Churchwardens after they had taken over the administration of the Poor Law contains a lot of interesting detail: the cost of law enforcement at the time, the £3 5s contributed by sabbath breakers to the rates, and the cost then of being a churchwarden (the account was indebted to Jonathan Smith to the extent of £73.)

BOROUGH OF *Newcastle.*

IT having been represented to me by some of the respectable Inhabitants of this Town, that it would be expedient to enter into a Public Subscription for the Relief of the Poor at this inclement Season. I do hereby call a Meeting of the Inhabitants to be held on Saturday next, the 18th inst. at Eleven o'Clock in the Forenoon, at the Public Office, to carry the same into effect.

RALPH CLEWS, Mayor.

Newcastle-under-Lyme, Dec. 15, 1819.

SMITH, PRINTER, NEWCASTLE.

The Mayor calls a meeting to secure additional support for the poor during the hard winter of 1819.

'Badging the poor' was an attempt in the days of outdoor relief to make the pauper feel a social leper. Newcastle introduced the practice in 1685: judging from the documents and other insignia of the time the badge would have looked like this.

Diet of Newcastle Union Workhouse
approved 27 January 1840

Breakfast *during week*
½ pint of milk porridge. Bread 7 oz for men, 6 oz for women.

Dinner *Sunday Tuesday Thursday*
6 oz of cooked meat for men, 5 oz for women.
Dinner *Monday Friday*
1 quart of lobscouse.
Dinner *Wednesday Saturday*
18 oz of cooked rice, 1 pint of milk.
Potatoes no stint.

Supper *Sunday Tuesday Thursday*
1 quart of broth with 7 oz of bread for men and 6 oz for women.
Supper *Monday Wednesday Friday Saturday*
8 oz of bread and ½ oz of cheese for men, 6 oz of bread and ½ oz of cheese for women. Children above 9 and women under 9 at discretion.
1 oz of tea, 7 oz of sugar, 5 oz of butter for old people if deemed expedient.

The distress of the heavy industry of the area in the early twentieth century drove many working men to eke out the little that they had by such devices as the coal-picking here depicted at Apedele in 1926.

The outward and visible signs of pauperism were to be continued. In September of the same year the Corporation ordered that all clothing issued by the town was to be made of blue cloth; the boys were to wear bonnets and the girls plain caps, an apparent reversal of the modern fashion. In 1742 the colours were changed, male paupers being required to wear green and females yellow, 'that it may be visible who are cloathed by the town'. The Corporation except for the special 'lunes' of 1630 and 1699 steadfastly avoided levying a poor rate, preferring to make do on the existing sources of income for the poor: borough charities, the profits of the borough mill, and sometimes burgess admission fees. Additionally they petitioned the House of Commons for an Act of Parliament, 'for inclosing such of the Townfields as is therein concerned in order to prevent a poor levy'. But it is not certain whether this scheme, which involved eight acres of the Marsh, was ever carried out.

Costs continued to rise. The increasing number of the poor made necessary the appointment of salaried officials. William Robinson, a staymaker by trade, was overseer in 1766 at a salary of £10 a year, but in 1772 the overseer, John Smith, was receiving £12 and 'forty shillings for his trouble in assisting to gather the toll corn'. The inevitable happened, as a Corporation minute sadly records: '1774 August 6th. Whereas for many years past not only the greatest part of the annual revenue of this Corporation but also several large sums of money raised by the sale of their estates and borrowed upon Bond have been expended in the maintenance of the Poor which at this time amounts to double the whole of the Corporation income and whereas there is now due from the Corporation a Debt of £1600 (as near as can be computed) chiefly incurred for the same purpose, and it being found impracticable any longer to support these expenses without the utter ruin of the Corporation which lays them under the necessity much against their inclinations of calling in the assistance of a Poor rate. It is therefore unanimously ordered that from henceforth no part of the Corporation revenue shall be applied to the maintenance of the poor except what is appropriated to that purpose by a decree of the High Court of

Chancery made upon 7th February 1740...'
The poor rate, levied regularly thereafter, realized £584 in 1775–6. But it had been applied too late to save the Corporation from debt.

A local man whose name is for ever associated with the Poor Law is Thomas Gilbert (1720–98), agent at Trentham Hall, MP successively for Newcastle (1763–8) and Lichfield (1768–95). He promoted an act in parliament in 1782 which, among other provisions, ended the hiring out of poor labour, tightened up the administration of relief, and allowed parishes to form unions for poor law purposes. It has been described as 'the most carefully devised, the most elaborate and perhaps the most influential for good and evil, of all the scores of Poor Law Statutes between 1601 and 1834'. There is no record of Newcastle adopting the provisions of Gilbert's Act but it is tempting to believe that his influence lay behind the reforms which led to the changes of the time. The church vestry of St Giles' took over poor law administration and applied themselves vigorously to economic management. The Vestry Minutes record the impact of the new hard line upon local and non-local poor:

'1783 June 26th. Ordered that the Act of Parliament respecting badging the poor be immediately printed and stuck up in proper places about the Town.'

'Take it poor boy!—you look so hungry'. The inspiration behind Sir John Millais' picture of Ursula March's compassion was Dinah Craik's Novel 'John Halifax, Gentleman'. She was born in 1826 at Longfield Cottage, Hartshill and lived subsequently in Lower Street and Mount Pleasant. Her father was a preacher and her mother belonged to the Mellard family, owners of the Newcastle Tannery.

The borough police force arrayed outside the old police station at the time of the Miners' Riots in 1909. The riots were caused by the worsening position of the miners in the early twentieth century and were typical of the unrest then existing in the country at large.

The Corporation handed over administration of the workhouse, also, to the Vestry Meeting in 1786. From 1809 the workhouse governor was also to take charge of debtors committed to the gaol, then part of the workhouse building. John Leach was appointed as overseer and 'Farmer of the Poor in the Workhouse' on a three month's contract in 1802. He had to provide for the poor in all 'necessaries' except clothing at three shillings per head per week.

But the problem of the rising costs of poor relief was not one that could be solved by any local administrative re-organization, no matter how effective. The numbers of paupers and the costs of their maintenance continued to rise during and after the Napoleonic Wars. The report of the overseers for 1835–6 tells its own story, a weekly average of 66 inmates in the workhouse costing £433, out-relief for 145 permanent and 109 casual paupers, costing £739, another 34 paupers living in other parishes for whose maintenance Newcastle paid £127, 26 children on the 'Bastardy List' (all girls, presumably the boys were in the workhouse or otherwise dealt with), costing £82. But neither public opinion in the country generally, nor governmental thinking, was yet ready to recognize that the causes of poverty lay deep in the fluctuations of a rapidly industrialising economy rather than in individual idleness or lack of thrift. Even before Shubotham and Sheppard, the Newcastle overseers, had presented their dismal report for 1835, the new Poor Law Amendment Act of 1834 had ushered in the age of the workhouse, the last and most sustained attempt to deal repressively with the problem of poverty that the poor had hitherto experienced.

In 1834 the Poor Law Amendment Act reinforced the deterrent character of poor relief. It was based upon the twin principles of 'less eligibility' and the workhouse test, that is, relief was only to be given inside the workhouse where conditions were to be 'less eligible' or congenial than those of the lowest paid independent household. By this act Newcastle became part of a union of nine parishes and townships: Audley, Balterley, Betley, Chapel Chorlton, Keele, Madeley, Maer, Newcastle itself and Whitmore, established in 1838.

After hearing a report on the state of the poor and the workhouses in each of the parishes the guardians decided to erect a new workhouse. Plans for a 300 bed workhouse, built in the 'Elizabethan' style, and designed by Scott and Moffatt, London architects, (the former later became Sir Gilbert Scott), were adopted in May 1838, and in June a tender by John Shawe to build it for £4,945 was accepted. In fact there were delays and the building was not completed until 1840. It stood in the Keele Road, and with alterations and additions functioned until its closure and demolition in 1938.

For a time the old workhouse at Audley was kept for old and infirm paupers, and even after the new workhouse was opened, the old Newcastle workhouse was still used; in 1849 it was sold to the Orme Charity, though in the summer of that year it was leased back to the borough as a temporary hospital for cholera victims.

The guardians also turned their attention to revising the lists of persons receiving outdoor relief in all nine parishes, for the abolition of such relief in 1834 had apparently not been implemented in Newcastle. Hundreds of summary case histories and the guardians' decisions are minuted. The records for a month in 1838 yield:

'1838 May 4th. Sarah Birchall widow of Samuel, 65, rent £4 Richard Birchall her son lives. a clockmaker earns 20s per week, has a wife and one child Harriet 26 years. Earns by plain sewing 1s 6d per week. Relief discontinued.

Mary Unsworth widow of Thomas, 70 years, earns by knitting 1s 4d lodges with William Wright a son by a former husband Joseph Lovatt clockmaker and beerhouse and has a wife and three children. Relief discontinued, her son must support her. Jane Russell spinster 78 years earns a little by knitting etc. 4 lbs of bread and 1s 6d.

John Plant 71 years shoemaker, earns 2s. Mary 65 keeps a school earns 1s. Rent £5. They have one son and two daughters unable to assist. 8 lbs of Bread.

PAWNED WITH

J. I. MEADON

1, Liverpool-road & Bridge street,
NEWCASTLE, STAFFORDSHIRE

April 1892

FOR THE SUM OF £ : :

4091

Money lent on plate, watches, jewellery, &c.

April 1892

4091

The poor man's possessions soon became familiar with the journey to the Pawn Shop. They became increasingly difficult to redeem.

The Duke of Albemarle bequeathed £6,000 in 1688 for the erection and maintenance of almshouses in Newcastle for twenty poor widows. The houses were not in fact built until 1743. Unfortunately this pleasant Georgian structure had to be demolished in 1964 to make way for the new inner ring road.

The Miners' Strike of 1912 produced such destitution that the miners and their families had to be helped through the erection of soup-kitchens in the streets. Here is a miners relief station run by St George's Church in Sidmouth Avenue.

11th May. Hannah Keen wife of Joseph 60, able to work. Matilda works at Silk, 25 years, earns 4s, Eliza 15, leather whipper, earns 2s. Rent £4 19s. Her husband is in Stafford Gaol. She has another son at Macclesfield, apprentice to a joiner, another daughter married. Matilda is a Bastard. 4 lbs of bread and 1s.

21st May. George Hassall, a bastard, and lives with his mother in Penkhull Street. Relief in the workhouse.'

year	no. of inmates	cost of provisions £ s d	cost of clothing £ s d
1839	86	100 8 ¾	15 17 ½
1840	91	98 10 3	16 8 4½
1841	103	104 2 4½	11 11 4½
1842	119	124 14 ½	22 0 1½
1845	99	99 16 2	14 5 2
1847	170	134 15 11¾	17 19 5½

By such strict means-testing the guardians reduced the costs of providing out door relief. The figure for such relief in Newcastle in 1835–6, exclusive of overheads, had been about £739. A sample quarter's costs in 1842 amounted to £141 6s 4d. Considering that the population was growing rapidly and that trade was slack the guardians were serving the ratepayers well, though at what cost to the poor can only be imagined. The number of persons relieved outside the workhouse was kept low: in 1847, one of the worst years economically of the decade 1840–50, there were only 277 paupers on out-relief, not many more than in 1835–6, twelve years before.

Inside the workhouse, the policy of 'less eligibility' led to a diet that was barely adequate, monotonous, and starchy, with only occasional minor luxuries dependent upon the good will of the master whose scope for exercising discretion was very limited. In fact this diet was probably no worse in quantity or nutritional value than that consumed by the lowest paid worker outside the workhouse, but the regimentation and discipline were strong deterrents to anyone applying for relief by the Union. On 21st December 1840 the guardians laid down a scale of punishments for paupers who did not observe the workhouse rules and were deemed disorderly:

A frequently suggested solution to the problem of poverty was the possibility of emigration. Chesterton Post Office about 1904 does its best to get the message across. How many, one wonders, responded to these overtures.

The former borough workhouse was demolished in 1938. On the same site the county has subsequently built an Old People's Home, some indication of the greater respect that our society has for its senior citizens.

NEWCASTLE FUND FOR CHRISTMAS DINNERS

1,200 Needy Families Assisted

APPEAL FOR SUPPORT

The need for increased support if the aid given to the poorer families of the town at Christmas time is to be on the customary scale, was emphasised at the annual meeting of the Newcastle Christmas Dinner Fund, which was held at the Municipal Hall, Newcastle, under the chairmanship of the Mayor (Alderman S. Myott), President of the Fund.

Others present were Mrs. D. E. Hollinshead, Mr. G. A. Heywood, Mr. J. H. Ramsbotham, Mr. S. Timmis, Mr. W. Evanson, Mr. A. T. Humphries, and Messrs. S. W. Carryer and J. L. Wellings (Hon. Secretaries). Alderman R. Beresford (Chairman) wrote regretting inability to attend owing to illness.

The report and balance sheet for 1935-6, which was approved, showed that last year the total receipts—from subscriptions and special efforts—amounted to £161 18s. 2d., compared with a total of £182 5s. in the previous year. The old people's treat was shown as having cost £16 8s. 11d., for 530 old age pensioners, compared with £35 12s. 6d. in 1934, when 475 people were entertained. Had not this cost been kept down, an adverse balance would have been shown for 1935.

FUND'S BOUNDARY

It was reported that last year for the Christmas dinner, one ton, 15 cwt. 3 quarters of beef, 1,300 loaves, two tons of potatoes, and 320lb. of tea in quarter lb. packets, were distributed. Approximately 4,000 people were provided for, representing 1,200 families.

The question of boundaries of the Fund's area of operation was discussed, in view of the removal of a large number of families owing to clearance orders, and it was decided that the Newcastle distribution should deal with all families in Newcastle south of St. Michael's-road, families living north of that line being dealt with by the separate Cross Heath section.

A letter was read from Mr. R. Holden, Joint Hon. Secretary, who was unable to attend, tendering his resignation, but it was decided to ask him to withdraw this in view of his long association with the work of the Fund. It was decided to appoint Mr. Holden and Mr. Carryer Subscription Secretaries, and to appoint Mr. J. Whitehurst and Mr. H. Skerrett as Assistant Hon. Secretaries.

A vote of thanks was accorded to all workers.

---

for such bread and water, and imprisonment in the 'refractory wards' were prescribed. The earlier guardians' minute books record frequent reports from the workhouse governor of such punishments being administered:

'1841 February 15th. Mary Myatt 22, bread and water for one day for swearing, 4th February, 12 hours on bread and water on 5th February for refusing to say grace and insulting the Matron.

1842 January 31st. James Horrobin for stealing 7 oz of bread, and Hannah Hopwood for making too much waste on oakum – bread and water for 12 hours'.

November 22nd. Joseph Lawton for taking another pauper's porridge, refractory ward and bread and water for 12 hours.

Picking oakum was the required occupation for paupers in the workhouse, as well as for convicts in prison. It consisted of teasing the fibres out of old rope, a hard, tedious task.

But the harshest workhouse regime was of no avail in stemming the rising costs and numbers of the poor. The quarterly figures in the guardians' minute books and ledgers show a general rise, with only occasional downward fluctuations. The standard of living of the poorer classes in the country as a whole began to rise after the turn of the mid-nineteenth century as they enjoyed some of the fruits of the rapid industrialisation and of sacrifices in consumption of the first half of the century. Much more research on the guardians' records for the period 1850 to 1900 would be needed to present a detailed picture of how the state of the economy generally throughout the country and particularly in the locality was reflected in the operation and administration of the Newcastle workhouse. Unfortunately the later minutes are not so full. Detailed decisions by the Board on individual allowances no longer appear, only a minute to the effect that they were approved. The costs of maintaining the poor continued to rise throughout the remainder of the century. This was due in part to the employment of extra officials to cope with increasing numbers, to the performance of more functions connected with the poor, like vaccination and the special provision for deaf and dumb children and for lunatics in Stafford Asylum. In 1842 a half year's poor relief for Newcastle parish cost altogether about £575, in 1869 the figure was £747, in 1882 £910 and in 1899 £1,728. These figures reflect in part the increase in the size of the population in the parish (the borough had 10,290 inhabitants in 1851 and 19,147 in 1901).

By the opening of the twentieth century public opinion was beginning to distinguish between poverty and pauperism and to see the existing Poor Law as inadequate to deal with both, or either. The 1834 act remained the basis of poor law administration until 1929 when the whole system was remodelled, but the harsh image of the Union Workhouse remained in the popular mind until after the Second World War. Changing conceptions of the causes and treatment of poverty and a changing political structure prompted the first social legislation of the early twentieth century, old age pensions, health and unemployment insurance, and the principles of a 'welfare state' were broadly accepted by all political parties after 1945, with the implementation of the Beveridge Report.

November 1936 saw a continued need to supplement national provision for the poor with more local and personal concern. The statistics are of interest: almost one and three quarter tons of beef, 1,300 loaves, two tons of potatoes and 320 lb. of tea were distributed to 1,200 needy families for their Christmas dinners.

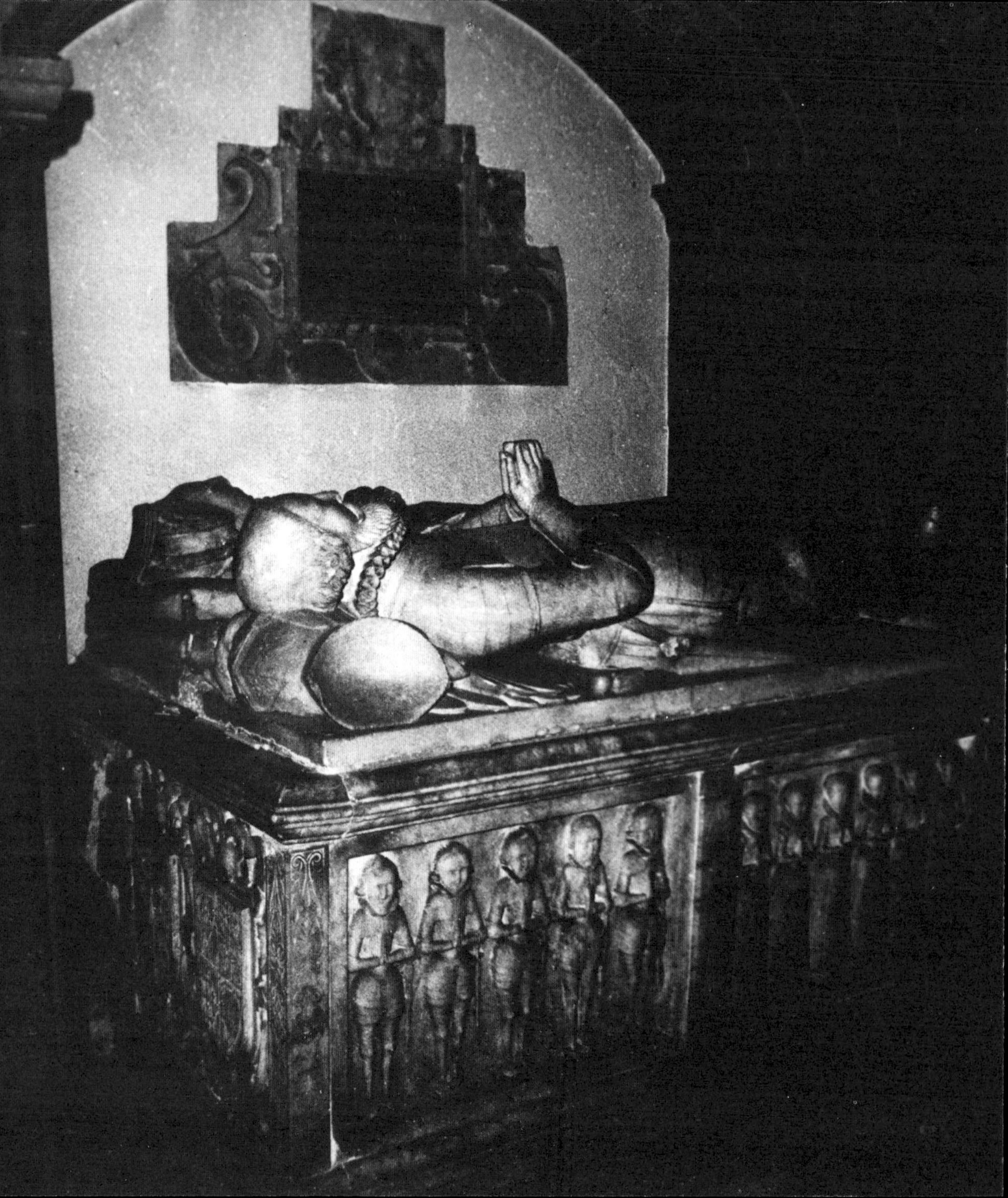

Reformers, Royalists and Roundheads

There is no evidence to show reactions in Newcastle to the religious changes of the Tudor period. The county of Staffordshire in general seems to have accepted the organisational changes carried out by Henry VIII quietly enough. The Bishops of the diocese, Lee and Sampson, were much used as Crown agents and civil servants. Though conservative in religious matters they accepted the change in headship of the church. The religious houses were dissolved without difficulty following the acts of 1536 and 1539; local Staffordshire men joined in the scramble for the spoils, and were ready to press their claims for consideration even before the suppression actually took place. In spiritual matters and doctrine Staffordshire seems to have been traditionally conformist, with only a few traces of Lollardy in the south. Yet at the same time there was no recorded opposition to the reforms of the reign of Edward VI. A few church wardens' accounts record costs of taking down and putting up roods and images in the changeable mid-century period but there is no evidence of local feeling, or whether townspeople or peasantry felt deprived of the colour and comfort of the old Roman Catholic faith. By the 1560s however the local bishops were complaining that attachment to the old religion in Staffordshire remained strong. The endeavour to enforce the Elizabethan settlement of religion met with passive resistance from numerous areas in the county where the presence of a local squire and landowner of Catholic persuasion provided a centre around which local Catholics could cluster with some degree of protection.

In the Newcastle area however there is evidence of Puritan sympathies by the seventeenth century, particularly amongst the Mainwarings of Whitmore. Episcopal visitations reveal evidence of Puritanism elsewhere in the locality, thus the Vicar of Wolstanton, in 1629, was charged with refusing to wear a surplice, and in 1628 the Newcastle Corporation decreed that church bells were to be used only sparingly. Certainly by the Civil War period the town was being served by Presbyterian preachers, and this continued during the Interregnum. George Longe, a man of strong Non-conformist views was ejected from the curacy of St Giles' after the Restoration.

Newcastle sources throw little light on the causes of the Civil War, still a subject of controversy among historians, nor is there much material to help show why men chose to support either King or Parliament. An explanation of the outbreak of the Civil War exclusively in terms of political and constitutional conflict has been found inadequate by many historians, who argue that the willingness of men to resort to armed conflict in 1642 suggests that there were deeper social and economic factors at work which caused stress and tension. Some historians have suggested that support for Parliament came from the class of 'rising gentry' hampered by the limitations imposed on them by the paternalistic government of the Stuarts. On the other hand it has been claimed that it was the 'declining gentry', hating the extravagances and financial powers of the central government, who fought against and helped to defeat the king. Another view stresses the decline of the local power and prestige of the aristocracy as a key factor in the general situation; their neglect by, and alienation from, the monarchy left the King and Church vulnerable when they sought to carry out unpopular constitutional and religious policies. A related theory argues that it was in the tensions between the local holders of power and the central government, tensions aggravated by the religious animosities of Puritan and Anglican, and by the problems of an expanding population, that the 'pre-conditions' of war are to be found. It is argued that this was a society 'coming apart at the seams' and that the dramatic events of 1640–42 merely triggered off the conflict.

The present state of knowledge about Newcastle's local history during the period is not sufficient to advance much argument either for or against any one theory. The rising gentry in the locality are found on both sides. The Sneyds of Keele Hall, who had made money in Chester in the 15th century, were prospering economically even if the peak of their political power had passed; Ralph Sneyd built Keele Hall in 1580; his grandson Ralph became a colonel in the royalist

Sir William Sneade's tomb at St Margaret's Church, Wolstanton, shows how prolific the late sixteenth century gentry were. Five sons and six daughters are depicted on the front of the alabaster tomb and four more daughters decorate the eastern end. The figure of Sir William's wife who accompanies him has been mutilated.

A principal source of the religious changes of the sixteenth century was the new concern to govern religious practice according to the Bible. The 'Breeches' Bible of 1560 here illustrated is so called because of the decent extent of the clothes that Adam and Eve made for themselves in Genesis 3 v7 in this translation.

of Esai.   lxxvi.

ng in my courtes, who hath required this
your handes?

Offer me no mo oblations, for it is but lost
bour: incense is an abominable thyng vn-
me, I may not alway with your newe
moones, your sabbothes and solempne mee-
nges, your solempne assemblies are wicked.

I hate your newe moones, and appointed
astes, euen from my very hart, they make
e weery, I can not abyde them.

When you holde out your handes, I wyl
me myne eyes from you: and though ye
ake many prayers, yet I wyl heare no-
ng at al, seeyng your handes are ful of
ood.

Wasshe you, make you cleane, put away
ur euyl thoughtes out of my syght: cease
m dooyng of euyl,

Learne to doo wel, apply your selues to
uitie, deliuer the oppressed, helpe the father-
se to his ryght, let the widdowes complaint
ome before you:

And then goe to, sayth the Lorde, Let vs
ke togeather: though your sinnes be as
as scarlet, they shalbe as whyte as snowe:
d though they were lyke purple, they shal-
as whyte as wool.

If ye be wyllyng and obedient, ye shal eate
e good of the lande:

But if ye be obstinate and rebellious, ye
albe deuoured with the Swoorde: for the
outh of the Lorde hath spoken it.

Howe happeneth it then that the ryghte-
s citie which was ful of equitie, is become
faythful as a whoore? Ryghteousnesse

22 Thy siluer is turned to drosse, & thy wine
mixt with water.

23 Thy princes are wicked, and companions
of theeues: they loue gyftes altogeather, and
gape for rewardes: As for the fatherlesse they
helpe hym not to his ryght, neyther wyl they
let the wyddowes causes come before the.

24 Therefore sayth the Lorde God of hostes,
the mightie one of Israel: Ah, I must ease
me of myne enimies, and auenge me of mine
aduersaries:

25 And I shal lay my hande vpon thee, and
purely purge away thy drosse, & take away
al thy tinne:

26 And set thy iudges agayne as they were
sometyme, and thy senatours as they were
from the beginning: and then thou shalt be
called the righteous citie, the faythful citie.

27 Sion shalbe redeemed with equitie, and
her conuertes with righteousnesse.

28 But the transgressours, and the vngodly, &
and suche as forsake the Lorde, shal altogeather be vtterly destroyed.

29 For ye shalbe confounded for the trees
whiche ye haue desyred: and ye shalbe asha-
med of the gardens that ye haue chosen.

30 For ye shalbe as a tree whose leaues are
fallen away, and as a garden that hath no
moystnesse.

31 And the very strong one of your idols shalbe
as towe, & the maker of it as a sparkle of fire,
and they shal both burne togeather, and no
man quenche them.

The.ij. Chapter.

1 A prophecie of Christe and his kingdome. 12 Pryde, couetousnesse, superstition, and ido-
latrie are reproued. 17 Gods terrible iudgement agaynst these.

He selfe same woord that
Esai the sonne of Amos
sawe vpon Iuda & Hie-
rusalem.

And this shal come
to passe in the later dayes:
b hyl of the Lordes house
shalbe prepared in the height of the moun-
tynes, and shalbe higher then the hilles, and
nations shal preasse vnto hym.

nd a multitude of people shal goe, spea-
ng thus one to another, Comme, let vs as-
nde to the hyl of the Lorde, to the house of
e God of Jacob, and he wyl instruct vs of
s wayes, and we wil walke in his pathes:
out of Sion shal come a lawe, and the
oorde of the Lorde from Hierusalem:
nd shal geue sentence among the heathen,
d shal reforme the multitude of people:

they shal breake their swoordes also into
mattockes, and their speares to make sithes:
And one people shal not lift vp a weapon a-
gaynst another, neyther shal they learne to
fight from thencefoorth.

5 Comme ye, O house of Jacob, and let vs
walke in the light of the Lorde:

6 For thou hast forsaken thy people the house
of Jacob, (b) because they be replenyshed
with euyls from the east, and with sorcerers
like the Philistines, and in strange chyldren
they thinke them selues to haue yenough.

7 Their lande is ful of siluer and golde, neyther is there any ende of their treasure: their
lande is also ful of horses, and no ende is there
of their charrettes.

8 Their lande also is ful of vayne gods, and
before the woorke of their owne handes they
haue bowed them selues, yea euen before the
thing

Kkk iiij

The restored Keele Hall that Plot recognized in the 1680s as 'the fair Mansion of the Worshipfull and judicious William Sneyd Esq', had been plundered during the Civil War when the Sneyds garrisoned it on behalf of the king. Plot seemed more interested in the making of frying-pans at the adjacent forge.

army during the Civil War. Similarly the Levesons (not yet Leveson-Gowers) may be classed among the rising gentry, they built the first Trentham Hall about 1633, and they too were active royalists. On the other hand another prominent local family, the Mainwarings of Whitmore, with their puritan sympathies and links by marriage to local and London merchant families, are found on Parliament's side. For the Newcastle area, as for the county of Staffordshire generally, no obvious material factors can be taken as determining whether the gentry supported King or Parliament.

There is some support from Staffordshire for the view that the power and influence of the aristocracy had declined. The great days of the Staffords, Dukes of Buckingham, were over long before the seventeenth century, and there was no one great peer of the realm in the county in the earlier seventeenth century so powerful and prestigious that he could sway the bulk of local opinion, as in some other counties in England. Most of the Staffordshire peers are found ultimately, if not immediately, on the side of the King. But Robert Devereux, 3rd Earl of Essex (the son of Elizabeth's favourite) of Chartley near Stafford, was the first Parliamentary commander-in-chief.

The history of the borough, so far as it is known, does not provide evidence to show any complete disruption of the traditional fabric of society. But there were signs of social change of such significance as to suggest a society in which authority in general might be challenged. Certainly there was a trend away from the practice of local gentry acting as mayors of the town. In 1624 there was a change in electoral practice. The hold of the close corporation, the capital burgesses, on the right to choose members of parliament was successfully challenged, and thereafter the whole body of town burgesses voted in elections. In the same year, John Keeling, member of a local family, disputed the election of Richard Leveson and Edward De Vere: here was a struggle for the social prestige that went with a seat in Parliament between two members of broadly the same social group: Richard Leveson, of a family that had 'arrived' at the status of gentlemen three or four generations before, and John Keeling, member of an up-and-coming family, who was to obtain his coat of arms a few years later. Personal and local rivalries may have been one of the factors in determining the choice of sides in the Civil War: the Keelings and Levesons are found on opposite sides of the fence after war broke out.

Another cause of social instability was the rapid growth of population. Sources of information about the population of the borough before the census of 1801 are scanty and unreliable. But such as they are they indicate that the population of Newcastle multiplied three or four times between the accession of Queen Elizabeth and the Restoration of Charles II. The detail of the problems of feeding, housing and administering this expanding population is largely unknown. But certainly the relief of the poor was becoming more of a problem, witness the special levy made in 1630.

The political and financial issues which led directly to the outbreak of war (the parliamentary subsidies of 1628 and 1629) provoked some opposition in the town. Some burgesses who had refused to pay were turned off the council, but the reason for their refusal to pay is not known. In 1635 and in the four years following the council paid the new tax levied by the King without Parliament, ship money, and there is no record of any opposition. The borough's share of the tax was £24.

Religious opinion helped to determine attitudes and may have acted as a precipitant of the Civil War, and there are hints that Newcastle's town council was influenced, if not controlled, by a small but active group of Puritans, led by the Mainwarings of Whitmore. Another Parliamentary family was that of the Terricks, of Clayton Griffith; a John Terrick was mayor of the town in 1610 and 1623, and his son Samuel, a member of the Parliamentary Sequestration Committee for Staffordshire in 1643, was elected as MP for the borough in 1645. The Keelings, mentioned above, provided the member for the borough in Cromwell's reformed Parliament of 1654. And there were the Harrisons. Little is

Edward Mainwaring (b 1577) was a member of an influential family who provided the borough with several mayors. Sympathetic to Puritanism (he was mayor in 1610 when the council fined an alderman for entertaining 'wandering players' at his house) he became an active Parliamentarian.

Colonel Ralph Sneyd (b 1612), a 'swashbuckling cavalier' fought for Charles I and plotted for the return of the exiled Prince Charles (later Charles II). Taken prisoner at the fall of Stafford in 1644 he died in the Isle of Man seven years later on royal service.

Major General Thomas Harrison (b 1616) also came of a mayoral family and himself served in that office. By 1653 he was the second most important man in England, but his enthusiasm for 'Fifth Monarchism' led to his downfall and banishment eventually to Newcastle.

John Bradshaw, (b 1602) Steward of Newcastle in 1614, was President of the Court set up to try Charles I. His remains were disinterred at the Restoration and exposed for public abuse along with those of Cromwell.

Harrison refused at the Restoration to flee to the continent. Captured in Newcastle, he was taken to London where he was hung, drawn and quartered as a regicide. Pepys witnesses to his bravery as he endured this hideous fate.

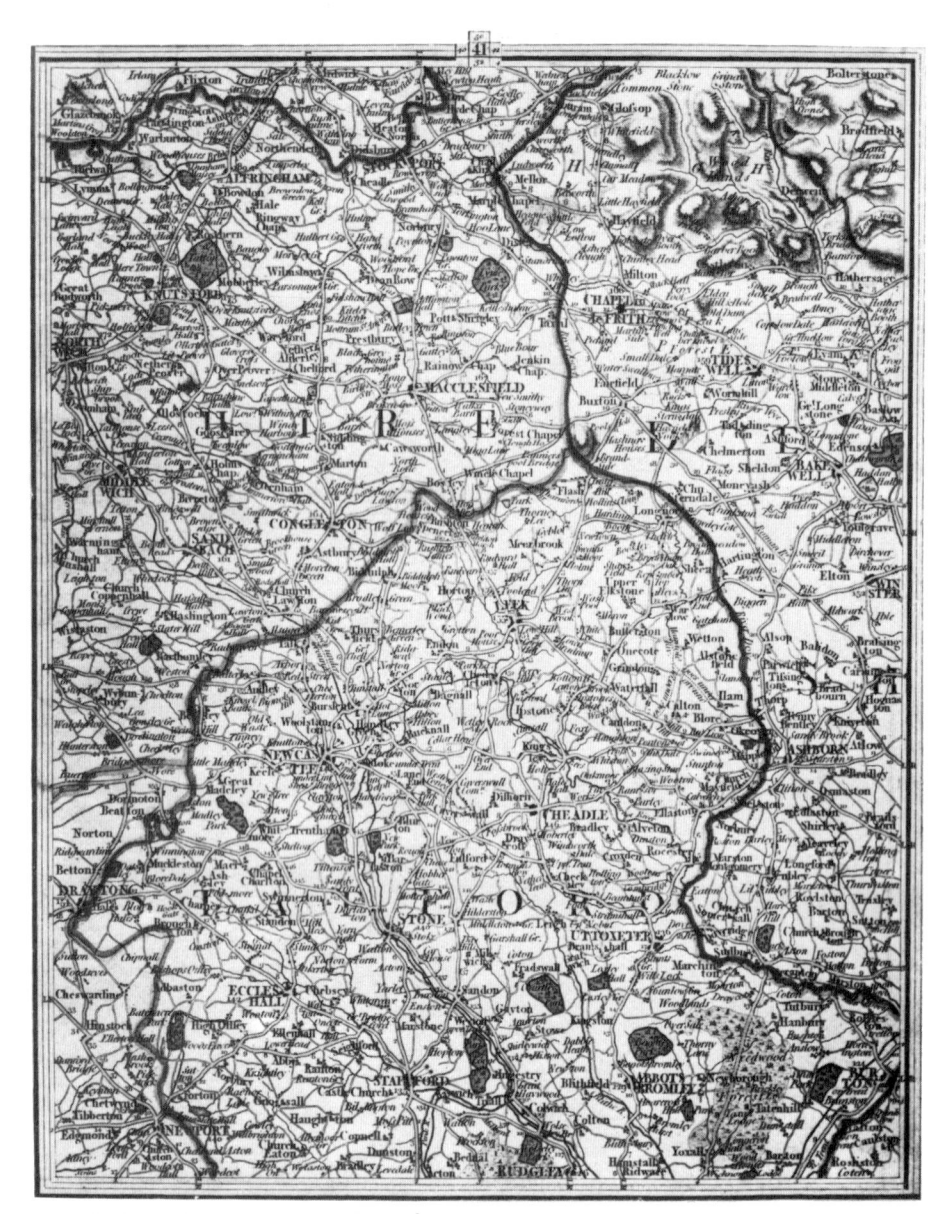

From the thirteenth century onwards Newcastle was the principal centre for the rural community of North Staffordshire. Situated on the road from London to Carlisle it was never in danger of becoming a provincial back-water, as is shown in Cary's map of 1794.

known of Richard Harrison, father of Thomas the regicide, and mayor of the town in 1626, 1633, 1643 and 1648. He may not have shared his son's views but he continued to sit on the Council until his death in 1653, as did another Thomas Harrison, and this suggests where family sympathies lay.

Seen in retrospect Charles I's main hope of winning the Civil War lay in using his immediate superiority in numbers, especially of cavalry, to achieve a quick victory. Parliament had somewhat greater potential resources and, given that these could be organised into military channels with effective leadership, it seemed likely to win in the end. Perhaps for lack of decisive leadership the king's forces failed to gain a speedy victory and the Parliamentarians, slower off the mark, began to organise themselves. Both sides face the same basic difficulty – the strong local feeling, centred on the county, that prevailed. England was in the mid-17th century a kind of federation of counties; it was difficult for either King or Parliament to win when the tendency of each shire was to organise and pay only for its own defence. In the end the victory went to that side which was first able to produce a professional army. The Parliamentary leaders like Fairfax and Cromwell found the military solution in a newly modelled, nationally organised army, and in the Battle of Naseby in 1645, which virtually ended the war, their organisation paid off.

After a slow start, when at first many Staffordshire men sought to stay neutral in the conflict, the military pattern began to take shape in the county of Staffordshire. A few people on both sides garrisoned houses, and sieges and forays constituted the main military activity in the county. There was only one battle in the county, a relatively minor engagement at Hopton Heath on 19 March 1643. Royalist forces under the Earl of Northampton had arrived at Lichfield too late to relieve the royal garrison there, which had surrendered and been allowed to leave for Stafford, also a royalist garrison. Northampton's forces encountered a Parliamentary army under Sir John Gell at Hopton Heath, not far from Stafford. Gell was saved from defeat by the timely arrival of Sir William Brereton from Cheshire, and the battle was indecisive. Stafford remained in royalist hands but not for long, for it was captured by Parliamentarians in a surprise night attack on 16 May 1643.

The importance of North Staffordshire for Parliament lay in the fact that it separated strong royalist concentrations in Cheshire and Derbyshire. So a good deal of defensive activity was put into the area, in which Newcastle was centrally situated, and an important communications centre, Caverswall House, was fortified and garrisoned with twenty men loyal to Parliament whilst Trentham Hall, the home of Richard Leveson, a royalist colonel, was seized so as to prevent the royalists from making it into a garrison on their behalf. The Sneyds had garrisoned Keele Hall on behalf of the king, but it was evidently not strong enough to survive in what was primarily a parliamentary area, and on 29 February 1643, the local Parliamentary authority, the County Committee, gave orders for its demolition. The order does not seem to have been fully carried out, and this illustrates one aspect of the local scene in the Civil War: it was a relatively gentlemanly affair and friendship and influence sometimes mitigated its consequences for individuals.

The area in which Newcastle lay was controlled for most of the war by Parliament, and in consequence the town had to find its share of the 'weekly pay' levied to maintain the Parliamentary forces in the neighbourhood. But Parliament's control was not continuous or complete and when on occasion large royalist forces marched through the county en route to rendezvous or engage in battles elsewhere, Newcastle like many other towns and parishes found itself taxed by the other side as well. It may have been in the spring of 1644 that a large royalist force under Lord Loughborough entered the town and exacted a fine of £200 for the king's service. Only £69 was collected, and the mayor, Richard Harrison, was carried away prisoner until he paid the remainder of the fine.

It is difficult to judge the economic effect of the war upon the town and its inhabitants. The

Retrospect

1590
Elizabeth's charter of incorporation granted.

1621
to 1629. Borough pays subsidies to Crown, granted by parliament.

1635
to 1639. Payments of up to £24 a year in 'ship money'.

1642
Civil War between King and Parliament begins.

1643
Sir William Brereton and Parliamentary forces in Newcastle.

1644
Borough contributes to costs of Parliamentary troops in neighbourhood. Parliamentary Committee in Stafford orders Keele Hall to be rendered indefensible as a garrison and later orders its demolition. Royalists levy £200 from borough to arrest the mayor for non-payment. **Battle of Marston Moor** – Royalist defeat.

1645
Battle of Naseby – final defeat of Royalists.

1646
Local Royalists pay fines to recover their sequestrated estates, Sir Richard Leveson of Trentham £6,000, Ralph Sneyd £2,026.

1649
John Bradshaw is President and Thomas Harrison is member of the court which tries and sentences Charles 1st.

1653
Newcastle sends one member to Cromwell's reformed Parliament.

1656
John Bowyer, MP for Newcastle, excluded from sitting in Parliament.

1658
Death of Oliver Cromwell

1660
Restoration of Charles II to Throne. Arrest and execution of Thomas Harrison.

1664
New borough charter requires royal approval of appointment of recorder and town clerk.

1675
William Leveson-Gower MP for Newcastle.

1684
Newcastle surrenders charters to Crown.

1685
New charter granted by King James II.

1688
The 'Glorious Revolution', William and Mary to throne. Newcastle recovers original charters.

One of the chalices in current use at St Giles' was presented by a Merchant Adventurer, 'the free gift of Thomas Lynnis, offered to Almighty God as a testimony of his humble and hearty thankfulness for his prosperous voyage and safe return from the East Indies, 19 October 1629'.

Corporation minutes only occasionally refer to the financial side. Probably Newcastle as a town suffered less than some country districts, whose population lived so close to the poverty line that the quartering and paying of troops and levies from both Royalists and Parliamentarians could be disastrous. Whether the interruption of trade caused by the Civil War outweighed the beneficial effects of the stimulus to the local economy provided by the war in other ways is unknown. The townspeople for their part must have welcomed the ending of the war. In 1646 the last royalist garrisons in Staffordshire surrendered and the war petered out.

But for royalists who had been on the losing side, the reckoning was still to come. The estates of those royalists who came from Parliamentary-controlled areas had previously been confiscated by a general ordinance of 1643, though wives and dependents of royalist 'delinquents', as they were called, were allowed up to one fifth of the value of the lands and goods seized for their maintenance. The administration of royalists' estates was sometimes left in the hands of their wives or other relations: thus in March 1644 Mrs Sneyd, of Keele Hall, wife of Colonel Ralph Sneyd, was allowed, whilst her husband was a prisoner, to keep and run the estate in return for a yearly payment to Parliament of £400. When the war was over, and even before all the fighting had ended, royalists who were prepared to take an oath of loyalty to parliament could buy their estates back in return for paying a fine. The fine was fixed in accordance with the degree of their 'delinquency' so that a man who had actually fought in the royal army would be fined more heavily than a man who was a less active sympathiser for the King. Of the royalists in the locality of Newcastle, Richard Leveson suffered most. He was fined £6,000 and had to settle annuities amounting to £380 on four ministers of religion in the county. Ralph Egerton of Betley escaped with a fine of £705 10s & annuities of £70.

Ralph Sneyd's fine was fixed at £2,026, to be reduced to £1,000 if he settled annuities of £50 on the ministers of Keele and Newchapel. The fines were not always paid in full. Even so, many royalist landowners had to sell part of their estates and raise loans on mortgage to recover their property. By and large, however, the bigger landowners managed to get back their estates. Good marriages and the development of their coal and iron interests enabled the Sneyds to recover from the financial consequences of their loyalty to Charles I in a generation or so, and by the opening of the eighteenth century they were buying land again.

The close corporation system of municipal government, as created by the 1590 Charter, operated throughout the earlier Stuart period. After the Restoration controls from the crown began to be added. In 1661, the Corporations Act gave the Crown power to appoint commissioners to remove and appoint corporation officials as 'expedient for the public safety'. In March 1663 the commissioners deposed 14 of the town's capital burgesses and appointed 12 others in their place. Then a new charter was granted in 1664 by Charles II, the most important innovation of which was that the Crown had to approve the appointment of the town recorder or steward, and town clerk. The intention was to ensure that the Crown could promote its interests through these two important officials, and in 1684 the town was forced to accept a royal nominee as recorder. Later that year Newcastle like other corporations had to surrender its charters to the Crown. A new charter granted in the following year reduced the number of capital burgesses to 15, added 12 aldermen to the new Council, and nominated them and the important town officials. However the uproar and unpopularity which James II created in the country by his policies resulted in a general restoration of all charters, including Newcastle's, in 1688.

So the close corporation, with its self-perpetuating and self-electing Council, renewing their numbers by co-option, remained in control of affairs until the changes introduced by the Municipal Corporations Act of 1835. There was no democracy. The town was controlled by a small oligarchy of wealthy or influential individuals even though when it suited their purposes they operated through householders of lowly rank in society.

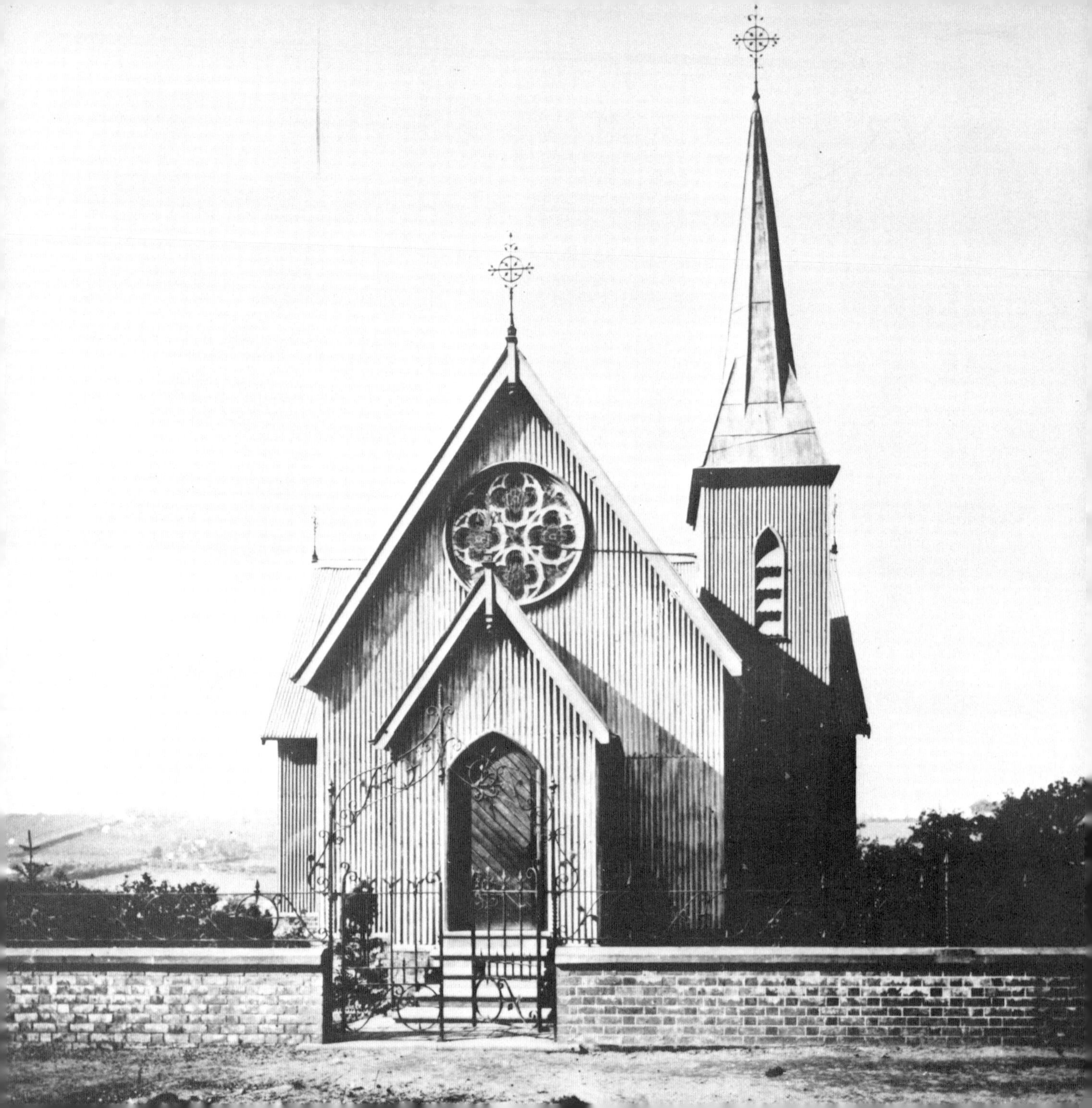

Hassocks and Harmoniums

From at least the time of Oliver Cromwell Puritanism in Newcastle could not be confined within the Church of England. Newcastle's most famous son, Thomas Harrison, was successively Independent, Fifth Monarchist (religious revolutionaries of the mid-century) and Baptist and it was to the latter two sets of belief that he owed allegiance when after 1654 he spent a considerable amount of time in exile in Newcastle before his arrest in Merrial Street and his execution in London at the time of the Restoration. It seems likely that a small group of Baptists who may also have had Fifth Monarchist tendencies met together in Newcastle in the later 1650s. When the early Quakers began to preach in the area in 1658, one of their missionaries who visited Newcastle wrote 'The people flocked in both nights to the house where I was and many of the town were forced to confess the truth, and have contended for it before the mayor of the town and withstood him and the priest who laboured to hinder our meetings there ... The Baptists ... are much dashed to hear of great meetings both in markets, towns and elsewhere, ... which is contrary to their expectations'. Certainly significant converts were made from among the Baptists including one of their leading men in Newcastle, Humphrey Woolrich, who sought to win over the whole of the Baptist community apparently with some degree of success. After the Restoration, Baptist and Quaker alike were driven out of the borough, though they survived in the surrounding villages into the eighteenth century.

The pulpit of St Giles' Church which had also proclaimed puritan doctrine reverted after the Restoration to the high church party. With the Reverend Egerton Harding as curate it shared in the religious renewal associated with the foundation of the Society for Promoting Christian Knowledge. At Newcastle Harding sought to revive the spiritual and moral life of the borough. With fifteen other clergy from the neighbourhood he met in conference every month at St Giles': on market days a popular service was held in the church which attracted large congregations leading to a 'visible increase of piety and morality' amongst the townspeople.

The preaching at St Giles' was not always so devotionally inclined. Whilst Harding was still curate, the Reverend John Naden on 24 June 1711, delivered himself of 'A Sermon to reduce dissenters' in which he followed the more famous Dr Sacheverell in using the position of dissenters in society to deliver a high Tory attack upon the Whigs. Convinced himself of the purity of the Church of England, he castigated schismatic behaviour as the most vicious of sins, unworthy of true patriots: dissenters were small-minded men, undeserving of office, those to whom toleration should only be sparingly afforded.

Under the influence of such preaching, which the local gentry willingly promoted, it is little wonder that the position of nonconformists became increasingly dangerous. George Long, the scholarly curate of St Giles' from circa 1659, who had previously been a Fellow of Trinity College, Cambridge, was ejected for his continuing Puritan loyalty in 1662. He continued to minister to Newcastle Presbyterians until persecution in 1665 led him to flee to Leyden in Holland where he qualified as a doctor of medicine in 1668. Another group clustered around the Machin family who for a century had been established in Seabridge on the western side of the borough. From the early 1650s John Machin was busy fostering missionary work in Staffordshire and Cheshire in the Presbyterian interest. He died in 1664, supposedly of a broken heart occasioned by the silencing of the preacher's voice by the Conventicle Act of the same year. His influence though was not dead, for when a Declaration of Indulgence was issued in 1672 allowing for dissenting services to be held in private houses, his widow, Jane, was amongst those who registered their homes for worship. So also did Susanna Sond, possibly a relative of another ejected minister, Joseph Sond of Swynnerton, who had been curate in Newcastle 1649–54. As soon as their right to exist was legally recognized, the Congregationalists and Presbyterians united to establish a Fund Board to foster church extension and ministerial training. To this body the Seabridge group applied in 1690 for funds,

The provision of churches for an expanding borough led to the use of the prefabricated buildings of the day—the 'tin tab'. This is the old Baptist Chapel in London Road. A similar building survives at the Church of Christ in Heath Street.

which were granted only on condition that they joined with the Newcastle group. In fact a separate group continued to meet in Seabridge into the eighteenth century. A meeting house to hold the church thus established was not completed until 1694, by which time George Long had returned to act as its minister.

The impact of the preaching of a man like John Naden was felt in 1715 when the Meeting House was burnt down by a church-inspired rabble, which the Presbyterians, loyal to the new king called 'a French and Popish mob'. One of the churchwardens is said to have 'delivered a great hammer out of the steeple to knock down the meeting house door'. The fire may well have got out of control since the nearby Parish Church was also reported as severely damaged in 1715. The Mayor, JPs and Ralph Sneyd, late MP for the county, were not only thought to be heavily implicated in inciting the rioters but unwilling after the event, to render justice. Two of Sneyd's servants appear to have been heavily incriminated but all townsmen and locals were cleared in the courts. Only two Irish fencing masters and two strangers, in Newcastle for a fair, were sentenced. So great, however, were the disorders that the government sent troops into the area and a further investigation took place at the next assizes where the mayor and magistrates, who were arrested and detained for some months, were specially reprimanded for their earlier judicial failures. Still the numbers of those punished remained small and the really guilty escaped without penalty.

Compensation for the meeting house was assessed as £310 and Henry Hatrell, an attorney, one of the members, received £100 for damage to goods and chattels. The riots of 1715 in the country at large led to a total compensation of £5,580, of which almost a third was distributed in Staffordshire, and just under a quarter of the Staffordshire total was expended in Newcastle. The heavy compensation paid to Hattrell is significant, for he had been one of the leaders of the dissenting group in the 1680s who successfully entered the borough council and was three times mayor in 1707, 1708 and 1709. Perhaps therefore the burning of the meeting house in 1715 needs to be seen as a last desperate action of the high Tories after 30 years' hostility to the Presbyterians, who were clearly men of high social and economic importance in late Stuart Newcastle.

The Old Meeting House continued to cater for a limited but distinguished congregation. From 1727–76 its minister was William Willett who married a sister of Josiah Wedgwood, whose family were supporters of this church throughout the eighteenth century. A close friend of Joseph Priestley, he built up a congregation of some 300 which, like many others, became largely Unitarian in sympathy. But not entirely so: there were some who hoped on Willett's death to bring the church back to orthodoxy. Of one possible successor Josiah Wedgwood wrote 'If we miss Mr Yates we shall very probably have some red-hot Calvinist or Methodist, which some of our flock are aiming at'. For forty years the orthodox tried to regain the chapel, but largely through the activities of the Wedgwoods, their efforts were frustrated. The contest of these years seems permanently to have weakened the congregation: four times during the nineteenth century the Meeting House was closed for a total of twenty years in all. In one period of closure the Trustees supported a congregation of Christian Brethren (a sect of dissident Methodists of Unitarian sympathies who followed Joseph Barker out of the Tunstall New Connexion Circuit in 1841) which then existed in Bow Street; between 1896–7 the Meeting House was used by a Labour Church.

The first association of the Methodists (so disliked by Josiah Wedgwood) with Newcastle occurs with a visit of John Wesley to the borough in 1768 when he preached to a large open-air congregation. Six years later he came again and stayed with the mayor. The first two Wesleyan Churches in Newcastle were built on a site opposite the present Catholic Church in 1777 and 1788 respectively. Eleven years later the Wesleyans built again, this time in Lower Street, a simple Georgian chapel that remained until 1960, though the Wesleyans left in 1861 for the more pretentious Brunswick Chapel. From 1790 Methodism was suffering from fragmentation: two splits were particularly important to the religious history of Staffordshire. In July 1797 the New Connexion of Methodists was established and between 1800 and 1810 the Primitive Methodists organised themselves separately. The New Connexion established a chapel in Newcastle within months of their foundation. The present school rooms built in 1799 were used as a chapel until the Ebenezer Church was built in 1857. The Primitive Methodists in the Higherland date from 1823 but never seem to have gained the strength in the borough that they secured in the northern pottery towns or in the surrounding mining villages. In his return to the government for the Religious Census of 1851 the correspondent for the Primitive Methodist Chapel in Silverdale embellished the statistics with the following comment: 'This place of worship his a credit to the nebroad (neighbourhood) and mainey soules have been saved and god will save money more. May his work be revived and all the place be saved is the pray (prayer) of your humbel servant, Joseph Platt, Leader, White Barnne Colery'.

Elsewhere within Newcastle Methodism the strains of class differences sometimes made their impact. In the Wesleyan Circuit there was no more famous local preacher than Sammy Brindley (1792–1874), the nailmaker of Bignall End. Some of the more respectable leaders of the circuit were rather embarrassed by the homespun theology of this ex-miner and complained about the broadness of his dialect, which they could not understand. Brindley replied to his accusers 'Well brethren if that's all, I'll confess. I know I am a rough stick, but I have put myself in the hands of Jesus the Carpenter, an' he has promised to polish me up a bit'. Brindley and his kind continued to bring the 'select society' of Wolstanton and Brunswick down to earth; they were also able to preach to their fellows in foul times as well as fair, such as on the occasion of the Diglake Colliery Disaster of 1895 in which 70 men and boys were caught by flood waters.

Methodism was not the only form in which the Evangelical Revival made its impact on Newcastle. A more local movement associated with the name of Captain Jonathan Scott brought to life Staffordshire Congregationalism. Scott's conversion led him to use his military appointment for evangelistic purposes to such an extent that his superior officers suggested that he resign his commission which he did, though he sometimes still appeared in uniform in the pulpit. About 1776 he began his first work in Newcastle in the open air leading to the formation of a congregation the following year. Scott's influence spread throughout North Staffordshire and South Cheshire and attracted the patronage of Lady Glenorchy. He used her benefactions to support an Academy at Newcastle between 1783 and 1792 during the scholarly ministry of John Whitridge who, it is claimed, established one of the earliest Sunday schools in the county. In 1784 his congregation built the Marsh Chapel which was rebuilt in 1859 and is today King Street Congregational Church.

William Smith's old St Giles', though despised by Sir George Gilbert Scott, is seen here as a pleasant Georgian brick structure built in 1721.

IN HEAVEN

William Willett who married into the Wedgwood family was minister of the old Meeting House from 1727-76. Friend of Joseph Priestley, he led this Presbyterian congregation towards Unitarianism.

The Old Meeting House was burnt down in 1715 but rebuilt by 1717. In 1926 an additional storey was added to it.

LOVE ABIDING

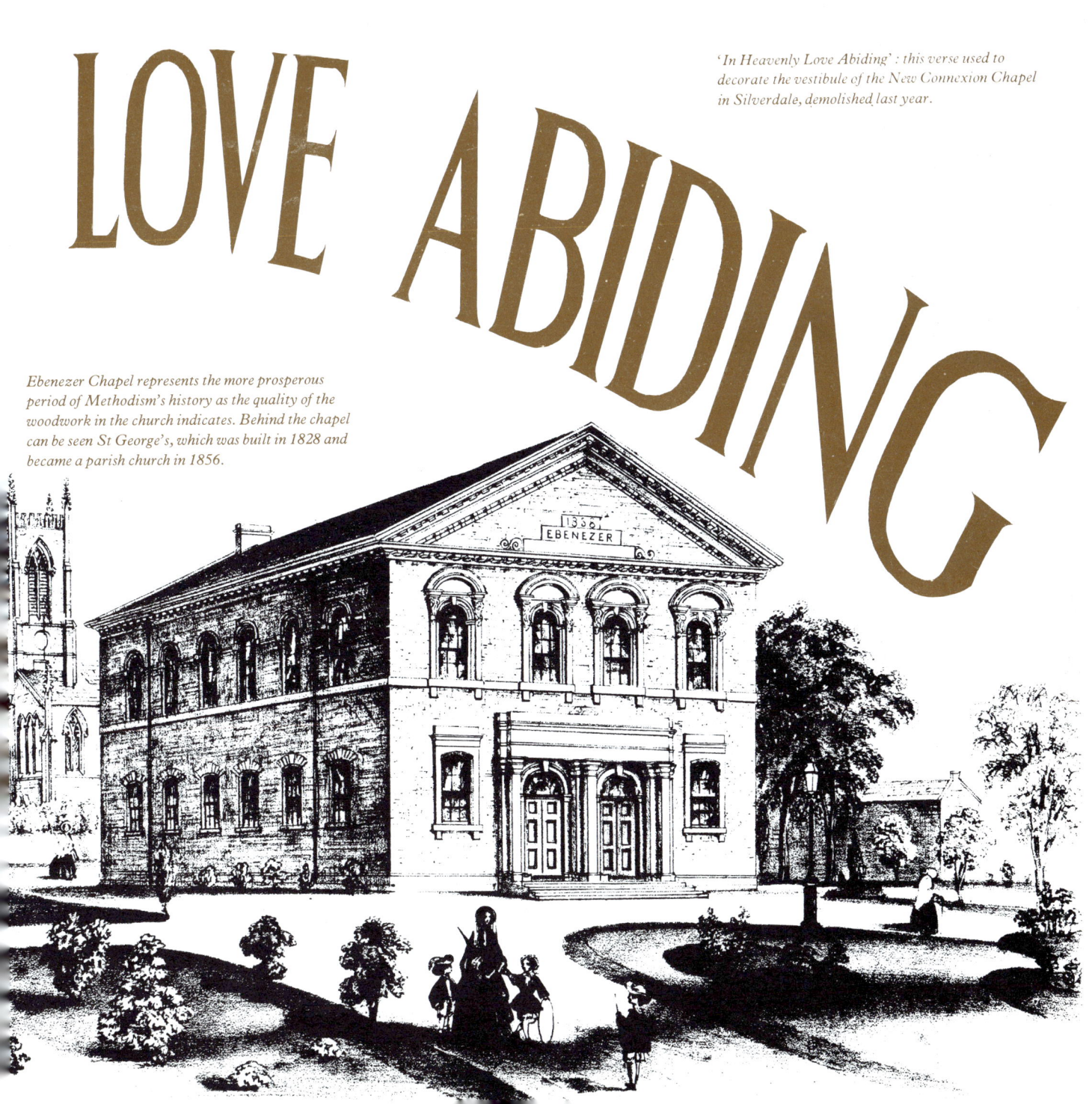

'In Heavenly Love Abiding': this verse used to decorate the vestibule of the New Connexion Chapel in Silverdale, demolished last year.

Ebenezer Chapel represents the more prosperous period of Methodism's history as the quality of the woodwork in the church indicates. Behind the chapel can be seen St George's, which was built in 1828 and became a parish church in 1856.

The Baptists found it difficult to re-establish themselves in the nineteenth century. In 1814 one of the town's brewers started a Baptist Church in Bagnall Street, but this seems to have lasted only about five years. In 1821 Thomas Thompson, proprietor of the Cross Heath Cotton Mill, who had preached in Newcastle in the late 1790s, began to hold services at the works, of which again there is only evidence for about five years. In 1832 a third attempt was made by Thomas Carryer, pawnbroker, to found a Baptist Church because, according to tradition, the cholera of that year made people more religious and the number of places was inadequate to accommodate all who sought them. Declining support led to the closure of their chapel which had moved to Bridge Street in 1854. The few shillings that they had on account were used however in 1867 to help restart Baptist activity and under the patronage of the proprietor of the Newcastle Sugar Refineries, an iron chapel was built on London Road in 1871. Its records speak of activities common to nonconformity at large. They witness to the frailty of the existence of all but the largest chapels: a constant round of teas and fruit banquets, sales of work and lantern entertainments, exhibitions of wax-works and bazaars were all necessary for solvency. In politics, the two great issues of the period 1870–1914 for most nonconformists were temperance and education: on one occasion it was recorded that the Rev A S Langley was absent from the pulpit because he 'was spending fourteen days at Stafford gaol as a passive resister', that is, opposing the government's supposedly pro-church educational policy, he had been imprisoned for refusing to pay his rates. On the positive side, Langley, like many of his contemporaries – nonconformist and Anglican – in the locality, sought to broaden the programme of the church's activities: there were tract and visitation societies, cottage meetings in different parts of the town, a 'Band of Hope' and a 'Christian Endeavour'. A 'Pleasant Sunday Afternoon' meeting,– brief, bright and brotherly– was introduced for the men who were also catered for in the Men's Institute, and the Young Men's Saturday Evening Society together with the chapel's own harriers and football team.

What is it? This plaque marks one of four pairs of cottages in Thistleberry Avenue, built, on land which belonged to the Reverend T Massey, before 1818. But who were the original inhabitants and why did they build their isolated settlement? So far the answers to these questions are unknown.

The Catholic Fife and Drum Band represents another example of the way in which the churches provided entertainment for young people in years gone by.

In the eighteenth century there was a Catholic worship centre at Chesterton Hall. Later a French priest, who because of the French Revolution lived in exile at Ashley, used to come over and say mass at the Shakespeare Hotel in Brunswick Street, as did the priest from Cobridge. From 1792–1809 a number of Catholics in the borough were given relief by the Quarter Sessions from the legal penalties which their religious beliefs then entailed. By 1826 Newcastle was a recognized mission and in 1831 James Egan moved from Ashley to Newcastle to superintend the work. Acting as his own architect, he planned the construction of the present Holy Trinity Church in 1833–4. At first the north aisle was a school and the south aisle the priest's residence. One of those participating in the opening was the notable Catholic convert, Father Ignatius. His presence was countered by lecturers from the Protestant Reformation Society who held a meeting in the borough attacking Roman Catholicism. A succession of Irish priests served the church, whose congregation by the mid-century was chiefly of recent Irish extraction. They needed not only a church but also schools for their children, the first separate buildings for which were erected in 1865. In 1892 the ministry of the clergy of Holy Trinity was supplemented by the arrival in the parish of the Sisters of Mercy who from the following year have operated from St Bernard's Convent on the south side of London Road. As with the Protestant Churches so also with Holy Trinity, the turn of the last century saw the development of a wide variety of church societies: the League of the Cross, the Catholic Young Men's Society and later Boys Clubs, the Society of St Vincent de Paul and a branch of the Knights of St Columba. After the first World War the position of the Roman Catholics in Newcastle was more assured: the partisanship of the last century was being forgotten, and the divide between Catholic and Protestant softened by mutual experience the one of the other.

Within the Established Church Newcastle finally became a parish on its own, separate from Stoke, in 1807. In 1815 the patronage of the borough was purchased by Charles Simeon of Cambridge and

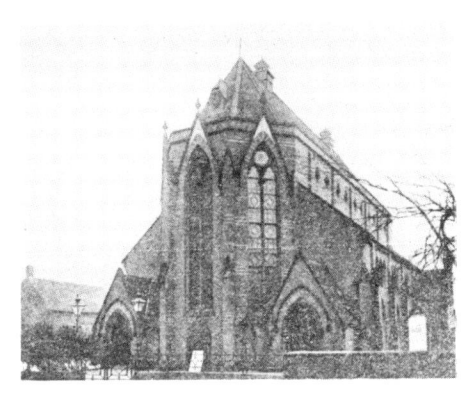

Brunswick Chapel 'a spacious and substantial building in the Gothic style of architecture with continental features', was erected in 1860 and represents the increased confidence of non-conformity in the second half of the nineteenth century.

Holy Trinity Church was designed by James Egan first Roman Catholic priest of Newcastle and built in 1833-4. One aisle was originally the presbytery and the other a school.

Lower Street Chapel was built by the Wesleyans in 1799. They occupied it until 1861 when the Methodist Reform Church took it over until it was demolished in the early 1960s.

put in trust so as to ensure that the Rectors of Newcastle would always be of the evangelical persuasion. In 1828 additional accommodation was provided by the building of St George's Church in the Brampton, the patronage of which was from 1856 vested in the Rector of St Giles'.

The Annual Reports of the two churches suggest that the two Newcastle parishes were very much typical evangelical parishes. The congregations were invited to contribute towards a variety of philanthropic and missionary activities including Missions to Jews, to Soldiers' Wives and Children, the English Mission to Romanists, the North Staffordshire Scripture Reading Association, the St Giles' Christmas Dinner for the Poor, the Parish Clothing Fund, the Indian Famine Relief Fund, the Lancashire Distressed Operatives' Fund and the North Staffordshire Infirmary, which derived a sizeable income each year from the churches and chapels of the area. As elsewhere there was concern that insufficient working men came to church, yet even so St Giles' had to abandon its Scripture Reader in 1854 for want of funds for his salary. Lack of accommodation seemed the great need: it was the vicar's 'firm conviction that if we prepared them a house of prayer, free to all who would come, marked by no vestige of exclusiveness, the poor man's church, and gave them a minister worthy of the name of the poor man's friend, we should see something like "life from the dead" among the labouring classes'. This programme was never realised though 'an Irish speaking Protestant Reader' was set at work visiting 'the homes of our poor benighted Roman Catholic neighbours' (1856). Lay visitors also took charge of visiting in the different districts of the borough. In 1881 a Bible woman was also working in the district at a salary of £30 per annum and together they distributed bread, coal and grocery tickets amongst the poor. At St George's which ran three missions at St John's Liverpool Road, Stubbs Walk, and Wilmore Row (Merrial Street), the early twentieth century saw a men's service on Sunday afternoons some thousand strong.

By 1872 the fabric of St Giles' gave serious cause for concern and Sir Gilbert Scott was invited to design a new church. In accepting the invitation Scott poured all the scorn of a Gothic revivalist on his predecessor's structure: 'a plain brick building without, and in style more like a Town Hall than a Church, within crowned up with high pews and galleries and without even a central passage'. Scott designed for Newcastle a church such as the medieval tower suggested Newcastle once had. The lowest tender was £15,000 from which £5,000 was lopped either by the deletion or postponement of aspects of the work. During the three years which the church took to be completed the congregation worshipped in an iron chapel. The internal arrangement of the new church conformed to the pattern common in English Churches from the time of the Oxford Movement. The church's liturgical tradition was however not changed. In 1883 the vicar was insisting that music should assist and not replace congregational worship: 'This I pen advisedly; for the tendency to assimilate the Protestant and Evangelical services of our Church, which we have inherited as a rich legacy from our martyred Reformers, to those of the Roman system is patent on all sides and the holy worship of the Lord of hosts has been degraded by some professors in our Church in many parts of our land to a religious musical and even a religious theatrical performance, the sensuous usurping the position of the spiritual worship and the gaudy attire and meretricious ornaments of the mystical Babylon being thrust forward and patronised, to the painful but necessary disappearance of the chaste and simple adornment ever worn by her, who is the Bride of Christ'. In everyday life the vicars counselled strict morality but always reminded their flock of the priority of the spiritual life: sabbatarian principles were upheld, the national involvement in the opium trade attacked,

A Sunday School Treat to Clayton Green in 1898; before the advent of the mass media and improved travel these occasions were red-letter days in a child's life.

materialism warned against and temperance principles championed, but when all had been said and done concerning social issues it remained that: 'Socialism is one thing; salvation by the blood of the cross, and fellowship in the gospel is another – a higher and a better thing'. (1857).

In the twentieth century a third church was added when St Paul's was built in Victoria Road. Designed by Scrivener and Sons of Hanley and generously endowed by the Coghill family it provides a pleasant focus to an attractive corner of the borough in association with the High School, Stubbs Walk and the modest town houses of Mount Pleasant.

In the last quarter of the nineteenth century and in the twentieth century most denominations have built additional suburban churches in the newer suburbs of the borough. The last fifteen years conversely have seen the disappearance of three ecclesiastical landmarks from the centre of the borough, Lower Street Chapel (on the site of the multi-storey car park), St John's Church, Liverpool Road, and Brunswick Church, next to the Swimming Baths. The scene of church relationships has changed also. The union of the Methodists in 1932 has caused widespread re-organization in North Staffordshire, with a large number of buildings becoming redundant.

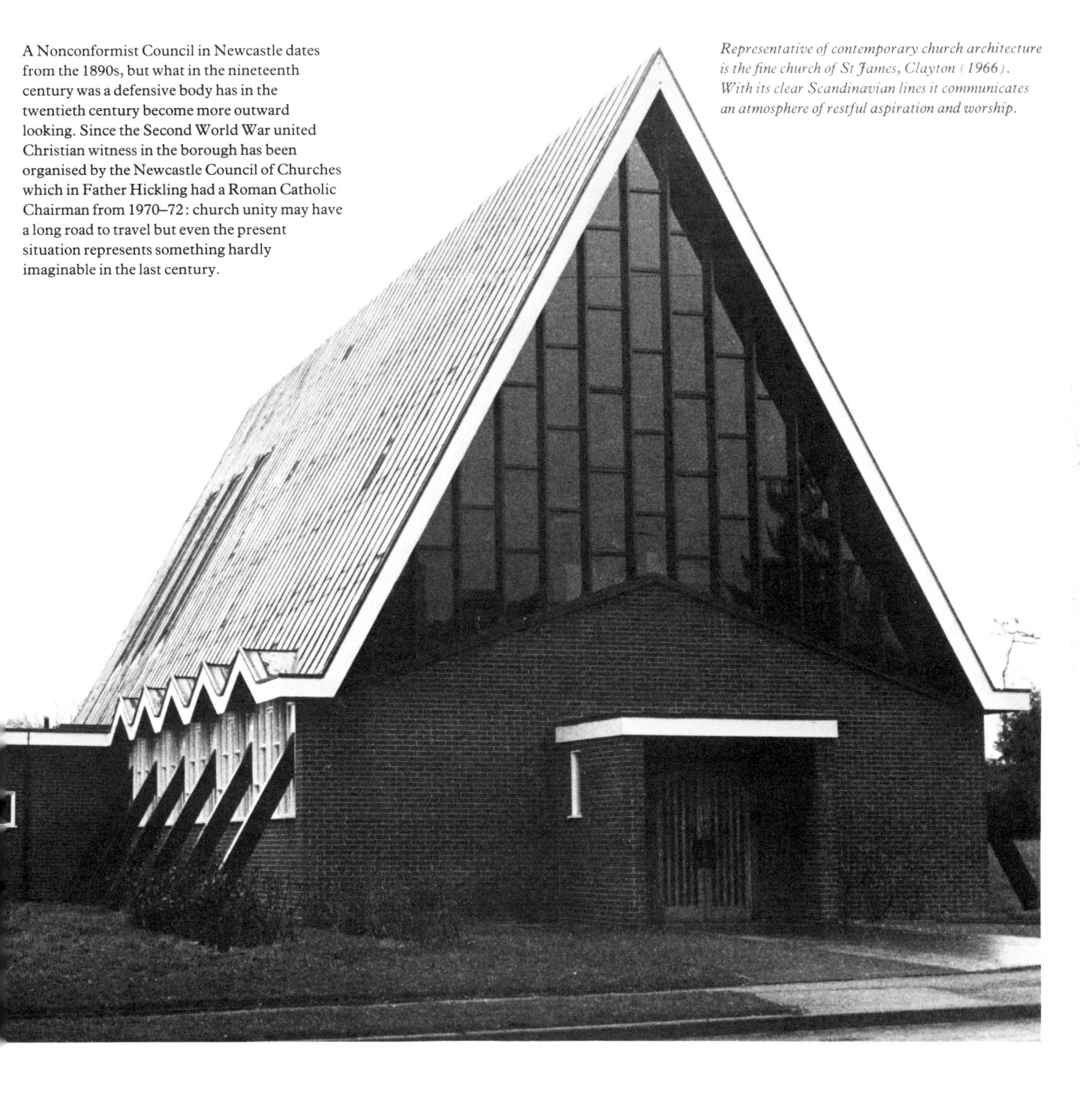

A Nonconformist Council in Newcastle dates from the 1890s, but what in the nineteenth century was a defensive body has in the twentieth century become more outward looking. Since the Second World War united Christian witness in the borough has been organised by the Newcastle Council of Churches which in Father Hickling had a Roman Catholic Chairman from 1970–72: church unity may have a long road to travel but even the present situation represents something hardly imaginable in the last century.

Representative of contemporary church architecture is the fine church of St James, Clayton (1966). With its clear Scandinavian lines it communicates an atmosphere of restful aspiration and worship.

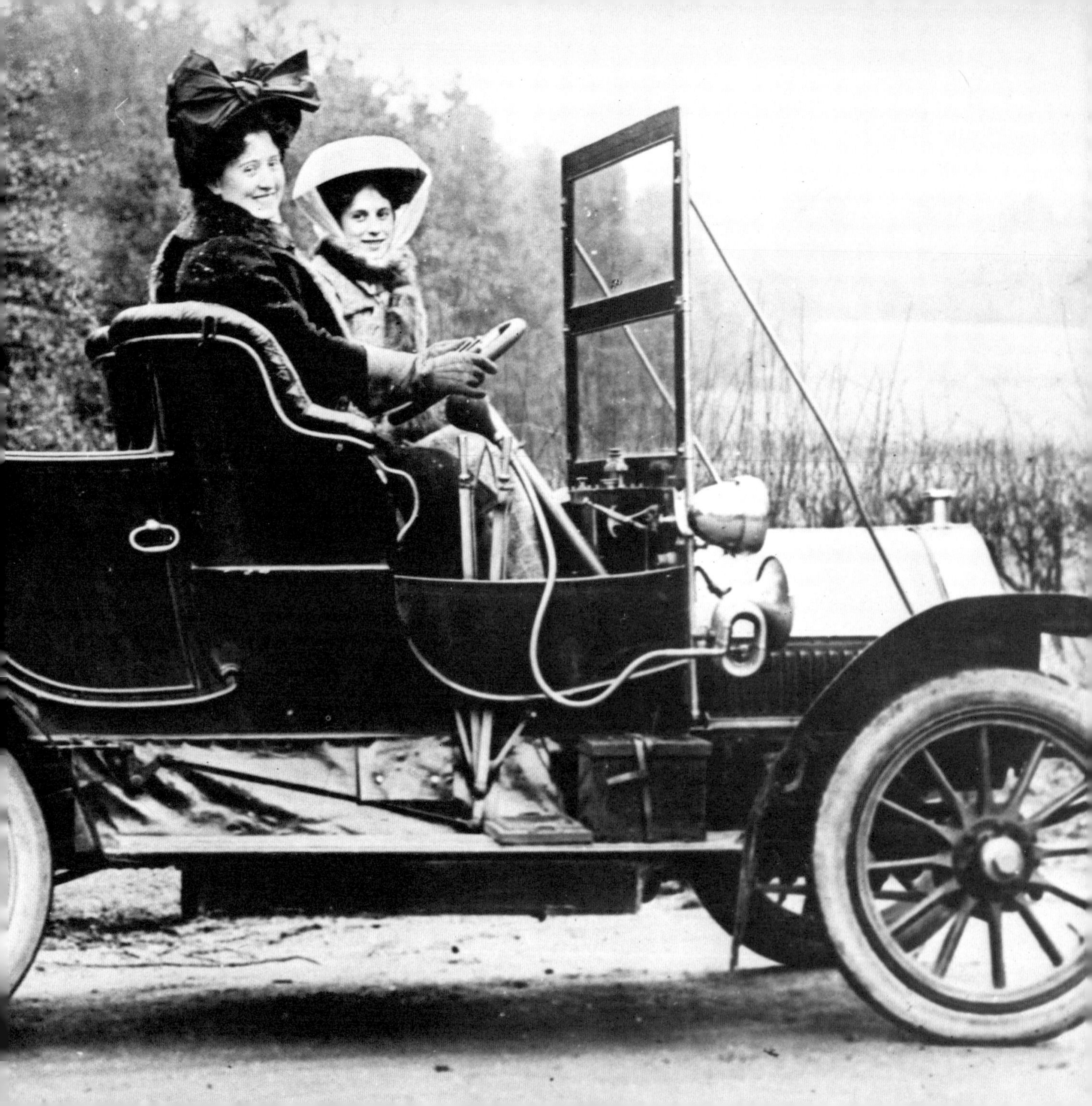

North, South, East and West

Although there is evidence for a Roman road between Derby and Rocester, with a possible extension through Holditch and on to Chester, Newcastle first became an important centre of land communications with the establishment of a castle to the north of the present Pool Dam. It was at this time that the road between London, Lichfield, Newcastle and the north was probably developed although documentary evidence for its existence dates only from about 1300. As the town grew in significance as an agricultural market other roads were built linking it with the neighbouring centres of Nantwich, Uttoxeter, Congleton and Market Drayton. In the late fifteenth century the Chester traffic was diverted from Newcastle onto a route passing through Woore and Nantwich (the present A51) but all northbound trade continued to use the Newcastle road.

As in many other parts of Britain the standards of road maintenance in North Staffordshire were very low in the fifteenth, sixteenth and seventeenth centuries and the routes approaching Newcastle faced the particular problem of negotiating the many small headstreams of the upper Trent. Bridges, either of wooden or stone construction, were in existence at Stoke, Hanford, Trentham and Strongford (Tittensor) by 1700 but the frequency with which such 'ford' names as Stableford, Meaford, Basford and Brindley Ford occur in the locality indicates the importance of crossing points on the streams. Many of the bridges remained as packhorse bridges until the introduction of turnpike roads, carts and coaches being obliged to ford the rivers.

Turnpiking a road involved the formation of a turnpike trust whose responsibility it was to keep a section of the highway in an acceptable state of repair in exchange for the right, as granted by parliamentary legislation, to charge for the use of the road. The first turnpike was set up on the Great North Road in 1663 and the advantages of the system over the traditional practice of piecemeal and haphazard road repairs were soon realised. Newcastle was one of the first towns in Staffordshire to benefit from turnpiking, the corporation itself being responsible for the trust established on the main highway between Tittensor, Trentham, Hanford, Newcastle, Chesterton and Talke in 1714. The tolls charged varied from a shilling for four wheeled vehicles to one penny for a horse and eight pence for a herd of twenty cattle, with local farm vehicles and coal traffic passing through without charge. In the south the Tittensor to Lichfield section of this main route between London and Manchester was turnpiked in 1728, in the north the Talke to Cranage portion in 1731 and the entire length of the road was improved and subject to toll by 1750. A turnpike trust on the Newcastle, Uttoxeter, Derby road was established in 1759 followed in 1765 by one on the Newcastle to Leek road and in 1769 by the turnpike on the Whitchurch road. Newcastle thus became the focus of a system of vastly improved land routes but its importance was soon to be challenged by the Pottery towns, whose growing needs for industrial transport were also met in the first instance by toll roads. The proposals for turnpike roads linking the Pottery towns with each other and with the London to Manchester highway were vigorously opposed by Newcastle Corporation, which benefitted from the tolls exacted on goods passing between the Tittensor to Talke road and Hanley, Stoke and Burslem. However, by 1791 a network of turnpike roads had been built which enabled the industrialists of the latter towns to distribute pottery to London and Liverpool without recourse to passing through Newcastle, which thus lost a substantial amount in tolls.

Although a stage coach service had been running on the London, Stone, Chester road since 1659, the widespread use of mail and passenger coaches dates only from the turnpike period. A list of coach and carrier departures from London in 1707 shows no coach link with Newcastle though a carrier left London for the borough each Monday. Regular services linking Newcastle with London and leading provincial towns were introduced in the second half of the eighteenth century, covering distances varying from about 30 miles per day in winter to 60 miles per day in summer. By the end of the century the 'Derby Fly' brought passengers to Newcastle from

The steam engine and the internal combustion engine have between them changed not only our working habits but our leisure activities as well. Mrs Beresford, later mayoress of Newcastle, is here pictured in her Ford Tourer about 1907.

74

75

Lincoln, Nottingham and Derby. Certain inns became important as posting houses, the leading ones in Newcastle being the 'Roebuck' and the 'Talbot' in High Street, the 'King's Head' in Penkhull Street and the 'Woolpack' in Red Lion Square. By 1818 about 40 coaches passed through the town each day, with ten daily coaches, including the Royal Mail, to London, four to Birmingham, six to Liverpool and four to Manchester, the last journey taking up to 22 hours. Goods transport was also organised on a more reliable basis, with scheduled wagon services to London (daily), Liverpool, Manchester, Oxford and Bristol and to the local market towns of Congleton, Wilmslow, Cheadle and Market Drayton.

By 1834, at the zenith of the coaching age, the frequency of services had increased and regular links with Shrewsbury were added. The Castle Hotel, the 'Globe' and the 'Three Tuns' had become posting inns and coaches, rejoicing in such names as 'The Duke of Wellington', the 'Eclipse', the 'Expedition' and the 'Bang-Up', had become a familiar feature of commercial life in Newcastle. Coaching collapsed abruptly with the coming of the railway however and by 1839, following the opening of the Grand Junction Railway between Lancashire, Crewe, Whitmore and Stafford, only about four long distance coaches passed through Newcastle daily. The Directory for that year advertises that an omnibus called at Newcastle at various hours 'on its way to the rails', that is Whitmore Station, some five miles to the west. With the opening of Stoke railway station in 1848, even the few survivors disappeared and by 1851 the long list of stages

E H Buckler's sketch of Newcastle drawn in 1853 views the town at a period when, with the old cottage industries in decline and the textile trade expanding, it was crucial that the town should have good transport facilities: in 1852 Newcastle was linked with the main railway system at Stoke.

that previously served Newcastle had been replaced in the trade directory for that year by the prosaic information that 'omnibuses left ten times a day from the Globe Hotel to meet trains at Stoke station'. Thus Newcastle lost its status as a focus for road transport in North Staffordshire and was not to regain it until the twentieth century development of motor vehicles which culminated in the opening of the M6 motorway and the building of the 'Post House' motel on the southern outskirts of the town as the modern equivalent of the Castle Hotel.

Although the improvement in roads brought about by the turnpike system encouraged the growth of the stage coach services, it could not satisfy the demands of the mining, ironstone and pottery industries of the area for the movement of heavy, bulky raw materials. These demands were met however by the construction of the Grand Trunk Canal between the Trent near Wilden and the Bridgwater Canal at Preston Brook, but this passed along the Fowlea valley close to Hanley and Burslem rather than through Newcastle. Sir Nigel Gresley secured parliamentary permission for the building of a canal to bring coal from his mines at Apedale to the borough in 1775: written into the Act was the condition that, for the first 21 years after the completion of the canal, coal was to be sold to the inhabitants of the borough at 5s a ton, and 5s 6d for a further period of 21 years after the completion of the first term, (though inflation caused the figure to be renegotiated at 6s a ton). The Nigel Gresley Canal was opened in 1775, two years before the completion of the Grand Trunk, but it was not until 1795 that the branch canal from the Grand Trunk navigation to Newcastle was built, giving the town its first link with the national network of inland waterways.

This branch canal, avoiding the ridge of high land between the Lyme and the Fowlea valleys, followed a circuitous course from Stoke along the Trent to its confluence with the Lyme at Hanford, then ran parallel to the latter stream, with a terminus in Newcastle near the present site of the Old Boat and Horse Inn in Brook Street. A proposal was made to link this canal with the Nigel Gresley navigation so that coal and iron-

One of the lost noises of town life is that of horses' hooves and the turning of solid wheels on cobbled streets. Gone too are the drinking troughs for the horses, familiar roadside landmarks until recent years. This carriage stands outside the old Globe Hotel.

The Newcastle to Hanley tram route passed over Hartshill and then to Etruria via Brickiln Lane, thus avoiding the steep gradients of Basford Bank. The photograph, taken at the scene of an accident in the early 1900s, also shows the old Hartshill station.

The Opening Ceremony for the first tram services to reach Newcastle. All the 100 trams in the Potteries Electric Traction Company's fleet were single-deckers because of the numerous low bridges in the area. Most of the 31 miles of the PET network was single track with passing loops, but the Ironmarket and High Street were equipped with double tracks to cater for the many services which terminated in Newcastle.

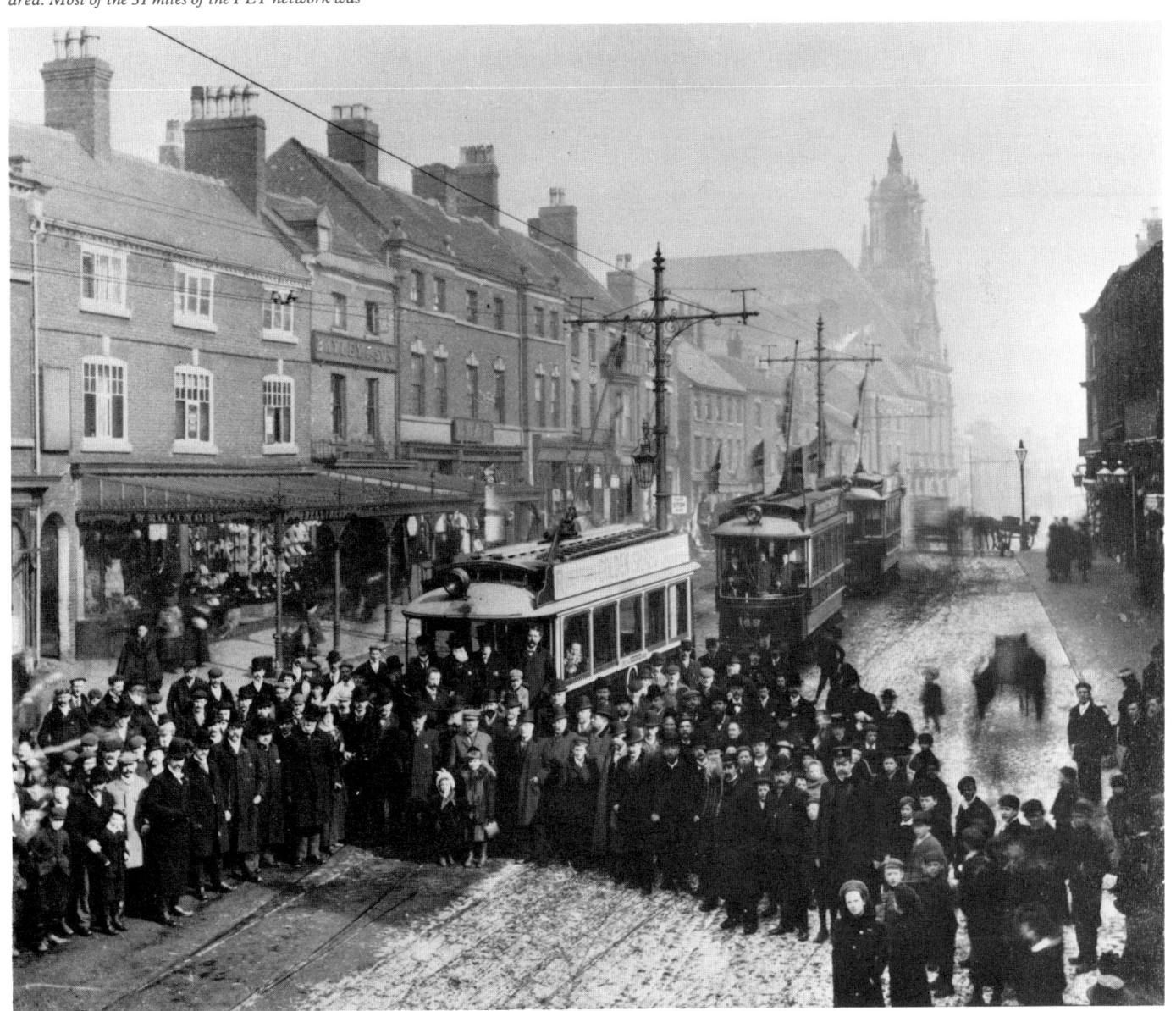

With its grand name, the charabanc, the aristocrat of all buses, brought fun and diversion into many drab lives as it made possible a variety of outings and excursions.

stone from the flourishing Apedale mines could be carried onto the national waterway network and in 1799 the Newcastle under Lyme Junction Canal was opened from the terminus of the Gresley Canal, near the PMT garage, as far as the present site of Stubbs Walks, with the provision of a wharf in Water Street to meet local needs for coal and iron. The level of this new canal was however about 60 feet above that of the Newcastle branch from Stoke and although various projects to connect the two with an inclined railway or canal boat hoist were put forward it appears that the link was never built, and Newcastle thus possessed two canals which were of only limited value because no through traffic could be carried. As a result the Newcastle branch was a commercial failure, and the first dividend was not paid until 45 years after it opened. Newcastle thus failed to achieve any importance as a centre for water transport.

Proposals to provide a railway system for the Potteries and Newcastle were first made in 1835, one of the original supporters being the owner of the Nigel Gresley Canal, but it was not until 1846 that the North Staffordshire Railway was incorporated. Just as the first canal to reach Newcastle was built to serve the Apedale collieries so the first railway was an industrial line connecting the Sneyd family's Silverdale mines and ironworks with Pool Dam, where freight was transferred to the Newcastle Canal. This line was opened in 1850, two years after the completion of the Congleton, Stoke, Norton Bridge railway but two years before the branch from the latter line to Newcastle was finished. Unlike their predecessors, the canal builders, the railway engineers took a direct route across the ridge which separated Newcastle from the main North Staffordshire line in the Fowlea Valley, although this involved steep gradients and the excavation of two tunnels 96 yards and 605 yards long through sandstone. Newcastle station was built

One of the many private buses operating in the Newcastle area in the 1920s. By 1939 most of the independent services had been absorbed by the PMT though a small group of private operators still remain in the district.

Taxis still play an important part in Newcastle's communications system. Here their predecessors ply for hire in the High Street of about fifty years ago.

on the north side of King Street and the railway was extended westwards along the bed of the disused Newcastle Junction Canal, under the Liverpool Road and across Lyme Brook to join the Silverdale line at Knutton Junction. Coal and iron from the Sneyd mines at Silverdale could thus pass directly through Newcastle onto the North Staffordshire railway and the old link with the canal at Pool Dam became of little use. Freight traffic on the Newcastle Branch was increased in 1856 with the opening of a line along the Lyme valley to the Apedale mines and the subsequent decline of the old Nigel Gresley canal.

In an age of fierce competition between railways the North Staffordshire Company was virtually unchallenged in the Potteries area, the nearest rival being the London and North Western Railway with its station at Whitmore, five miles from Newcastle. In 1859 however the Sneyd family was given permission to operate public passenger services on their Silverdale–Newcastle mineral line and in the same year the London and North Western Railway proposed to build a branch from their main line at Madeley to the Sneyd line at Silverdale in order to attract some of the potteries traffic away from the rival North Staffordshire system. This move was countered by the latter company, who leased the private Sneyd line and took over the running of trains on it, and in 1871 the extension of this branch to Market Drayton was opened, providing the North Staffordshire network with a link with the Great Western Railway.

In addition to the passenger service operated by the North Staffordshire Railway on the Stoke, Newcastle, Market Drayton branch, and from 1881 on the Leycett loop to Alsager, several local mining companies ran workmen's trains between Newcastle and Apedale and freight trains on the Knutton and Pool Dam lines. Newcastle was however never able to rival the position of Stoke on Trent as the principal rail centre within the Potteries area.

One interesting project that would have altered the railway map of Newcastle had it materialized was the proposal to continue the Trentham branch (opened in 1910) across the Lyme valley and northwards to join the Pool Dam branch near the site of the old gasworks. This line would have served Clayton and the other growing residential areas south of Newcastle but the scheme was abandoned because even in the early twentieth century the rail services were beginning to suffer from the effects of tram competition. This was particularly true in the case of the Newcastle–Stoke railway and in 1905 the North Staffordshire Company decided to introduce rail motor services and establish new halts at Hartshill, Brampton and Liverpool Road in an

A skilled eye can still detect the course of the old Newcastle Canal as it ran parallel to the London Road past the City General Hospital.

effort to prevent capture of its passenger traffic by the trams. These measures were not sufficient to stave off road competition however and with the introduction of bus services in the 1920s the rail passenger traffic between Silverdale, Newcastle and Stoke continued to decrease. By the late 1950s, when British Railways began their investigation into the unprofitable sections of their network, only twelve trains daily used the Newcastle branch and Sunday services were abandoned. The passenger services between Silverdale and Market Drayton had been withdrawn in 1956 and the surviving Stoke–Newcastle–Silverdale service was condemned in the Beeching Report of 1963 as uneconomic and unworthy of retention. In the following year all passenger services between Stoke and Newcastle were withdrawn and two years later the line between Newcastle Junction, on the main line, and Brampton was abandoned, with the subsequent demolition of Newcastle station and the infilling of the Hartshill tunnels with colliery spoil. The Apedale and Pool Dam branches were closed in 1967 and all that remains of the Newcastle and Market Drayton branch is the link between Silverdale and Holditch collieries and the main Stafford to Crewe line at Madeley.

From the coming of the railway to the end of the nineteenth century, road transport made very few contributions to public passenger services in the Newcastle area. Although horse trams were introduced between Hanley and Burslem in 1862 it was not until the application of steam and later electric traction that the tram was able to offer any serious challenge to the railway in Newcastle and the Potteries towns. Steam trams began running between Stoke and the other centres in the 1880s and in 1898 the Potteries Electric Traction Company was formed to take over the North Staffordshire Tramways Company and develop an electric tram system within the built-up area.

This new network was installed between 1899 and 1905, with Newcastle as the centre of routes in the western section. In 1901 services along the Liverpool Road and onward to Chesterton, and alongside the Pool Dam railway to Silverdale were begun, and Newcastle was linked to Hanley by a route through Etruria and to Stoke upon Trent by a service passing over Hartshill. From Nelson Place another route led northward to May Bank, Wolstanton, Longport and Burslem, where connections for Tunstall were available. Only to the south of Newcastle was there a gap in the network, the High Street being the tram terminus with a reversing loop at the Well Street intersection with Penkhull Street. Although an extension tramway from High Street along London Road to link up with the Stoke to Trent Vale line was authorised in 1902, it was never built and it was not until the introduction of buses in the 1920s that this growing part of Newcastle was adequately served with public transport.

With the development of the Westlands and Clayton as residential areas after the First World War and the building of the municipal housing estates at Knutton and Chesterton it became clear that the existing tram services were inadequate to meet the increasing demands for passenger transport. The tram routes were supplemented by a large number of bus services, often operated by very small companies, and by 1924 over 90 bus undertakings were running buses in the Stoke and Newcastle area. The Potteries Electric Traction Company also began to introduce motor buses and the tram routes linking Newcastle with Chesterton, Silverdale, Stoke, Hanley and Burslem were gradually replaced by buses, all trams being withdrawn by 1928. Bus services between Newcastle, the Westlands, Trentham, Poolfields, Leycett and Halmerend were begun in the late 1920s and outlying villages such as Pipe Gate and Hill Chorlton were also provided with buses at this time. Predecessors of the Crosville company also operated services in the districts to the west of Newcastle and by the beginning of the Second World War most of the present day routes had been established.

After the war the growing popularity of long distance coach travel gave Newcastle an opportunity to regain some of the importance as a road transport centre that it had lost with the demise of the stage coach a century earlier. The town's position on the A34 trunk route connecting the north west with the midlands and the south attracted many coach operators and the 'Four in Hand', which dates as a refreshment centre from 1932, became a well patronised halt for both regular long distance services and for summer season excursions. By the mid-1950s it was possible to travel directly by coach from Newcastle to London, the south coast, the south west, North Wales, Liverpool, Manchester, the Lake District and Scotland with a wide range of connections at Cheltenham for other destinations. Coach journey times were cut substantially with the completion of the M1, M5 and M6 motorways, the fastest timing to London, for example, being reduced from 7 hours 26 minutes to 4 hours 11 minutes. Newcastle has thus achieved a new status as a focus for coach services and offers facilities that none of the Potteries towns can rival.

A view of Newcastle railway station: passenger services began on 6th September 1852 and the one and three-quarter mile journey through the Hartshill tunnels to Stoke station took about five minutes. The through services between Newcastle and Market Drayton took 35 minutes and there were also through coaches between Newcastle and Birmingham. Only the goods shed remains and much of the former railway property is now occupied by a car park and scrap metal yard.

Postal services must not be forgotten in the record of Newcastle's communications. Is this wall post box in King Street in fact the oldest surviving in the borough?

83

Although the opening of the M6 motorway through Cheshire in 1963 reduced much of the long-distance traffic passing through the High Street section of the A34 in Newcastle the town continued to be faced with several problems created by the heavy volume of private cars and commercial vehicles using the centre. Most of the north south traffic was diverted to the western by-pass in 1966 and by 1968 the High Street had been closed to all through traffic and reverted to its function as a street market. The difficulties associated with the east to west traffic using the town centre remained however and in 1971 a series of proposals designed to relieve this pressure were made by the Borough Engineer and Surveyor. These proposals were made the subject of widespread consultation, with the public invited to participate in a discussion of policy. In the event, none of the routes proposed were accepted by the Council. The problem of the volume of traffic passing through Newcastle, however, remains: some solution must be sought which preserves both the existing appearance of the town centre and the attractions of the High Street as a market. It is to this task that the new Highway Authority must address itself in 1974.

The only railway lines left in the borough are the colliery lines that help to take the coal production of Holditch and Silverdale Pits all over the country.

Second Eddition!!

WANTED.

Twenty Journeymen Hatters, for Twenty-eight days, apply at the Workshop of T. & G. Kristie, Hatters, MARKET-LANE, *Newcastle Staffordshire, or their Bailiff on the premises.*

N. B. They will be required to wear White Hats, with black Crape.

The Men who where advertized for in the Manchester Newspaper, *to lower prices* shall be discharged during the above time, and no work sent to Manchester.—Those men who now come, shall be certain of *some* work for 28 Days, without alteration, and they shall be afterwards *as a special favour,* be sent back to their old Masters W. W. & Co. and Strangers *taken in* as usual.

Newcastle, February 25th, 1820.

Hats, Pots and Clocks

Newcastle enjoyed a virtual monopoly as the chief trading centre in North Staffordshire, maintaining its position as the area's principal market town from medieval times until the second half of the nineteenth century, though from the second half of the eighteenth century the 'Pottery' towns were slowly becoming self-sufficient.

This primacy in trade dates back to the grant of the Charter of the Gild Merchant in 1235 which provided the basic legal rights whereby the burgesses of the town could form their own Gild Association. This in turn empowered them to regulate trade and industry within the borough for the good of the community as a whole. It also gave them the right to trade freely throughout the land, exempting them from tolls, except within the City of London. This encouraged the growth of industries in the town, but few details of their character prior to the Stuart period survive.

Obviously one important industry was the servicing of local agriculture: a mill for grinding corn is first mentioned in 1193. Tanning was carried out in Newcastle from at least the sixteenth to the nineteenth centuries, as were a variety of trades concerned with iron working. There can be little doubt that the most important of the small scale industries that developed in the seventeenth and eighteenth centuries was felt hatting. Evidence of hat making can be traced from Elizabethan times to the last decade of the nineteenth century. It was during the seventeenth century that the home market expanded with the aid of a heavy tariff against imported hats. By the first half of the eighteenth century a large export trade had developed between England and most European countries. France, with access to the North American beaver lands, was the only serious rival. By 1763, the fortunes of war had transferred Canada to the British Empire and secured for the English hatting trade an adequate supply of best quality beaver skins whilst at the same time depriving her chief rival of raw materials.

During the first half of the eighteenth century trade developed and a large proportion of the working population was employed in this industry. By 1790 there were twenty seven hat manufacturers in the town, whilst in 1822 nearly one third of the working population was connected in some way with the hatting trade.

The town's principal master hatters appear to have employed an average of eight or ten journey-men and workpeople in what remained a cottage industry: nineteenth century property sales show that a large proportion of the premises up for sale combined dwelling houses and hatting workshops. Much work was 'put out' to the smaller manufacturers: the large internationally known London firm of Christy's are known to have been supplying basic raw materials to commission firms at such towns as Macclesfield, Oldham, Stockport and Newcastle under Lyme. It was at Newcastle that Christy's advanced John Mason some three hundred pounds to build a new factory.

Although in 1844 the chief manufacture of the town was still described as that of felt hats, the labour was now confined to preparing articles for finishing by the London hatters. This was done, it seems, so that a London label could be used on the finished hats. Competition from the increasingly popular silk hat for the upper and middle classes and the cloth cap for the industrial worker evoked a decline in the demand for felt hats, and by 1851 there were only nine hatters in the town. By 1892, G R Turner appears to have been the only hat maker left in the borough. The gradual transition from hatting, which can be detected from the end of the eighteenth century, was also due to competition resulting from the establishment first of a cotton mill at Cross Heath and then, in the following century, of four silk mills in the area.

The manufacture of clay tobacco pipes in the borough was at one period in its evolution second only to hatting in economic importance to the town. During the second half of the seventeenth century the town's pipemakers shared equal fourth place with Chester, York, and Hull as the major producers of clay pipes in England.

The extent to which hatting as an industry had developed by the 1820s is reflected in this squib—one of the less outrageous political broadsheets of the period.

The Pipes of Newcastle and their Marks

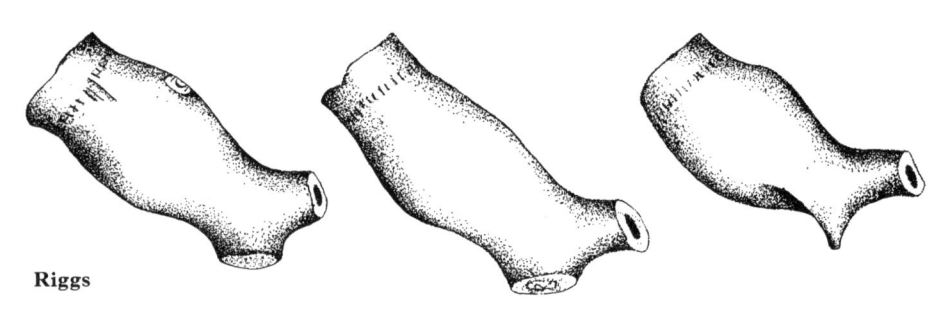

Riggs

Riggs c.1649–76

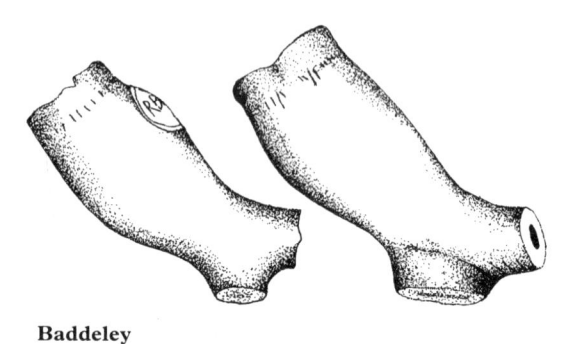

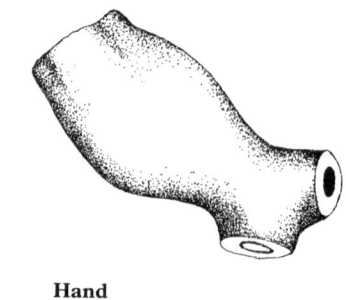

Baddeley

Hand

Baddeley c.1676–1730

William Hand c.1780

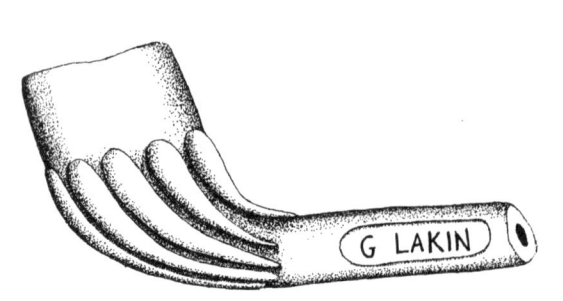

Jones c.1670

Catherall

G LAKIN

Catherall c.1637

R MORGAN NEWCASTLE

Ralph Morgan c.1780

Pomona site type

The site of the Borough Hotel, King Street, was formerly occupied by a potworks and then a brewery.

The Water Street brewery as it appeared in Ingamells' 1881 Directory; by this time it was owned by C H King and traded under the title of the North Staffordshire Brewery.

Almost the whole of one side of Water Street was occupied by brewing interests here shown as they appeared before demolition in about 1893. The present County Court buildings occupy much of the original area.

The Guildhall, where, from the early eighteenth century onwards, decisions concerning the regulation of trade and industry were made by the borough council, is probably the first building constructed with bricks from the corporation brickyard.

Between 1637 and 1680 there were at least seventeen master pipemakers operating in the town and of these perhaps the Riggs, Baddeley, Ball and Fox families were the most prolific manufacturers. It was to Charles Riggs that the eminent seventeenth century historian, Dr Robert Plot, gave the credit for being the first Englishman to use a simple form of machinery to mass produce his tobacco pipes. Pipe making continued well into the nineteenth century and such families as the Morgans, Bloods and Tittensors were producing pipes on an extensive scale. By 1850, however, there was a general decline in the demand for clay pipes due mainly to the increasing competition from Meerschaums, Cheroot holders, fruitwood pipes and finally the vastly superior briar pipe. This, and the increasing demand for labour in the adjacent pottery towns, which seems to have absorbed more and more of the borough's indigenous clay workers, meant that by 1850 there were only some five master pipemakers left in the town. The last recorded pipemaker was George Lakin who is listed as a manufacturer in 1881.

Newcastle was as much a commercial as a manufacturing centre: it enjoyed many social and business connections with the pottery towns, particularly during the latter part of the eighteenth century. Recent discoveries show that a considerable amount of capital for setting up many new pottery ventures originated from Newcastle. Josiah Wedgwood's first partnership was with a potter named Thomas Alders of Cliff Bank and with John Harrison, a Newcastle tradesman who invested capital in Alders' potworks. Such links are not uncommon and connect many historically important North Staffordshire potbanks with Newcastle entrepreneurs.

Recent archaeological discoveries have proved that the town's own potters made a distinguished contribution to the evolution of the industry especially between 1724–54. High quality table wares were first produced at Samuel Bell's manufactory in Lower Street (now Messrs Placemate) between 1724–54.

The founder of this potworks was the eldest son of Samuel Bell Senior who was by profession a saddler. Like his father, he was an active member of the town council and held many important posts over a period of years. On purchasing the Lower Street property, however, Samuel Bell ceased to play an active role in council affairs, being fully occupied in running his newly founded pottery.

Samuel Bell commenced his potting career at the age of forty; he was a senior contemporary of John Astbury, the famous Shelton potter, and outlived him by twelve months. The similarities between the wares of these potters are quite remarkable and it is not unreasonable to suggest that they were acquainted with each other, and that there may even have been some form of co-operation between them. There does not appear to have been any tradition of potting in the Bell family, nor is it known where Samuel obtained his potting knowledge. Judging by the extent of the output from the pottery, there can be no doubt that he employed several potters to produce wares for him. Nevertheless, he must have been a potter in his own right, since, as an experimenter in improved wares, in May 1729 he took out a patent claiming the discovery of a new method of producing a marbled red ware pottery. Red earthenwares were produced by Bell from the commencement of the potworks in 1724 until his death in 1744. These wares consist mainly of high-quality thrown and turned table wares: teapots, cups, saucers, mugs, tankards, and bowls, all beautifully finished, showing a remarkably high standard of workmanship.

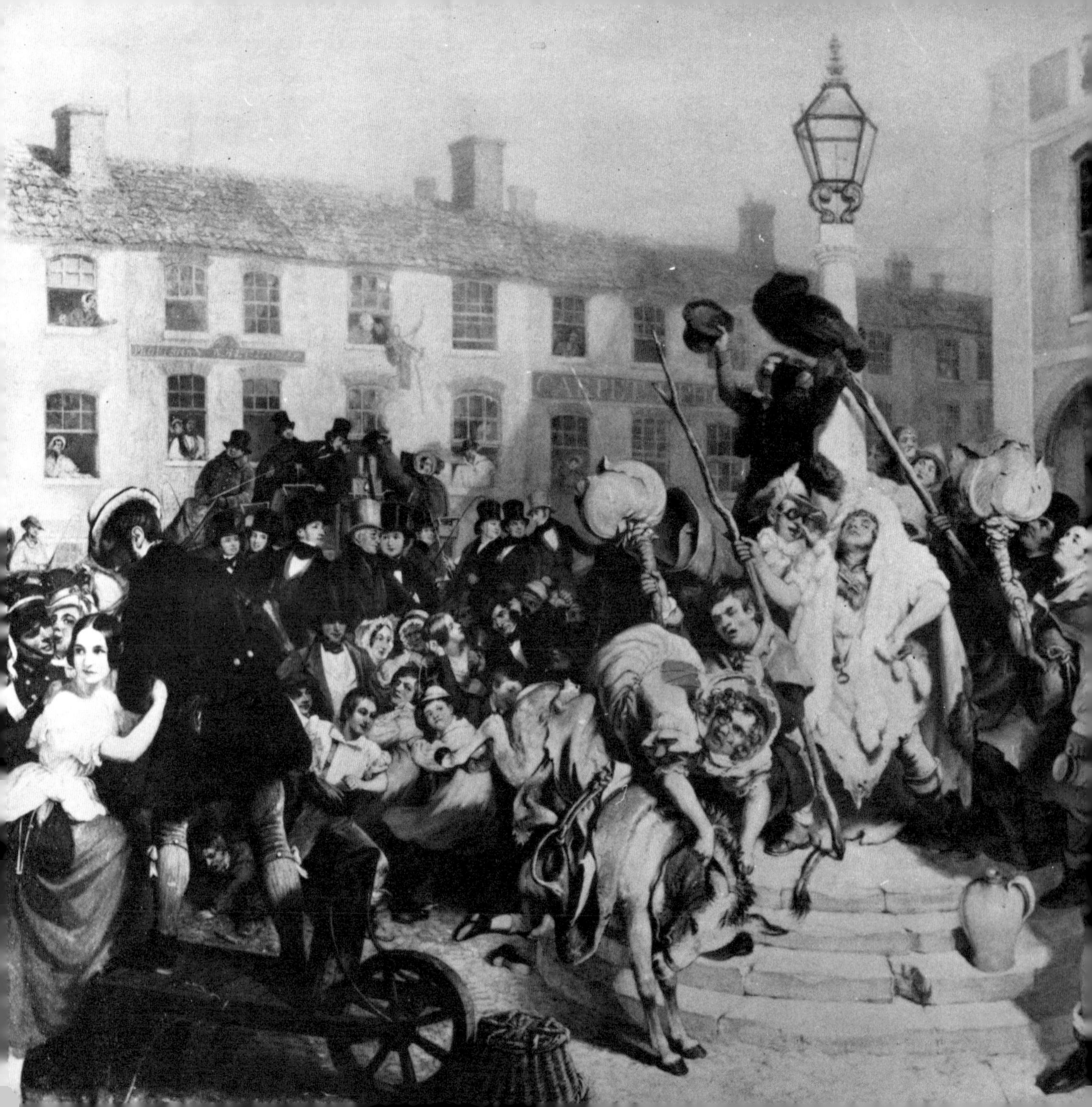

After Samuel's death, his brother John, a London broker, appears to have let his brother's potworks to a London potter, William Steers, who was experimenting in the production of porcelain on the site from his arrival in 1744 until about 1748. Recent discovery shows that Newcastle was the first town in North Staffordshire to produce porcelain on a commercial scale and further suggests that the Lower Street potworks was making these wares at the same time as the earliest productions of the London manufactories of Chelsea and Bow. The pottery appears to have continued to produce earthenwares in addition to porcelain, but since redwares were out of fashion, white earthenwares were made in their stead.

From about 1748 until its final demise in the following decade, the potworks appears to have been managed by yet another London potter named Joseph Wilson. Even though this manufactory appears to have ceased production by about 1755, there is strong evidence to suggest that some at least of the potters from the Lower Street site removed to Liverpool and were employed by the firm of Reid, Baddeley and Company.

It was not until some three decades after the closure of the Lower Street potworks that potting emerged again as one of the town's industries. The re-establishment of this trade was brought about by the formation of a somewhat unusual partnership between two Staffordshire businessmen, one from Newcastle, the other from Cheadle, neither of whom, unlike their predecessor Samuel Bell, appear to have had any experience of potting before they established their short lived potworks in the town. This firm, known as Bulkeley and Bent was founded either in 1790 or 1791, and remained in business for about seven years until the partnership between James Bulkeley and William Bent was dissolved in November 1797, after what appears to have been an unprofitable business association. Of the two partners it was William Bent of Newcastle who seems to have been responsible both for the foundation of the potworks and also for its administration. Bulkeley, on the other hand, seems to have been a sleeping partner throughout the firm's life. William Bent's interest in the pottery trade may be explained by the fact that his elder brother James associated with several master potters including Josiah Wedgwood.

It was not until the firm had been established for over twelve months that the partners drew up their first apprenticeship agreement; this was between themselves and a young man named John Rowley. The agreement gives no clue as to what type of pottery was being produced at the works. The only other apprentice indenture, dated 1794, does however specify that a youngster by the name of Samuel Scarlett is to learn the particular business of on-glaze painting and 'blue' painting. Only one example of the products of this firm has so far been discovered. This, surprisingly, is not decorated by any of the methods described in the second indenture, but takes the form of a sprigged stoneware jug, similar in style to those made by such potters as the Wedgwoods, Turners and Adams. On the failure of the pottery Bent adapted the defunct potworks into a brewery. His second adventure into the field of commerce eventually led to the establishment with his five sons, of the Bent brewing empire which had capital assets of over a quarter of a million pounds in 1890. Bent's new liaison in the brewing business was with John Barrow and James Caldwell. Caldwell was the Recorder of Newcastle from 1800–37 and had for

R W Buss's painting of the mock mayor making ceremony illustrates well the type of head gear made in the town; many of the spectators can be seen smoking clay tobacco pipes manufactured by the local Morgan family.

Samuel Bell, who founded the Pomona potworks in Lower Street, was responsible for the manufacture of beautifully made red earthenwares such as these. His products were identical in style to those of his better known contemporary, John Astbury of Shelton, and were made between 1724-44.

Newcastle can justly claim to be the first town in the county to have produced soft paste porcelain; the group of table wares depicted here, made about 1745-6, typify the wares being produced for the middle and upper classes.

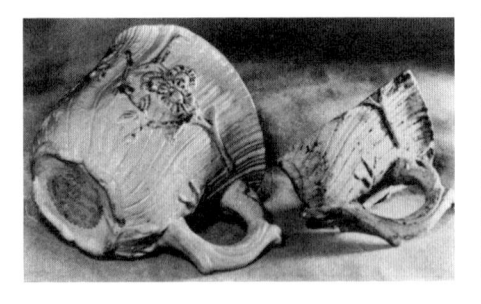

Porcelains such as these appear to have been made during the late 1740s; they were based on Oriental designs which had become very popular in Europe by this time.

Although it is known that Bulkeley and Bent produced a form of china ware, the only known marked piece of their pottery shows that they also made relief decorated stonewares such as this jug.

some years been a partner of Enoch Wood, the potter. They traded under the name of Wood and Caldwell. This second venture was not without its catastrophes for on September 15 1806 the brewery warehouse suffered devastating damage by fire. The ready assistance given by the Volunteers and others who put out the conflagration did not go unrecorded; Bent and Caldwell expressed their thanks in a hand bill published the following day: 'Mr Bent and Mr Caldwell are desirous to lose not a moment in returning their most hearty thanks to the Volunteers, their friends and neighbours and to the inhabitants of the town of Newcastle and the Potteries in general, for their kind and ready assistance, as well as great and efficacious exertions in the calamitous accident which happened last night; and of which Mr Bent and Mr Caldwell beg to assure them, that they shall ever retain the most grateful remembrance. BREWERY. Tuesday morning, September 16th 1806'. The fire consumed one thousand and eighty bushels of malt which would have produced about five hundred barrels or eighteen thousand gallons of beer.

The Bent brewing business had it seems been transferred to Liverpool by 1836 since by this time the premises were occupied by three other Newcastle brewers, Messrs Rogers, Hindle and Baker who by 1839 were known as 'Ale and Porter Brewers' at the North Staffordshire Brewery, Water Street. At this time there was one other brewery operating on a large scale in the town owned by Richard Baddeley whose premises were next door to the North Staffordshire Brewery.

A long-case clock by John Redshaw about 1690 is thought to be the oldest surviving example of Newcastle's clockmaking industry.

One other Newcastle craft which grew to be a profitable industry was that of clockmaking. Between 1734 and 1832 no less than eighty watch and clock makers can be found listed in the Corporation Apprentice and Freeman Books. This industry was at its height during the Georgian period although one of the oldest of the Newcastle clockmaking families, the Redshaws, are known to have been active during the reign of Queen Anne. Other early manufacturers include the Beech and Nickisson families.

The products of the Newcastle clockmakers reflect the national pattern of the industry's development. The market for clocks in the Stuart period had been confined and elitist, with production dominated by craftsmen-shopkeepers who made clocks to sell to a limited number of clients. A rising standard of living in the eighteenth century expanded that market but caused a fall in standards of craftsmanship. Machinery came to be used on an increasing scale for the manufacture of such components as geared wheels, fusees and pinions. Though some craftsmen still maintained high standards, an increasing number of movements were made, which, though adequate for time keeping, did not manifest the skills of the earlier period. So in Newcastle, the hand made brass-faced clock set in a 'country style' case of the pre-1730 period gave way to the mass assembled product. Also whereas in the earlier period a number of 30 hour clocks had been made for a country market, these after 1750 yielded to the almost universal production of 8 day clocks in oak or mahogany cases. By about 1775 brass faces with spandrels and silvered chapter rings were being reserved for only the most expensive clocks. The enamelled dial was by then well established. Newcastle clocks abound with such faces which were obviously being obtained ready painted from either London or Birmingham workshops.

This bracket clock, made by Francis Chambley about 1800, represents a typical country product of the Newcastle clockmakers.

The chief provincial clock making centres of the eighteenth century were Liverpool, Derby, Leicester, Newcastle upon Tyne and Bristol, whilst Prescot and Coventry vied with each other as watchmaking centres. Newcastle under Lyme as a clockmaking centre was never in this class; nevertheless its clockmakers played an important part in the town's economy. Because of the borough's virtual monopoly over the adjacent pottery villages and its service of the agrarian communities of North Staffordshire and South Cheshire, it produced a wide variety of clocks and watches: examples of long case and bracket clocks and the verge pocket watch are all in existence bearing such local names as Nickisson, Chambley, Massey and Bloor.

One of the most important aspects of the Industrial Revolution was that it gave a new emphasis to time, not now the clock of nature, of sunrise and sunset, winter and spring, but the man made clock with hour and minute registered in fine precision. The lives of working men were becoming increasingly regulated by the clock and in consequence a demand for cheap mass produced movements was created. This, however, was largely met by the import, in free trade conditions from the 1840s, of vast quantities of European and American clocks. The cheapness of these imports eventually undermined the products of the native clockmaker to such an extent that, as Benjamin Vulliamy, the most eminent of the surviving members of the old school of London horologists, wrote to a customer in 1849, 'The new Free Trade system is daily throwing thousands of operatives out of employment, increasing the Poor Rates and diminishing the means to pay them'. Thereafter Newcastle clocks were to be sought in antique shops, no longer in the market place.

The domed enamel dial of this Nickisson clock indicates a much later date: the nobler brass-faced clocks, previously the mainstay of the trade, were now being produced in only limited numbers for the wealthy.

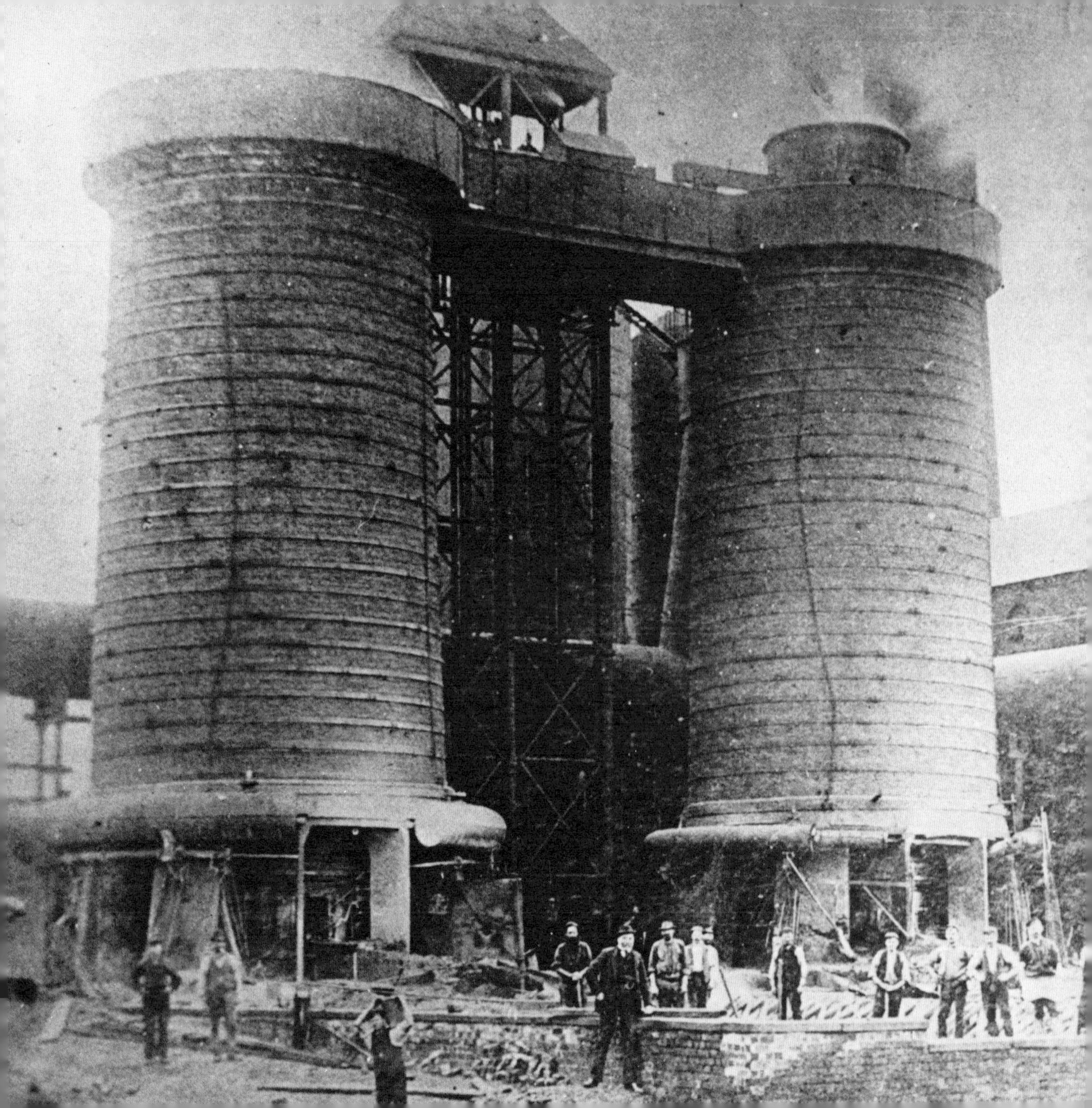

Mines and Mills

Newcastle's older business undertakings were, almost without exception, cottage industries of limited size and scope, hatting, potting and clockmaking. They served the surrounding area and exploited Newcastle's favourable position as a communications' centre. Unlike either the semi-mechanized iron and steel industries of the Black Country or the rapidly expanding textile production of Lancashire and Yorkshire, they did not depend upon vast imports of raw materials or the availability of a single source of fuel. And yet, the rock formations of the north and north west of the borough were early found to be rich in mineral resources: ironstone, coal and clay were all there to be exploited. The time was to come when new extractive industries were to compete with the old cottage industries and to attract labour away from the older forms of employment.

Archaeologists excavating the Romano-British settlement at Holditch in 1960 found indications of the exploitation of coal and iron dating from the second century AD. Apart from the occasional artisan's exploitation of resources for his own use, there is little evidence of further activity in this field until the fourteenth century, although a 'manufactory of iron', existed at Madeley in 1293 and coal was being worked in the manor of Keele by 1333. Newcastle itself had established a reputation as a centre for the marketing of iron by the mid-fourteenth century. Surnames and descriptions of trades in fifteenth century records indicate that ore was being smelted locally and the resulting iron used for local manufactures which included not only black smithing and gun smithing but most importantly nail making. The prominence of this trade is sealed in the name of the Ironmarket which, in 1608, had an 'iron hall', possibly the meeting place of a gild of ironsmiths. John Smith's will of 1612 refers to both his furnace and his forge: in 1671 Newcastle had a pan forging manufactory, the second to be established in England. By 1642 there is evidence from the Sneyd papers of iron ore being mined at Apedale and Silverdale where a small forge, probably fuelled by charcoal, was apparently supplying South Staffordshire with pig and bloom iron: later in the same century comes evidence of trade with Ireland. Newcastle was, then, well sited in relationship to mineral resources. The exploitation of these resources required, however, a communications' system better than that which sufficed for the town's cottage industries. The absence of navigable rivers meant that in the eighteenth century other areas developed as centres of iron production, and Newcastle's early industry was left at a primitive craft stage. Sir Nigel Gresley's canal of 1775 only partly remedied the situation, because it did not give clear access to the main canal system of England.

In the last third of the eighteenth century landlords like the Bowyers, Heathcotes and Sneyds became increasingly conscious of the mineral resources which lay under their land. In 1768 the first coke burning furnace in the area, at the Springwood site, Apedale, appears in the Excise Returns. Seven years later Gresley built his canal to bring Apedale coal to the borough. In 1785 a new furnace was built lower down the valley on the canal side. By 1788 the returns show that Silverdale also had a furnace producing 1,100 tons of pig iron per annum. The ore and coal for both these ventures were obtained from the clayband ironstones of the main coal measures and were extracted by means of shallow or 'footrail' workings in close proximity to the furnaces. Whereas the Silverdale furnace was founded and controlled until 1851 by the Sneyds of Keele Hall, the Apedale ironworks were rented by the South Staffordshire firm of G Parker until about 1815. In 1842 the works were leased from R E Heathcote Esq. by Thomas Firmstone, who also leased furnaces at Madeley. John Ward significantly comments that the region's iron ore had been 'only sparingly raised until the recent demand for iron for the railways'. In this respect the railways went beyond the canals; not only did they provide for the transport of heavy goods, they themselves also consumed iron and coal. Some of the pig iron produced was processed by the great ironmasters of Stoke and Biddulph, but a sizeable proportion was transported to the Black Country. In 1851, the year of his election as Mayor of the Borough, Francis Stanier took over the Silverdale furnaces (in which he had had an

Perhaps one of the most impressive views of the Silverdale ironworks as it appeared toward the end of the nineteenth century. The furnaces had by this time passed their peak output and were eventually forced to close down in 1901.

The Apedale furnaces as they appeared shortly before their demolition in the 1930s.

interest since 1848) rebuilt them and further extended the works output by the addition of a forge; six years later he founded a new forge at Knutton which consisted of sixty puddling furnaces and five rolling mills. The climax of Stanier's empire building was reached in 1864 when he took over control of the Apedale works, thereby making himself the head of the largest iron company in North Staffordshire whose plant comprised ten furnaces and two forges. By 1870 Silverdale was on the decline whereas Apedale had not reached its peak output: yet by 1880 only two of the six furnaces there were in use. Shortly after his death in 1882 his industrial empire was dispersed. In 1885 the Silverdale works and mineworkings were purchased by the Derbyshire Company of Butterley but closed in 1901, while in 1890 Apedale was taken over by the Midland Company and closed in 1930.

The Podmore Hall and Upper Silverdale valleys were extensively mined for coal from the late eighteenth century. The earliest mines were situated in the upper valleys or on the ridges between the valleys where there were few drainage problems. At first the coal was obtained by surface mining, leaving a barren and uninhabited landscape, but as the nineteenth century progressed so the workings became deeper and deeper. By 1833 the Apedale coal was being worked at a depth of over 2,500 feet: though the shaft was only sunk to 720 feet, a steam engine hauled coals up an inclined plane of 1,800 feet to the shaft bottom, one of the technological marvels of the times. Names like Nelson, Victory and Blucher attached to the early workings at Leycett indicate the industrial expansion taking place in England from the end of the Napoleonic Wars in 1815.

With the introduction of hot-blast furnaces to the iron industry between 1840 and 1870, the demand for coal, which had hitherto been confined to the needs of the potters' kilns, increased rapidly. Although in 1862 it was noted that the workable seams in North Staffordshire extended for 147 feet (25 feet more than anywhere else in Britain), the significance of this was not realised, for the pig iron manufacturers despised the local coal and, at first, preferred imports from Derbyshire. But at the end of the nineteenth century it became clear that few fields yielded coal of such variety, coal which would serve the potter, the iron founder and the railway operator.

Conditions down the mines before 1850 were primitive: with the establishment of the North Staffordshire Institute of Mining and Mechanical Engineers in 1872, improvements were made in haulage, ventilation and propping devices. Machine cutting was only slowly introduced, though by 1938 over 90% of North Staffordshire coal was mechanically cut and extracted.

The physical character of the workings meant many hazards for the miners, principally gas and water, and later faulty machinery, particularly in the shafts. A further hazard was the economics of the butty system with its disastrously heavy emphasis on speed and haste. A sad record of mining disasters on the west side of the North Staffordshire Coalfield has to be chronicled: at Talke 91 men lost their lives in 1866 and 18 in 1873, at Silverdale 19 in 1870, at Bignall Hill 17 in 1874, at Bunker's Hill 43 in 1875, at Apedale 23 in 1878 and 10 in 1891, at Holditch 30 in 1937, whilst the three great disasters at Madeley and Leycett (62 men in 1880), Diglake, Bignall End (77 in 1895), and at the Minnie, Halmerend, where 155 men lost their lives in 1918 still haunt local memory.

Tom Smith's early seventeenth century cast iron gravestone can still be seen in St Giles churchyard and remains a grim reminder of what could be cast in iron.

The hazardous nature of mining demands careful attention to safety and the availability of appropriate rescue services. Here a pre-war Holditch rescue team display their newly-provided life support equipment.

The possibility of disaster and the general condition in the pits, together with the vulnerability of the miners to the fluctuating world demand for coal early led to primitive forms of unionism and strike action. Until the establishment of the North Staffordshire Miners' Federation in 1869 this was, however, intermittent. Even so, the Staffordshire miner was difficult to enrol as a trade unionist until the beginning of the twentieth century; since then the only mining strikes involving North Staffordshire have been national ones. In a mechanised age improved conditions and industrial harmony have led to increased output: Silverdale mine currently holds the European record for the tonnage of coal per man per shift extracted.

A third natural resource of the area is the existence of clay measures. Once again the Holditch excavations indicate some Roman exploitation of these resources for the making of bricks and tiles. In the late seventeenth century Plot noticed 'brick-earth' between Newcastle and Keele, and commented in some detail on the tile manufactory (on the site of 'Bookland') of Thomas Wood who was mayor in both 1656 and 1662. In 1710, when William Lawton was mayor, the corporation itself successfully began

Ponies and horses were used extensively in the mines, below and above ground. The collier's horse shown here was engaged in haulage duties at a pit head in Silverdale.

brick making at Kingsfield. Indeed it is probable that one of the first buildings to be constructed with corporation bricks was the Guildhall when it removed to its present position in 1714. After the mid-century the activity was ceasing to be profitable, so the corporation withdrew, levying a charge on individuals who still wished to dig clay at Kingsfield. The last brick manufactory on the site appears to have been that of William Gibson, who was working the clay deposits in 1871. Brick and tile manufacturing is, however, still carried out by Walley's Tiles Co at Silverdale, and by G H Downing at Knutton and Chesterton.

From the last decade of the eighteenth century Newcastle was also involved in textile manufacture. On the banks of the Upper Canal at Cross Heath was a multi-storey cotton mill. The owner-founder, Richard Thompson, a typical example of a mill manager who became a successful factory master, was an employee of Peel, Yates and Co's cotton manufactory at Burton on Trent and rose to become, first, superintendent and then a partner in Sir Robert Peel's business. Thompson opened his own mill in 1797 and also spent £500 in erecting apprentice houses and mill workers' cottages, where, it seems, some domestic processes were carried out alongside the production of the factory.

The cotton mill has the longest record of continuous textile production in the town. The factory seems to have been well equipped to spin cotton from the outset since an agreement drawn up in 1801 between Thompson, Walker and Ward shows that machinery and tools had been specially built for this purpose; additionally the firm had also installed an 'Improved Boulton and Watt' steam engine of forty horse-power. In addition to the suitability of the climatic conditions Thompson's siting of the cotton mill must have been influenced by the availability of cheap fuel and the proximity of the canal which was used not only for the transportation of goods but also to supply water for the steam engine. In 1836 the Blue Book on Textile Factories showed that at least 200 employees were operating the machines: the impression conveyed by the company's answers is that of a paternalistic organization, much respected by its employees, which was quite sure that any government interference in regulating conditions would lead to a loss of competitiveness in the market. Thompson refused to employ young children (the youngest he employed was 12), or to use corporal punishment; he opposed night work and was proud of a record of 20 years free of accident in the factory.

Thompson and his son were in charge of the mill for over 50 years, but by 1864, James Whittaker Evans had apparently bought out their interests. The factory was acquired in 1896 by A & S Murray Ltd and operated by them with further extensions until the 1960s when it was taken over by Messrs English Electric who in turn have been succeeded by Messrs Swift Hardman, distributors of electrical equipment.

Silk throwing as an industry appeared in the town during the early decades of the nineteenth century. The first factory to commence production was founded by William Henshall and Thomas Lester during the early 1820s. The building (now occupied by Messrs. Gill Insulation Ltd), was situated in Marsh Parade near to the banks of the Upper Canal. Although the partnership did not flourish, the Henshall family remained in the business until at least 1839. Thomas Lester had in the meantime joined Richard Faulkner and operated the silk mill in Friarswood Road, known to the mill workers as the 'Flying Horse', until the

Although only one pit survives, Silverdale in the nineteenth century, affectionately known as 'jamland,' was the centre of a cluster of surrounding collieries. The busy-ness of the pithead scene is well captured in this photo of about 1900.

A group of furnace-workers pictured at the Apedale Blast Furnace about 1895: the only protective clothing appears to be the ubiquitous cloth caps and mufflers.

dissolution of their partnership in March 1830. By 1829 capital amounting to some £30,000 had been invested in the town's silk industry. In 1828 and 1829 petitions were sent from the borough on behalf of 700 employees in what had become four mills to seek more protection for the industry against foreign competition. In 1833 a spokesman for the Newcastle mills argued that free trade had devastated demand: 'We are so afraid of competition that we work day and night to be first in the market, which creates an overstock, and then we are not able to work above three or four days per week'. The additional mills were the Brampton Mill in Hempstalls Lane and the earlier of the two silk mills in Silverdale.

The Friarswood Mill was probably the largest silk manufactory in the town. By January 1834, the firm was trading under the name of Thomas Lester and Sons, but in 1861 the mill was under the management of the Brocklehurst family of Macclesfield. This firm had converted to fustian cutting by 1891 and the mill was demolished in the early 1950s. The Silverdale mills had a long history of child employment. The principal employer in the second half of the century was George Walker, first as partner in the family firm and, from the early 1890s, as manager of the Silverdale Silk Throwing Company. Even as late as 1874 George Walker and Co were still employing children under the age of nine.

Brampton Mill, which was operated by Bridgett and Co by 1861, had, by 1875, ceased silk throwing and had become a boot and shoe factory. Like the Friarswood Mill, it was taken over by the United Velvet Cutters Association and about 1900 was converted to the production of fustian. For a number of years after the later 1920s the mill fell into disuse, but in 1958 the premises were acquired and adapted by Photopia into a photographic and electronics agency.

In the early twentieth century six fustian mills were being operated by the United Velvet Cutters Association in Newcastle. In addition to the Friarswood and Brampton Mills, there were also the Albert Mill (now Dean's Colour Works in Silverdale Road), Bratby's Fustian Mill in Stanier Street, now demolished (the site today forms part of the Placemate carpark), the Pool Dam Fustian Mill, and the Albion Mill at Silverdale. These mills were operating into the late 1920s, but the introduction of automatic cutting machines into the larger textile manufacturing areas replaced the hand cutting of greycloths, and the local trade was gradually discontinued by the Association.

These cottages, now sadly gone, were built by Thompson opposite the mill for his workers and apprentices at a total cost of £500.

Nothing is now left either of the original cotton mill or the workers' cottages but this contemporary view of the mill site relates well to the previous picture of the old building.

Richard Thompson's original cotton mill at Cross Heath, built in 1797, was positioned close to Gresley's canal which not only served to bring in fuel but also supplied water for the forty horse power Boulton and Watt steam engine.

Key

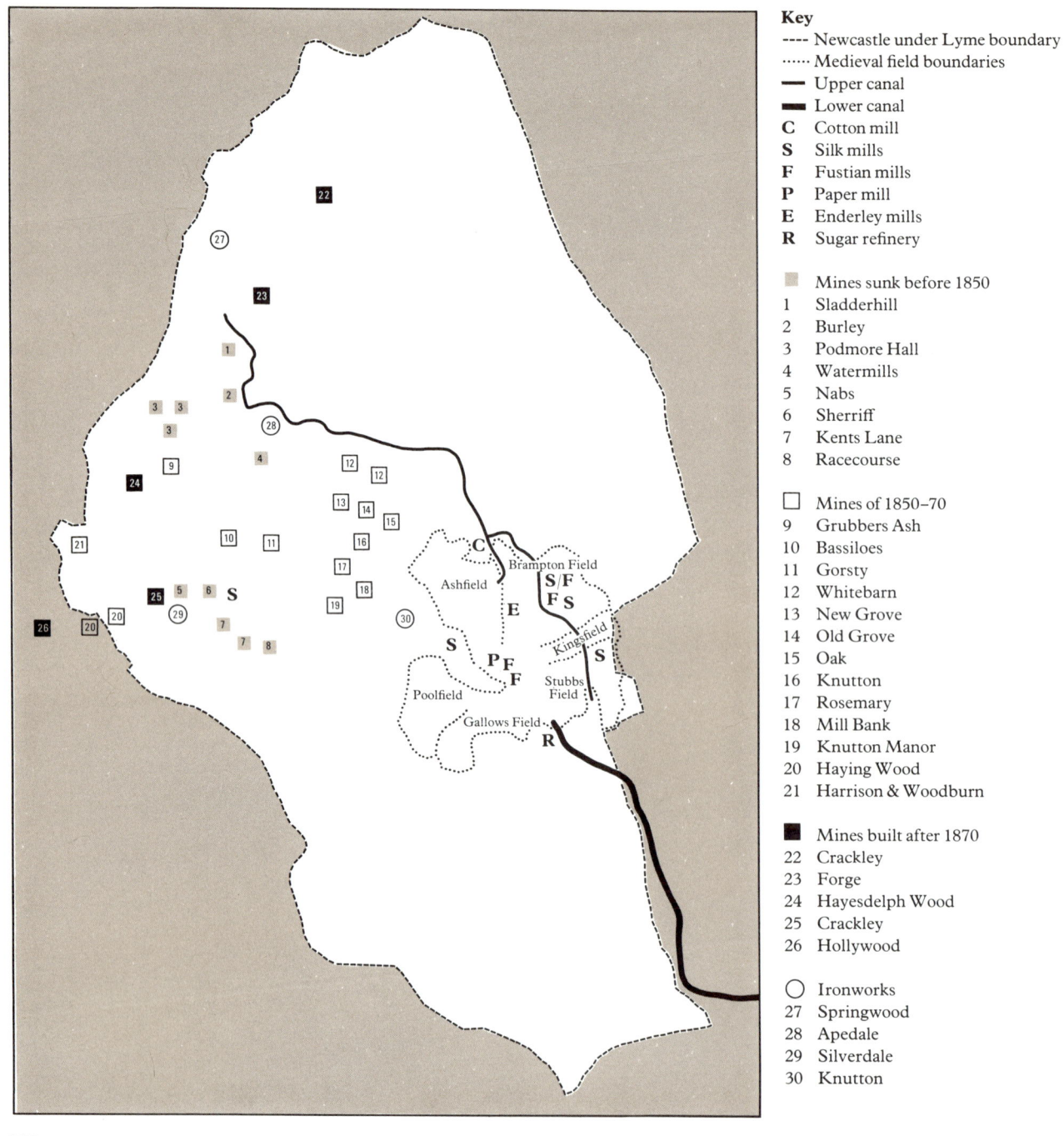

---- Newcastle under Lyme boundary
······ Medieval field boundaries
——— Upper canal
▬▬▬ Lower canal
C Cotton mill
S Silk mills
F Fustian mills
P Paper mill
E Enderley mills
R Sugar refinery

▨ Mines sunk before 1850
1 Sladderhill
2 Burley
3 Podmore Hall
4 Watermills
5 Nabs
6 Sherriff
7 Kents Lane
8 Racecourse

☐ Mines of 1850–70
9 Grubbers Ash
10 Bassiloes
11 Gorsty
12 Whitebarn
13 New Grove
14 Old Grove
15 Oak
16 Knutton
17 Rosemary
18 Mill Bank
19 Knutton Manor
20 Haying Wood
21 Harrison & Woodburn

■ Mines built after 1870
22 Crackley
23 Forge
24 Hayesdelph Wood
25 Crackley
26 Hollywood

○ Ironworks
27 Springwood
28 Apedale
29 Silverdale
30 Knutton

The latest mills to be built in the town were the Endersley Mills which remain in current operation. Founded by Richard Stanway in 1881 as a model factory, it included a surgery, a crêche, a nursery department, a reading room, and a savings bank. Prizes were given for good work. It was taken over by John Hammond and Co on Stanway's bankruptcy in 1884. It is now operated by Messrs Briggs, Jones and Gibson, who are maintaining the traditions of producing military and service uniforms.

Other industries include the Lower Street paper mill and the town's former sugar refinery. Paper has been made at the Holborn Paper Mill since about 1811. Little is known of its early history but it is known that the Lamb family owned the mill for much of the nineteenth century and continued in ownership until about 1928. The firm is now occupied by Messrs. Deeko Ltd who process paper for the food industry. After the large scale fire of 1967 they extensively rebuilt the factory. Refinery Road indicates the location of the one time Victoria Sugar Refinery, which was owned by L J Abington and was in operation in the last third of the nineteenth century. Little is known of the extent of the trade, but it must have been reasonably extensive because between 1874 and 1876 no less than eight reports of nuisance were submitted to the local Board of Health by residents, leading to the regular inspection of the premises. The firm became Bostock and Abington in 1882 and was known as Bostock and Company in 1884. It appears to have ceased production about 1890.

Increasingly in the early twentieth century Newcastle was becoming a place in which to live rather than a place in which to work. With, however, the decline of the staple industries of the area Newcastle began to attract a range of new technological light industries. These have the double advantage of offering good employment in wholesome surroundings without doing violence to the environment as the older heavy industries so often did.

The Brampton Mill, Hempstalls Lane, originally built as a silk mill, was adapted into a boot and shoe factory in about 1875 and then converted for fustian cutting in 1900. It is now owned by Photopia.

The partners of Henshall and Lester's silk mill, Marsh Parade, were the first to establish a silk throwing manufactory in the town in the early 1820s. The Henshall family appear to have remained in business until about 1840.

The partnership did not last long and Lester soon joined Richard Faulkener in founding the largest of the town's silk mills, known as the Friarswood Road Silk Manufactory. This recent view shows the original mill site. The building was demolished soon after World War II.

This busy shopping corner in Merrial Street was once the site of Thomas Wood's tile manufactory. Wood, who operated in the late Stuart period was commended by Plot for the excellence of his garden tiles.

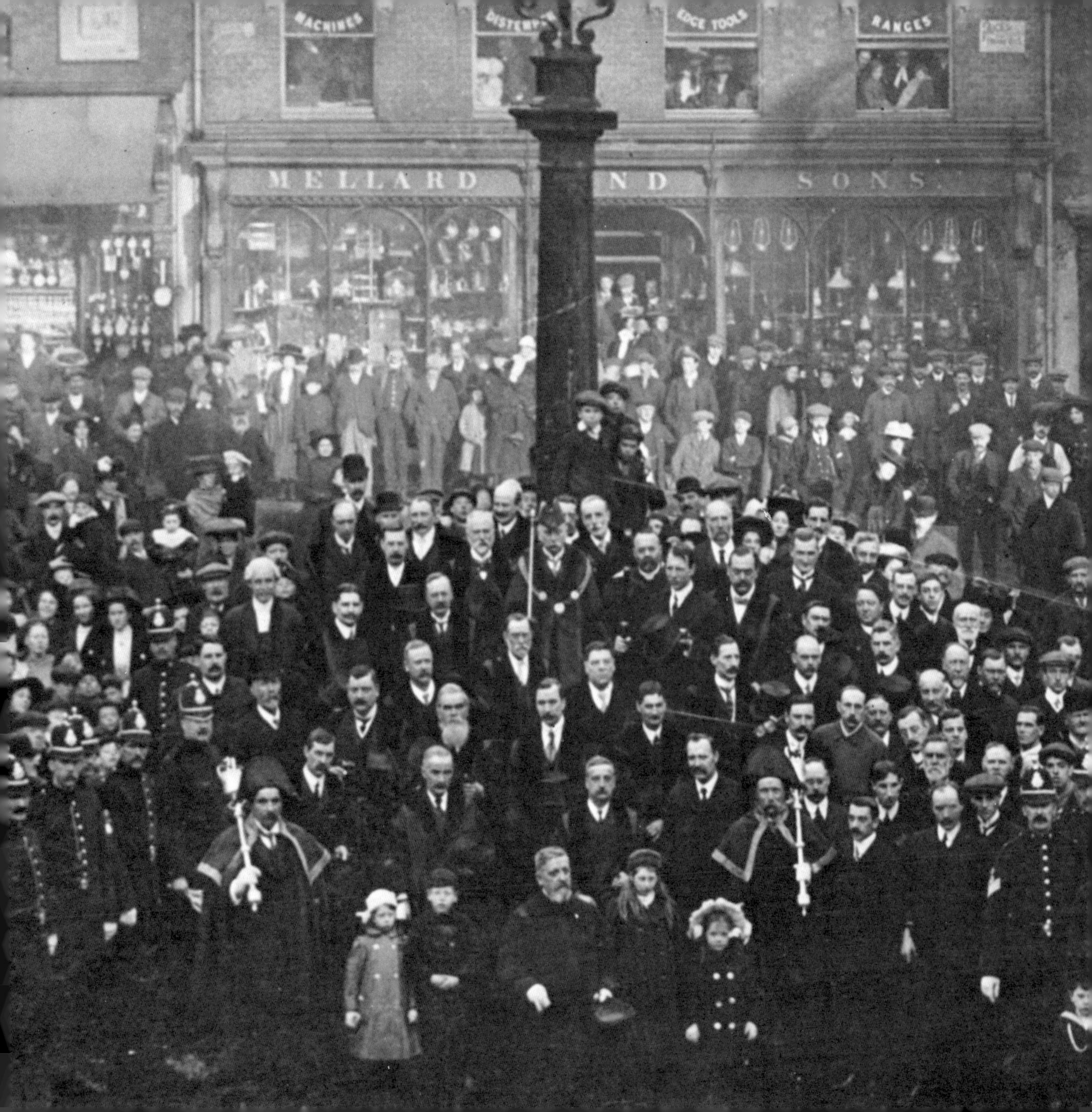
MACHINES
EDGE TOOLS
RANGES
MELLARD
ND
SONS

From Bribery to Ballot Box

Until the end of the eighteenth century Newcastle was governed by the old medieval system of mayor and burgesses, as revamped by the Stuart Charters. With the growth in size of the borough these agencies appeared increasingly antiquated, inefficient and elitist.

In 1819, because the borough was 'very populous, a place of considerable trade and also a great thoroughfare for travellers', Parliament set up a body of Improvement Commissioners who were authorised to levy a supplementary rate for the purposes of paving, lighting, watching, cleansing, regulating and improving Newcastle. On the Commission, which employed its own clerk, treasurer and surveyor, sat most members of the unreformed council together with its officers.

Even before the changes brought about by the Municipal Corporations Act of 1835, therefore, new agencies like the Improvement Commission had come into being with some power to improve the environment of the borough, providing the reformed corporation with a stock of useful expertise. The establishment of the new Council did not, however, lead to the liquidation of the older body and in the early years of its administration there was constant friction between earlier private bodies and the new bureaucracy.

As in so many other unreformed boroughs, Newcastle Council had by the late eighteenth century become principally an agency for manipulating the electorate for the purpose of electing the two borough MPs in the interests of the Gowers of Trentham. The electorate in Newcastle was limited to resident burgesses, but many of these were tied to the Gowers who during the eighteenth century bought up property in the borough for this purpose. At the same time the Fenton family, whether as mayors or town clerks or Gower agents cemented the alliance between Trentham Hall and the borough. In 1792, a Commons Committee accepted evidence that: 'The greater part of the borough was the property of the Marquess of Stafford whose influence directed the choice of the electors; and that it was customary for the burgesses who were the electors, to live for ten, fifteen or twenty years in their respective houses without paying any rent'.

In the context of the increased political consciousness within the nation in the 1790s, the first breach in the alliance between the Gowers and the corporation is witnessed, when W S Kinnersley, a member of a corporation banking family which normally supported the Gowers, stood as an Independent and forced an initial defeat for the Gowers. Their candidate was, however, re-established after the votes had been scrutinised, but in 1812, Sir John Fletcher Boughey succeeded in snatching one of the seats from the Gowers, thereby heralding the period of crisis and contest that marked the last twenty years of the unreformed borough.

The 1812 defeat caused the Gower agents to look to their mettle in a last attempt to retain power. In 1815 when Granville Leveson-Gower who sat for the county became Earl Granville, the family decided that his nephew George, then MP for Newcastle, should succeed him. This they contrived to effect with secrecy and speed in order to confound the opposition. In addition they planned to lend their support to Robert Wilmot-Horton, campaigning under the blue banner of independency, rather than finance a pink and white candidate of their own. But Gower support for Wilmot-Horton, a man of genuine independency of mind, was all too thinly veiled: on the other hand, he was unable to treat the electorate as custom required, for this would have confirmed the burgesses' suspicions of Gower influence. Meanwhile, his rival, Sir John Chetwode, Boughey's father-in-law, distributed largesse from the Roebuck Inn without restraint, so that Horton, thinking the task hopeless, left Newcastle. Overtaken at Stone by the pink and whites he was persuaded to return to no avail.

This second defeat drove the Gowers to even more frenzied action: they attempted to weight the number of electors whose loyalty could be assured by creating a new category of towheads or honorary burgesses, who only exercised burgess rights at the polls. The activists in this

The Mayor and Council assembled at the market cross for the annual mayor-making ceremony (1910). The police here appear to have little difficulty in disciplining the spectators. In the general election of 1910, however, there was considerable violence. Colonel Wedgwood said of it 'Old men still tell with awe of that great free for all fight. It took the place of Agincourt'.

Trentham Hall, the seat of the Leveson-Gower family who controlled the Newcastle constituency from the late seventeenth century until 1825, by which time the process had become too expensive and too uncertain. The engraving shown here depicts the hall in the early nineteenth century.

process were Alderman Robert Fenton, agent of the Gowers and sometime Mayor of Newcastle, and his brother Thomas, clerk to the Turnpike Trustees and subsequently Town Clerk. In the three years following 1815 they added 202 names to the electoral roll or something under a third of those voting in 1818, some of them within a week of the poll. Well might an anonymous pamphleteer write of the influence exercised by the pink and whites through the agency of the corporation: 'That nothing might be wanting to fill up the black catalogue of their enormities, they have determined that the men who in 1812 freed themselves from the shackles, and the Corp...n from the Pap of Trentham, are unworthy to enjoy the elective franchise, and the consequence is, they have robbed you of your and your children's right'. But this extension of the franchise was self-defeating; the cost of success was becoming too high. Wilmot-Horton went on record that the 1818 election had cost him 8,000 guineas.

In 1825, the Gowers began to sell up their property in Newcastle, symbolising their abdication of control of the constituency. A lot of it was bought by Richard Borradaile, a London furrier, who became the champion of the Blues with a wealth of popular support, demagogically cultivated by his studied anti-Catholicism. In contrast, part of Wilmot-Horton's independence consisted of advocating Catholic emancipation, a stand which both deprived him of office and eventually contributed to his losing his constituency. His position was too insecure to accept the seats in the Cabinet offered him in both 1827 and 1828, for this would have necessitated his obtaining a new mandate from the borough and this, even with Thomas Fenton as Town Clerk, could no longer be guaranteed. In 1830 rather than contest another election Horton accepted office as Governor General of Ceylon. In a speech in 1826 he confessed that two courses lay open to him: either to give all his time to courting the electorate or to accept that the Gower-Corporation agency ensured a quick route to Westminster conserving his energies for the discharge of his parliamentary duties: he unashamedly chose the latter.

Meanwhile in 1827 the reforming independents of Newcastle challenged at law the voting rights of the honorary burgesses and for six years this issue and the conduct of affairs in the old unreformed borough was the subject of scrutiny in the Court of the King's Bench. These proceedings cost the corporation over £4,000: in consequence when the reformed council came into being in 1836, it started its work with a credit balance of only 2s 10½d. In the meantime the 1832 Reform Act had become law, reducing, on the expiry of life interests, the electorate of 800 resident freemen to some 360 £10 freeholders.

This new council set about its work by establishing an array of committees needful for it to discharge its new responsibilities: first, a Watch Committee and then a Markets and Tolls Committee (heir of the old gilds merchant) and a Highways Committee. Others followed, especially in the last quarter of the century. Municipal reform in Newcastle was slow to advance: since it was a borough without large-scale industry, its council fell under the control of a 'shopocracy', or group of small traders, whose general concern was to save the rates and avoid expense. The borough electorate was after 1835 smaller than before: the new ratepayer franchise produced an electorate of only 533 voters or about 1 in 4 of adult males, first because 2½ years of residence was necessary for enfranchisement and secondly, because many of the poorer classes did not themselves pay rates.

Some professional men and manufacturers entered municipal politics after 1835, but in general the new council was very like the old. Even after it was nominated as the Local Board of Health in 1850, the council was still divided into those who saw the need to make provision for the development of the town and those, who, opposed to all expenditure as rash, were supported by the Burgesses' Trust. Administering the old town fields they refused to release land for the sewerage scheme shown to be so crucial by the cholera epidemic of 1849. The activists came together in the Newcastle Freehold Land Society (which secured elective trustees to the Burgess Trust by Act of Parliament in 1859) and in 1851,

for the first time, a 'Workingman's Candidate' stood, albeit unsuccessfully, for the Council.

The principal opposition to reform came from the main body of small ratepayers, who after the modest reforms of 1852 (a primitive sewerage system and the building of the first Public Baths), elected their own representatives to oppose this 'injudicious and uncalled-for expense'. This led to the foundation in 1866 of a Newcastle Ratepayers' Protection Association, which used the over-expenditure on the rebuilding of the Smithfield market to sweep the board in the elections of 1870.

The Ballot Act of 1872 and the Municipal Electors Act of 1875 did not entirely eliminate alcoholic persuasion: in 1902 one of Newcastle's prominent citizens said he could buy 'hundreds of votes' at the price of a pint of beer apiece, and five years later one of Newcastle's public houses was still providing free beer on polling day. It is perhaps not surprising that 'drink' represented one of the most important interests amongst the councillors (nearly one fifth of those elected between 1872–1914 were associated with the trade). Led by Samuel Hyslop, proprietor of the Borough Arms, mayor in 1872, a respected Liberal and Wesleyan Methodist, they secured a high number of Aldermanic elections (from whose number JPs were often selected) and also contrived to pack the Watch Committee, a potential source of criticism of the moral standing of publicans. So successful were they that they could dispose with ease of the services of any dissentient voices on the committee.

In the early twentieth century, temperance opposition was organized by the three brothers Myott, Evangelical Anglicans, and G Scott, a Methodist, who constituted themselves the guardians of the town's morality, opposing for example the introduction of mixed bathing at the Public Baths: they remained a vocal minority.

The Guildhall as it appeared in the late eighteenth century was the centre of local politics. The key men here were often members of the Fenton family who also acted for the house of Gower at Trentham.

The principal division in borough politics was, as earlier in the century, between those whom Professor Bealey calls 'Economisers' and those he calls 'Improvers'. The small shopkeepers led by William Mellard, the ironmonger, championed economy with the support of Hyslop and the drink interest, and, in latter years, of Ralph Ratcliffe who marshalled the often decisive working class opposition to expenditure, whilst W O Briggs, a draper led those who campaigned for improvement (from 1877 as the Municipal Reform Association) with, it must be said, little success.

In view of the strength of conservatism, only modest changes were accomplished in the 1880s, and these at the cost of increased opposition. In consequence Briggs' followers changed their name to the 'Ratepayers Association' in an attempt to secure support but to no avail: the municipal gospel of urban improvement made little progress in late Victorian Newcastle. The opposition was formidable, in Professor Bealey's words it consisted of 'complacent shopkeepers, rascally innkeepers and hostile working class voters'. Reform failed, 'not because of the absence of democracy, but because of its presence'.

The organisation of Labour as a political force resulted in the election of J Mayer, a bricklayer from the West Ward, in 1905: ten years later he was able to initiate the first municipal housing in the borough. After a further period of ten years Ellis Roberts, a railwayman, became Newcastle's first Labour mayor. Later both Mayer and Roberts gravitated towards middle class status. Labour was slow to make its impact on borough politics in part because the Miners' Federation and the Silverdale Co-operative Society, the two most powerful forms of Labour organization at the time, tended to concentrate their energies in the Wolstanton UDC. In part it was because partisanship was suppressed by the concern of all classes to resist municipal takeover by Stoke which threatened the 'ancient and loyal' borough in both 1920 and 1929.

In 1932, supported by 96% of the voters of the UDC, Wolstanton, although larger in population than Newcastle, amalgamated happily with the Borough in order to protect itself against Stoke's imperialism. Niceties of political boundaries, though, were of small import as compared with the grave economic condition of the times. 8,000, or nearly half the insured workers of the combined area, were unemployed in this era of soup kitchens and allotments. All were united in opposing the Means Test and the introduction of government economies. Ironically only the threat of a second World War, the opening of the armaments factory at Radway Green and the subsequent opening of two munitions factories within the borough changed that situation.

In national politics, Newcastle was solidly Conservative from 1831 until the disruption of the Conservative party in 1847, principally Liberal from 1847 to 1859, and generally was equally divided between both parties from 1859 until 1885 when the borough lost one of its two representatives. From 1885 until 1910 the borough returned either Liberals or Liberal Unionists and from 1906 for almost half a decade the borough's representation was associated with the personal biography of Colonel Josiah Wedgwood who, first elected as a Liberal, sat from 1919 to 1942 as a Labour member. 'The last of the Radicals', with his blunt and

The Council of 1888 seen on the occasion of the laying of the foundation stone of the Municipal Hall by Henry Coghill, a wealthy benefactor of the town's cultural life.

'*The Baronets Bargain, A Scene at N-----e. 1815*'. *An electioneering print which seeks to expose the corruption of the day. Outside the Cock Inn Sir John Fenton Boughey tempts the electors, 'Take the £1,000 it is a liberal offer, and then you will belong to me'.*

This Will Dyson cartoon in the 'Herald' commemorates Wedgwood's harrassment of the government's Mental Deficiency Bill whereby subnormal children could compulsorily be placed in homes against their parents' consent.

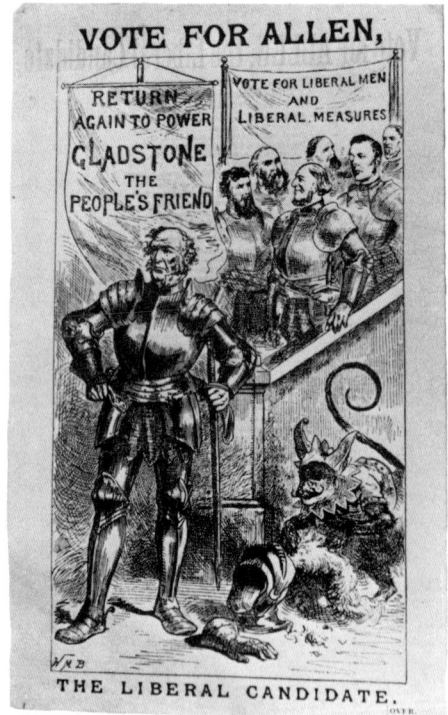

A propaganda cartoon for the 1885 election. W S Allen who had represented the borough for twenty one years made a special appeal to the newly enfranchised working men 'Many of you are now for the first time entrusted with political power. Take care that you use that power wisely and well'.

'The Battle of the Pamphleteers or Newark Versus Newcastle.' Robert Wilmot-Horton, Newcastle's MP, here seen astride his (hobby) horse, was a keen advocate of emigration as a remedy for unemployment. Sadler by contrast advocated agricultural expansion at home.

conspicuous concern for justice for all was a popular MP, not to be dislodged in the affections of the people of Newcastle by an untimely ecclesiastical attack upon him when his divorce was announced (later he became the first 'guilty' party in a divorce to sit in the cabinet). In a foreword to Wedgwood's *Memoirs* Churchill wrote 'The distressed of the world have learnt to look to him, and through him to Parliament, for a patient hearing and the redress of wrongs'.

Although three times elected unopposed, Wedgwood had on other occasions to fight for the votes of the borough, as for example, in the two elections of 1910 when his opponent was Captain Grogan, a Tory racialist. Wedgwood wrote of the first election 'Grogan's colours were red, mine blue... All the school children painted blue, with tin cans and other things, came in from Silverdale and drove the red children in rout through the Ironmarket. We both moved from meeting to meeting with our bodyguards. From one meeting my football team threw his forty out after a long and bloody fight. Thereafter neither side was allowed to address anything but a sea of fists and I was bombarded on the Market Cross, with shop-soiled produce... Old men still tell with awe of that great free-for-all fight. It took the place of Agincourt'.

The social balance of the constituency combined with Wedgwood's own personal following in the borough meant that after 1910 he was supported by a safe majority of voters. Only those far out from the centre of politics opposed Wedgwood, among whom must be numbered the colourful Fanny Deakin. Born in 1883, she joined the local Social Democrats who had existed in Silverdale from the 1890s. When they broke up, she joined the ILP in 1919 and four years later the Communist party. Twice between the wars she visited Russia on the sponsorship of the people of Silverdale. She knew from personal experience the destitution of working people, particularly those who lived in the Wolstanton UDC to which she was first elected in 1923. A determined campaigner for free milk for mothers and babies, for the raising of the public assistance scales of the borough

Wolstantion Urban District Councillors, in 1924-5. Seven years later Wolstanton Council decided by only the casting vote of the Chairman to unite with Newcastle; in a subsequent enquiry, however, 96% of the electorate voted in favour of amalgamation with Newcastle.

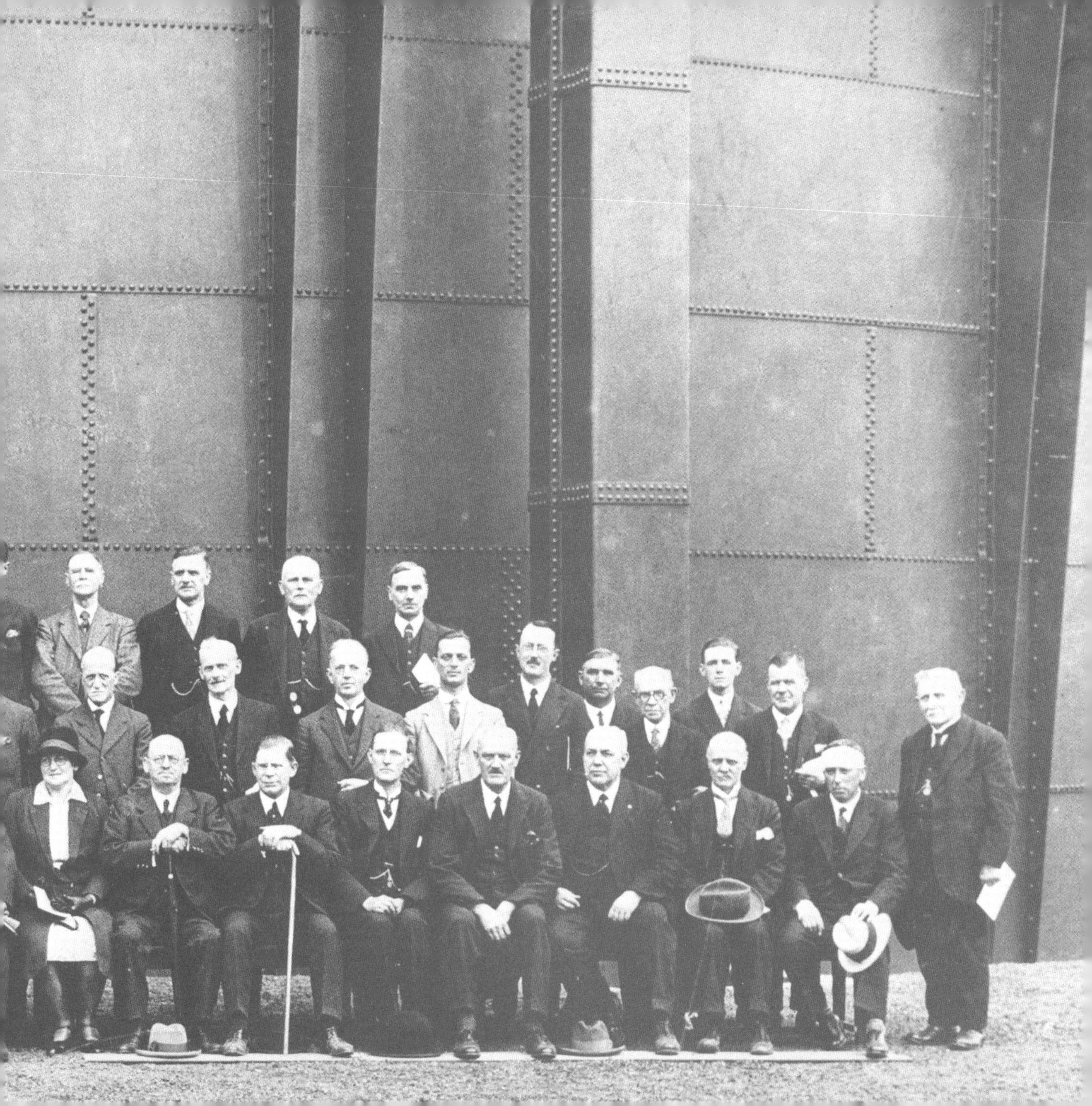

The Maternity Hospital, campaigned for by Fanny Deakin, was opened in 1947. Since 1971 it has been a home for the chronically sick.

Since 1967 the Council Chamber has been located in the Civic Offices in Merrial Street which will continue to be the focus of administration after the implementation of the 1972 Local Government Act.

Population Growth 1801-1931

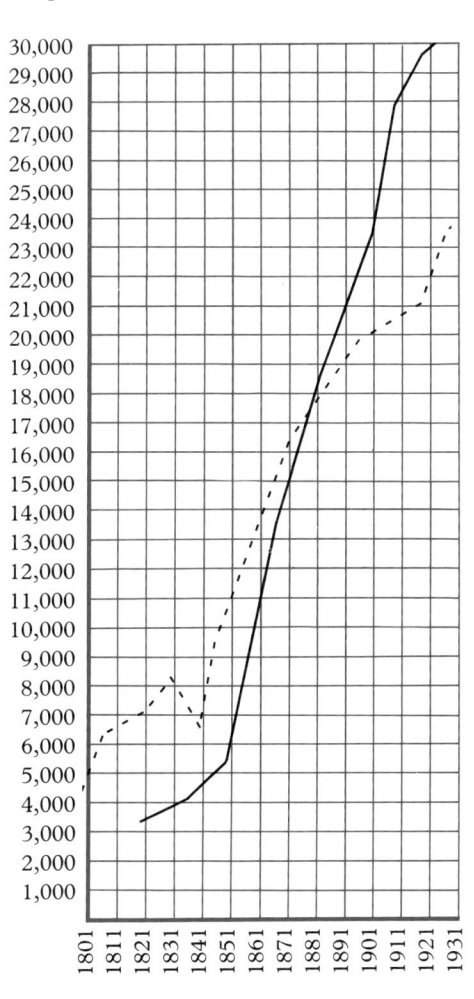

—— Chesterton, Knutton & Wolstanton
- - - - Newcastle Borough

This graph shows the relative population growth of the borough and of Wolstanton UDC prior to the amalgamation of 1932.

from second from the bottom to the highest in the country; she also campaigned for higher wages for council workmen. The pressures of poverty she knew all too well. When she married a miner in 1901 his average wage was 18s a week. Almost continuous short time working brought with it the chronic poverty that made this Silverdale mother a political activist. Leader of strikes and hunger marches, it was appropriate that when the maternity hospital for which she had campaigned was opened in 1947 it should be named after her.

This protest, though often more fervent than tactical, was important in so far as Wedgwood's support, which was personal rather than partisan, tended to have a moderating effect upon local politics. The borough, grateful for its MP's championship of its cause against Stoke's attempt at a take-over in 1929 elected Wedgwood mayor for the two years 1930–32 and returned him unopposed to Westminster in 1931 and 1935. In the House, Wedgwood took a distinctively personal line and often diverged from the official policy of the Labour Party. In his constituency, though assiduous in cultivating good personal relationships with men and women of all stratas of society, he did little to encourage the growth of a local Labour Party. At the same time the respect in which he was held in the borough also inhibited the organization of Liberals and Conservatives as campaigning parties. Politics in Newcastle, on the eve of the second world war, with only marginal exceptions, were not ideologically polarised.

With the appointment of Wedgwood's successor in 1942, the local Labour Party came to new life and entered upon a most significant period of expansion which secured a huge majority for John Mack, the new MP, in 1945. Changes also occurred in local government when the newly organized Labour Party took control from the independents in 1947: from that date onwards there has been an increasing tendency for the independents to suffer at the hands of the greater political self-consciousness of all three main political groups.

By the early fifties the local Labour Party was finding it increasingly difficult to sustain the expansion of the immediate post-war years. It was this situation that confronted Stephen Swingler when he agreed to defend Newcastle in the 1951 General Election. A former WEA lecturer in the area, he had sat for Stafford from 1945–50. As MP for Newcastle from 1951 until his untimely death in 1969, he was above all a good constituency member. This secured him not only respect but also support which extended beyond party limits. His obituary in the *Times* summarised his career as that of 'the rebel who became a first class administrator'. Standing to the left of the Labour Party he was one of Aneurin Bevan's ablest lieutenants and subsequently became the first chairman of the Victory for Socialism group. In Mr Wilson's administrations he became Minister of State first in the Ministry of Transport and subsequently in the new Ministry of Social Security.

During the period when he represented the borough at Westminster, Newcastle was made the subject of a major investigation of constituency politics. This analysis, published in 1965, concluded 'The whole constituency is characterized by a lack of extremism ... there are elements in common on both sides of the political fence, a circumstance which hardly predicates a "class struggle". Class "consciousness" there certainly may be in Newcastle, but class hatred is very uncommon.' Changes in the social balance of the constituency together with boundary changes and the impact of the Welfare State have led to a constituency in which the division of allegiance between the two largest political parties is more evenly divided than it was before 1949. In times when nationally the tide was running against Labour, Mr John Golding, the present MP, was returned to Westminster with only modest majorities, 1,042 at the 1969 by-election and 2,106 in the subsequent 1970 general election.

REYNOLDS,
CARVER
AND
GILDER,
PICTURE FRAME
MANUFACTURER

PRINT SELLER
& c.

Law and Order

A medieval borough with a population of less than eight hundred needed very little by way of law-enforcement machinery. From at least the sixteenth century, however, there was confusion as to whether the borough was a separate manor (with separate powers of jurisdiction) from the manor of Newcastle. This held court at the castle until on its decay it moved to Stoke. From the 1580s the sessions were normally held at Penkhull where the court house was incorporated in the Greyhound Inn. Surviving cases illustrate this confusion of jurisdiction. In 1608–9, for example, Ann Sneyd was unable to defend herself against her brother-in-law Ralph Sneyd, when he sued her for not sending her corn to his mills to be ground. She attempted defence along the lines of the borough being distinct from Newcastle Manor. The court could find no grounds for sustaining this distinction, though on the grounds of compassion (Ann Sneyd was both poor and old) they allowed her to maintain her own hand mill for her life time only.

From 1664, the mayor and two capital burgesses of the borough were appointed JPs. Thus the borough court of Quarter Sessions was established, which by the nineteenth century was supplemented by weekly Petty Sessions meeting at the Police Office. The Municipal Corporations Commissioners in 1835 recorded contemporary judgment that the bench was tainted with political partisanship and as a consequence recommended an increase in the number of justices (four additional JPs were in fact added including the ex-mayor of the borough). In 1847 a County Court for Newcastle and district was formed which by 1851 sat monthly at the Guildhall where Quarter Sessions also took place. By the Courts Act of 1971, Quarter Sessions were abolished and replaced by a Crown Court.

A borough prison is first mentioned in 1490–1: by the early seventeenth century this was the Stone House at the junction of the Ironmarket with the High Street. There was also a 'cage' or temporary lock-up in the seventeenth century borough. By the beginning of the nineteenth century the borough had two gaols, one for debtors, and one for criminals, both located in the Workhouse Garden. Unfortunately, parties going to the prison from most parts of Newcastle had to pass through a detached part of Stoke parish where the borough constables had no power to act; consequently rescues and escapes were easily accomplished. The prison itself was hardly more secure, and so commitment to the county gaol was secured as soon as possible. This, however, involved a charge of 6s 6d per head per week to the county magistrates as against the 3s 6d per head per day costing for prisoners at Newcastle Gaol. Plans to build a new prison in Friarswood in the 1840s seem not to have materialized; presumably thereafter Newcastle, apart from the lock-up attached to the Police Office in the High Street, used the County Gaol for its prisoners.

From the 1490s the superintendence of the gaol was committed to the borough sergeant(s) assisted by two constables. Later the security of prisoners was entrusted to bailiffs. From at least the fifteenth century, then, the borough had some 'professional', even if part time, law keepers. Yet the responsibility for securing peace, a community task, was more widely spread: for example, in 1607, every burgess was required to carry a club or 'good balke staffe' to enable him on all occasions to assist the authorities in keeping the King's peace.

Even the modest expansion of the eighteenth century put these minimal provisions for law and order under pressure. The first response to the new situation came with the Improvement Act of 1819. The lighting of the streets for which the Act provided was principally to aid the borough's security. More specifically the new commissioners were 'empowered and requested as they think expedient to provide and set up watch houses, watch boxes, and to employ watchmen and night patrols'. The duties of the night watchmen were to prevent fires, murders, burglaries and robberies, and disorders. They were to arrest and apprehend night walkers, felons, vagrants and disturbers of the peace and to lodge them in the borough prison. In fact, the first watchmen were not appointed until 1831 when four night patrols furnished with staves,

The volunteers, predecessors of the Territorial Army, process past the old St John's Church, Liverpool Road on the occasion of the opening of the Municipal Hall in 1890.

An Ancient Bridle
USED IN THE
BOROUGH OF NEWCASTLE-UNDER-LYNE,
FOR THE
TAMING OF SCOLDS.

NOW IN THE POSSESSION OF
SAMUEL MAYER, ESQ., MAYOR.
1833—34.

The scold's bridle was supposedly invented to deal with the nagging women of the borough. It was argued that it was superior to the ducking stool which gave the woman's tongue 'liberty between every dip' whereas the bridle secured both humiliation and silence.

lanterns and rattles were appointed. Such minimum provision however proved inadequate. So in 1834 the continuing high crime rate, (the citizens of Newcastle believed a gang of determined and undiscovered 'banditti' were operating in the town), led to the consideration of the establishment of a police force. Isaac Cottrill was appointed chief officer and he set up the Newcastle force, in accord with what he knew of the Manchester system of police which he had observed when he was Superintendent of Police at Pendleton (Lancs).

The new force was to consist of a constable and two under-constables, paid for by £78 from the Improvement Rates, £52 from the Highways Rates (on condition that the constables supervised paupers from the Workhouse in cleaning the streets) and £78 from the poor rates (so long as the constables acted as 'market lookers'). Some services were to be paid for by the public and any remaining deficit was to be provided from the borough's general revenue account. Some of the early offences on which the police secured convictions make interesting reading:

'1838 September 22nd. 13 year old boy – deserting the Workhouse with clothing and shoes belonging to it. Stafford House of Correction. 3 months (14 other cases of this kind 1838–9).

17 year old boy – idle and disorderly and refusing to work 14 days with hard labour at the House of Correction. (3 other cases 1838–9).

1839 January 16th. Two men charged with contemplating a cock fight. Bound over to keep the peace for 12 months.

1839 January 31st. A man charged with being in a house which contained an illicit still. £30 fine with commitment to Stafford Prison in default of payment (1 other case 1838–9).

GALLOWSTREE LANE

'Gallowstree'—the name of the reputed 'gallows' field' is preserved in a modern street name.

**BILLY PUNKIE,
NEWCASTLE-UNDER-LYME.**

Billy Punkie who features in the Mock Mayor painting was reckoned to be a notorious footpad in London around 1843.

The problem of public order involved not only the disciplining of minor crime and what was taken to be social deviance, but also the control of agitators like the Chartists. The psychological impression formed upon the mind of the local establishment by such forces may be gauged from the following account in the *North Staffordshire Advertiser* for August 1842: 'The Rioters did not actually visit Newcastle, but from Monday, noon, excitement had been at fever pitch. Newcastle was the headquarters for the magistrates and troops, it being well known that the mob would put their threat into execution to visit the town and destroy property'.

'On Monday, the Mayor, W O Lester, Esq, assisted by the other magistrates and aided by our excellent head police officer, Mr Cottrill, lost not a moment in making the best preparations for the protection of the town. They augmented the special constable force to 800 strong. The working classes came forward and volunteered in great numbers. The Specials gave confidence to the town. A good many arms were placed in the hands of this force and two pieces of canon belonging to the town have lain in front of the Police Office since Monday ready for instant use'.

Isaac Cottrill, painted a year before his dismissal as Chief Officer of Police. He established the borough police force in 1834, wrote a useful directory of the town in 1836, and defended the town against the Chartists in 1842.

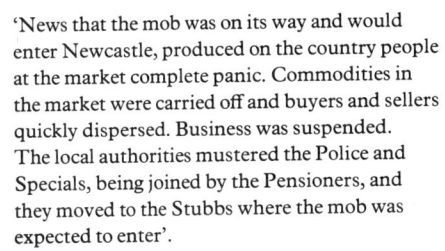

'News that the mob was on its way and would enter Newcastle, produced on the country people at the market complete panic. Commodities in the market were carried off and buyers and sellers quickly dispersed. Business was suspended. The local authorities mustered the Police and Specials, being joined by the Pensioners, and they moved to the Stubbs where the mob was expected to enter'.

'The mob, perceiving the opposition, thought it prudent to turn aside, thus preventing bloodshed. A government proclamation, offering a reward of £50 to anyone by whose information any rioters might be apprehended and convicted, and pardon to any accomplice, impeaching, was published throughout the district'.

'At 9 pm, twenty prisoners were escorted into the town by the military. The night was passed in great disquietude due to the prisoners being drunk and unruly. The Specials remained on duty throughout the night'.

'On Tuesday, disquietude remained when knowledge of what had occurred at Hanley was made known. A reinforcement of the military took place...'

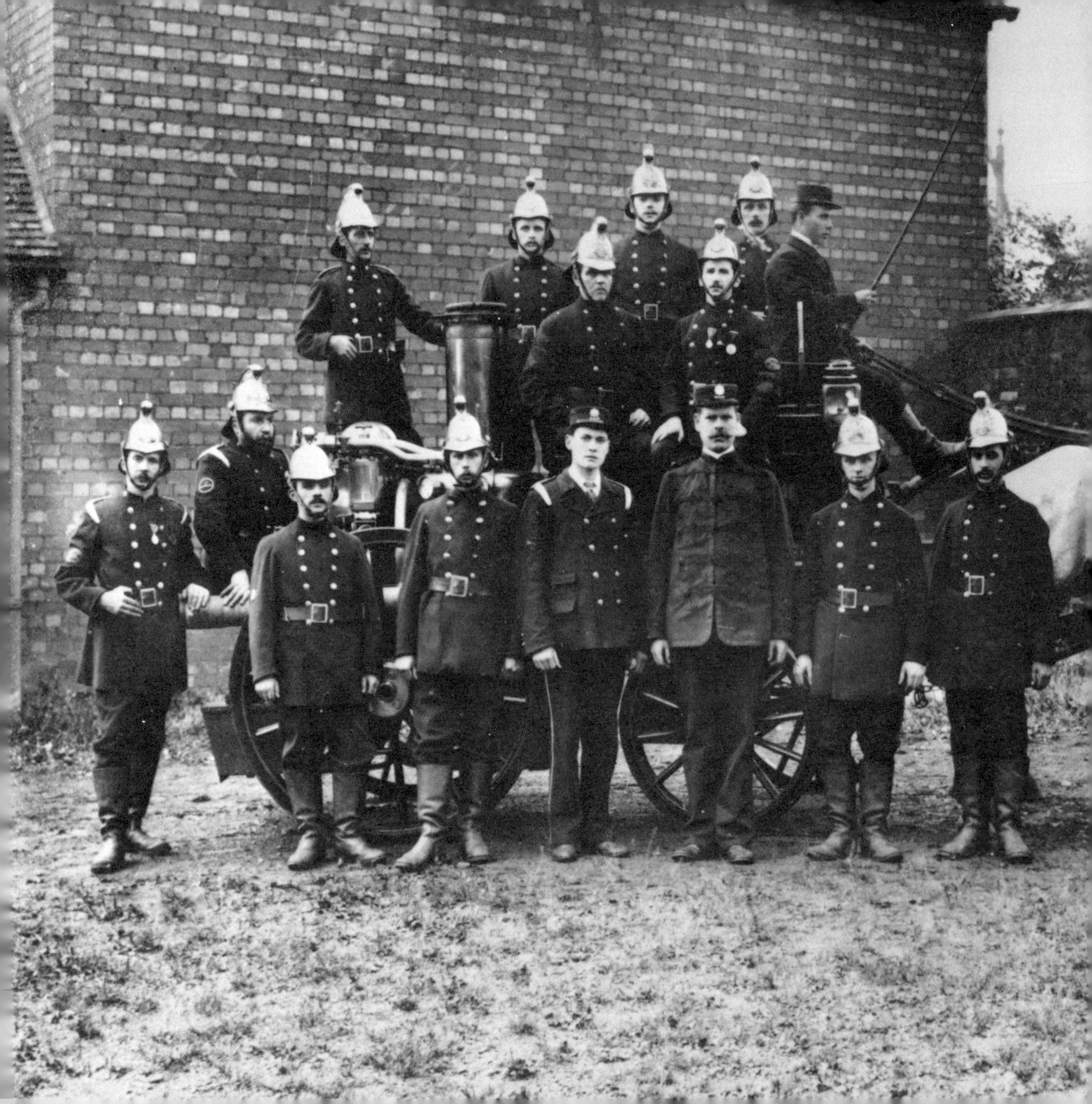

Captain Bayley and the fire team posing with their new steam powered fire engine about 1901.

Captain Bayley, who when first appointed was the youngest officer in command of any fire service in England, is seen here in 1910 with his company and engine.

Newcastle fire-men during the Second World War dressed in preparation for a gas attack.

The borough water cart seen at the rear of the Barracks in 1894.

The character of 'our excellent head police officer, Mr Cottrill', defender of the borough against the wild forces of Chartism, seems not, however, to have been impeccable. At the end of 1849 he was dismissed for two incidents involving drunkenness and absence from duty. Even the gift of £50 associated with his dismissal in respect of 'the extraordinary exertions used by him in the preservation of the peace of the borough at the time of the riots in the Potteries in 1842' was subsequently withdrawn when it came to light that he had been misapplying fire service funds over the past twelve years.

With Cottrill's defection and dismissal in 1849, the council decided that closer supervision of the police service was necessary. The government's model rules were adopted for use in Newcastle and the Watch Committee resolved to keep the force under close superintendence. In February 1850 J T Blood of the Uttoxeter force was sworn in as Superintendent with an additional constable added to his force at the end of the following year. Blood, who apparently had too much of a taste for bureaucracy, was difficult to entice out of the Police Office: he claimed that his occupation there was inevitable because of the illiteracy of the three constables. The council resolved to give him more help in the office so that he could be seen more in the town. Significantly, he believed that policemen should of preference be 'strangers' to the borough, presumably because local connections were full of potential for bribery; in fact the commonest cause of dissatisfaction in the early years was not corruption but drunkenness on duty. At this time the officers wore frock coats and silk hats though later a rather unpopular helmet was introduced which became compulsory after 1869. For protection they carried only a truncheon or staff, and exceptionally a cutlass, and at night a lantern. The Superintendent only may have carried a pistol.

Sergeant Thomas Maskery, shortly before his retirement after twenty-two years service in the 1st Volunteer Batallion of the North Staffordshire Regiment which he joined in 1876.

The militia of about 1875: notice that their rifles are muzzle loaded and not cartridge fired.

In 1856 Lord George Grey's Police Bill was passed by Parliament. This required all counties to set up rural police forces, established an inspectorate of police, and provided exchequer grants of up to 25% of the costs of salaries and uniforms to all forces certified efficient (excepting boroughs of less than 5,000 population). Newcastle was one of those many small borough forces, eligible for grant, but failing to secure it through lack of efficiency. Part of the difficulty was that the inspector considered the Newcastle force too small; part the lack of co-operation that existed between the Newcastle and the county police, who, not exemplary themselves, presented the borough force as inefficient men merely content to drive criminals off their own patch into areas for which the county force was responsible. It was not until 1873 that the borough was willing to expend sufficient funds upon the police force for it to be recognized as efficient and worthy of government grant. The failure of the interim years represents the stranglehold of ideas of economy, in the hands of a 'shopocracy', upon borough politics.

Between 1873 and 1947 the borough police force continued to expand so that on the eve of the Second World War the force, which now had to superintend a much larger area, numbered about 60 men. These operated from the recently completed Police Station in Merrial Street, which in 1936 replaced the old Police Office pulled down to make way for the redevelopment of the Lancaster Building site. In 1947 the county council became the police authority.

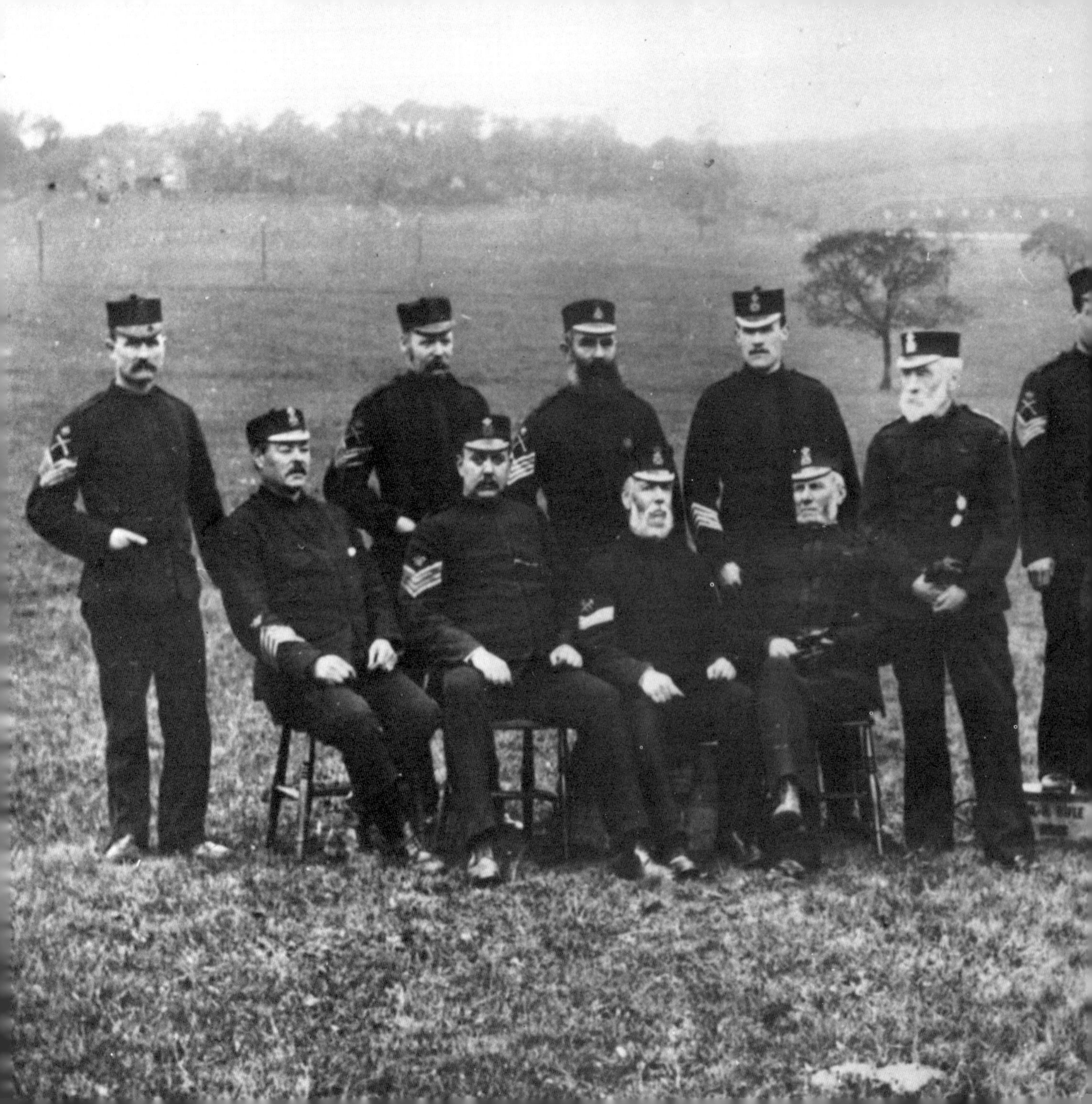

The volunteers on exercise at the Butts beyond Zoar Village about 1890. Much of this area is now occupied by the Westlands Farm Estate.

130

Built in 1855, the Italian styled Barracks, were the headquarters of the militia and of the fire brigade before the old fire station was built in the last decade of the nineteenth century.

Isaac Cottrill's downfall, it will be remembered, arose out of his misapplication of fire service funds. Newcastle's fire conscience dates back to 1623 when, in the thatch roofed borough, every capital burgess was required to equip himself with a leather bucket. In 1666 three 'fire-lookers' were appointed, and in 1689 a 40s fine was to be levied on citizens who failed to keep good chimneys. In 1734 the first manual fire pump was secured and in 1819 the Improvement Act forbade any further use of thatch. (The equivalent date for London is 1212). The superintendent of police in the 1840s had two fire engines and 24 firemen under his control, and this provision seems to have limited the number of fires breaking out in the borough. More modern machinery was bought in the mid-century but it was not until 1888 that a volunteer brigade was formed which became separate from the administration of the police. This force used the old militia barracks built in 1855 as their headquarters. Garrison-like with its grim brick frontage onto Barracks Road, it encloses a drill square approached through a castellated tower. Used by the King's Own Staffordshire Rifle Regiment until 1880, it has since been used by successive volunteer forces until in most recent years it has been occupied by Remploy Ltd. Once an efficient and nation wide police force had been established, small provincial barracks lost a large part of the reason for their existence. In the twentieth century this obsolescence has been confirmed by the contraction of the Territorial Army.

Old and new: a Newsham engine of about 1740 (the town's first manual fire pump) alongside a tender of 1964.

Modern fire tenders at the new fire station in Knutton Road. Built in 1965 the station now attends to between six and seven hundred calls a year, a good proportion of which are concerned with road accidents. Last year 118 people were rescued from vehicles as compared with 9 from fires in buildings.

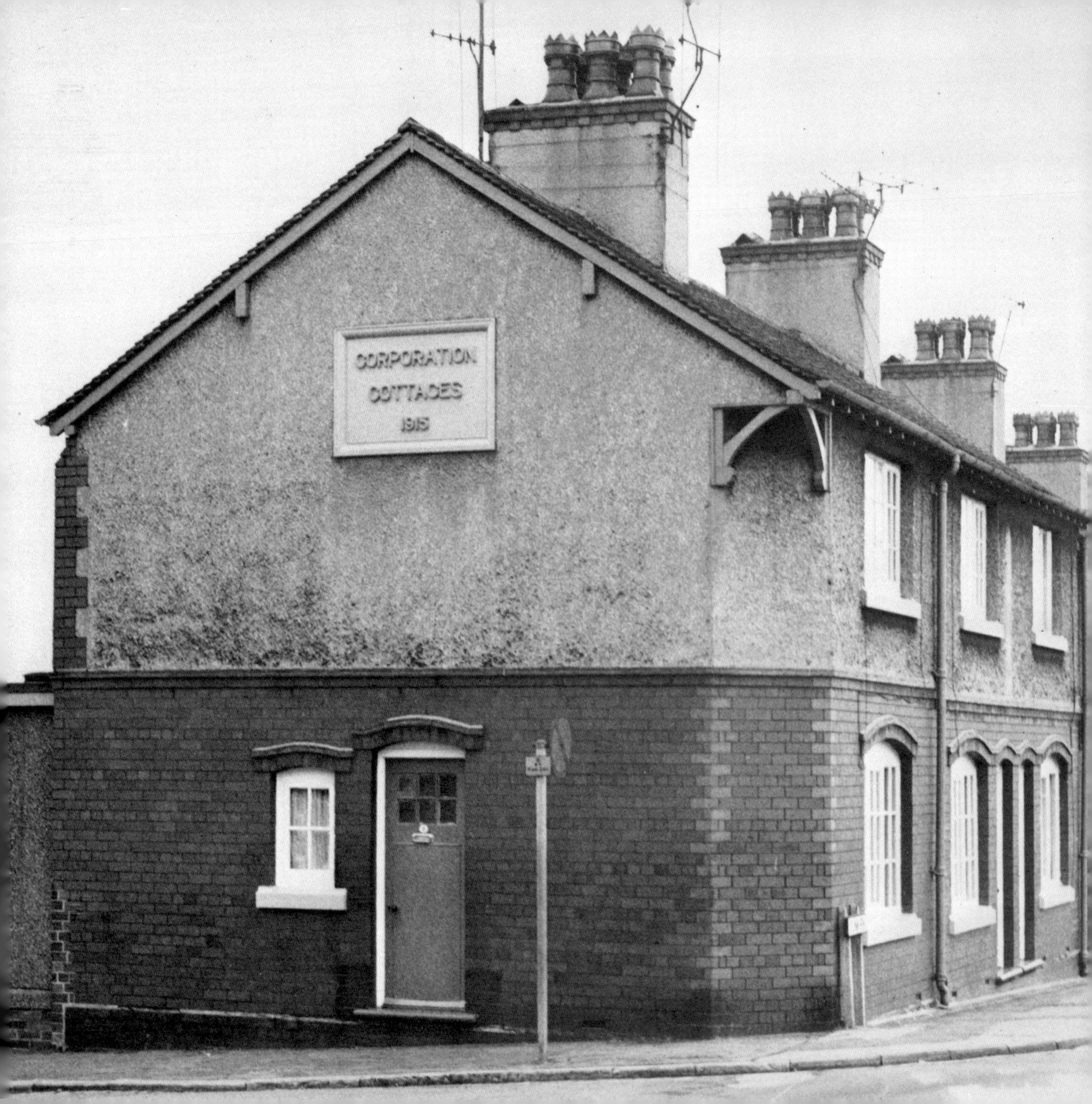
CORPORATION
COTTAGES
1915

Clean and Decent

Conservationists are properly indignant at the way in which the demands of the motor car and modern commerce rob us of much of our priceless urban heritage. Care needs to be taken to avoid sentimentality with regard to the past. Newcastle may have lost too much by way of coaching inns, town houses and civic buildings, but this loss must not blind us to the altogether desirable passing of those dark insanitary courts that too often lurked behind the austere but elegant houses of the principal thoroughfares, or of the wretchedly inadequate housing in the low lying and, in the nineteenth century, unhealthy areas around Lower Street, Pooldam and Holborn.

The borough shared to the full the consequences of sanitary neglect with other British towns, though in her case neither the growth of factories (which were too few and too small rather than too many and too large) nor the coming of the railway can be made the culprit. Instead the growth of commerce in the borough centre and the stranglehold of the Burgess Trustees upon expansion must bear heavy responsibility.

From 1635 the borough had had a common warder, whose duties amongst many others included that of acting as borough scavenger and removing refuse from the central streets. It was not until 1682 that the first common scavenger as such was appointed though the post had been advertised since 1670. In 1685 the borough resorted to self help, each inhabitant being required to clean the public areas surrounding his house twice a week, the savenger acting in cases of default, a charge of 4d being levelled on the offending householder. The prohibition, in 1726, of the making of middens (or dunghills) in the street indicates just how rudimentary was the sanitary state of the town in the eighteenth century.

The first significant reforms awaited the appointment of the Improvement Commissioners of 1819, who had special responsibility to keep the streets free of nuisances (a polite word for all forms of obnoxious accumulations including piles of human sewage). This, however, tended to become a matter of window dressing with the main streets cared for but not the courts and alleys where the poorer people lived. There everything depended on the inclination of the landlord, whose first priority was usually maximising his profits. One important change made by the 1819 Act was however the prohibition of thatched roofs in the borough, at once eliminating an important cause of urban fires as also a ready home of town vermin.

Throughout the century the story was the same: improvement meant expenditure, meant pressure on the rates, meant popular and petit-bourgeois opposition. Little by little improvements were made even though the expansion of the town was constantly throwing up new problems: in 1801 the first municipal contribution towards the establishment of a town sewerage system had been made but when the Commission of Enquiry into the Sanitary State of the Large Towns and Populous Districts reported in 1845 it presented a grim picture of public health in Newcastle.

The retention of human sewage in the town was still commonplace; of solid materials the report says: 'In many of the neglected courts and obscure places, there are collections of refuse dung and dirt brought in from the highways and heaped up in some corner till sufficient for sale;' of liquid sewage, 'The fluid contents are dammed up to irrigate meadows or gardens in the vicinity of the town, exhaling a pestilential smell in hot weather.' Nobody locally, apparently, undertook any comparative costings: the cost of lost life against the miserly pence secured by selling manure to the local farmers.

Particularly ill served were the working class areas. R A Slaney, the Commissioner for the area, always backing up his censures with particular example, reported: 'Little is done for the health or comfort of the majority of the poorer inhabitants. The main streets are generally open and well drained but there are many narrow entries, alleys and courts quite neglected. Some new streets of sufficient width are unpaved and undrained and although the water is generally good in quality, frequent complaints were made by the poor women, that

Corporation Cottages, now modernised to include a Bathroom and internal WC were Newcastle's first council houses, built in 1915 as the result of a campaign undertaken by John Mayer, the first representative of organized Labour on the Borough Council.

135

Most of the cholera cases were buried in St George's churchyard since St Giles' was already too full. Even today a walk around the gravestones of the reduced burial ground indicates how short a life span could be anticipated in the 1840s and 1850s.

Newcastle is fortunate in having in its archives a Cholera Map, which carefully locates every house in the borough where a fatal case of cholera occurred in 1849.

the public pumps from which many were supplied were out of order or gave an inadequate supply. Part of the town is supplied by pipes and the whole might in the same way be easily furnished with this indispensable necessary at a moderate cost from an unfailing source.' In fact, of the town's 2039 houses in 1845, over half of which had been built in the nineteenth century, only 215 had tapped water inside the houses whilst a further 168 had access to street stand pipes, that is less than 19% of the town's housing had access to piped water of any kind. There were no public baths but there was 'every facility for public bathing in our canals, without being a nuisance'. The widespread existence of open drains, in-town pigsties, open privies, overflowing cess pools, back to back houses (though the absence of cellar dwellings is noted) are all complained of and related to a 2·88% annual mortality rate. The national average was 2·1% with the most unhealthy towns as high as 3·0% or 3·1%. The Public Health Act of 1848 required all areas with a mortality of more than 2·3% to establish local Boards of Health. It is clear, therefore, that Newcastle with a figure of 2·88%, before the ravages of the 1848 cholera outbreak, stood near to the most unhealthy towns in Britain in respect of annual mortality.

The standard of the housing was generally reasonable in the first half of the century, though the houses of the poor tended to be very small: only 3% of the householders were estimated to be in a position to supplement family incomes by taking a lodger, and 40% of the town's houses were let at a rent of 1s 6d a week or less. In general there was little overcrowding, the principal difficulties being the absence of ventilation and sanitation. Overcrowding did, however, occur in the lodging houses where most of the town's 6–800 Irish lived in wretched and dirty conditions. They were in the main recent arrivals; Joseph Mayer could remember a time when there was only one Irishman in the town, and he lived as a servant to an English family.

More important probably than government reports in prompting reform was cholera, the second great epidemic of which, three times more fatal in its influence than the 1832 outbreak, hit Newcastle in 1849. In August a public meeting was convoked and the General Board of Health was almost unanimously petitioned to take action on account of the escalating mortality rate. John Hallam, who forwarded the motion to London, had been re-elected mayor for 1849 when his predecessor (as also the latter's nurse and washerwoman) died of the cholera; clearly the disease was no respecter of class and status, hence the middle class alarm of 1849. And yet the cholera, the most dramatic of the nineteenth century fevers, has to be seen in context. In 1849 it claimed 234 victims in under nine weeks, pushing the death rate up to 5·2%. Taking the evidence of John Smith Mayer, that the death rate in the working class parts of the town was double that in the better drained areas, this statistic means that about 1 in 10 of Newcastle's working class population lost their lives in 1849. But even two years earlier the death rate soared 170 above the annual average, typhus claiming 100 deaths, and measles and scarlet fever 70 between them. In other years influenza and smallpox were the killers.

As a consequence of the Newcastle petition, William Lee, Superintending Inspector of the General Board of Health held an investigation into 'the sewerage, drainage and supply of water, and the sanitary condition of the inhabitants of the borough of Newcastle under Lyme' in October 1849, only forty days after the petition had been received in London, the report going to the General Board before the end of the year. This document is of crucial importance in depicting the state of Newcastle at this crisis in her history, and corroborates much of what was reported four years earlier, yet indicating that things were moving from bad to worse. In particular the report witnesses the alarm felt by local doctors, some six of whom with very little disagreement gave evidence as to the state of the borough. Once more the Irish, who apparently made Newcastle a base for peddling activities in the Potteries, were distinguished from the 'native inhabitants of the town': 'their habits are very filthy and that has tended to produce and disseminate disease when any epidemic has existed in the town.' A doctor with experience in Calcutta thought Newcastle suffered from the

The earliest water pipes in the borough were made of wood: those here seen at the Museum date from the eighteenth century.

same defects: filth and nuisances, bad water courses and inadequate burial places.

Such was the impact of disease in 1849 that many of the town's friendly societies with over 30 years existence collapsed under the strain: even the prosperous Oddfellows had to raise their subscriptions by twopence per member per month. William Hallam noted that if these same monies had been applied to sanitary improvement the societies would have flourished on two thirds of the original subscription. The doctors did not always arrive at proper diagnoses of the causes of disease: they correctly diagnosed the cruciality of the presence of nuisances and the absence of a proper water supply but only in as far as these contributed towards the presence of matters which 'pollute and poison the air. The inhabitants are compelled to breathe – and inhaling poison they die'. Tarmacadamed roads were held to be unhealthy as absorbing dirt and as giving off an unhealthy vapour. Of course the source of disease was not so much the air the people breathed, but rather the water that they drank.

With more justification the state of the burial grounds was diagnosed as a primary cause of ill health, and these became the subject of a separate report the following year, which underlines the worst aspects of small-town administration in the nineteenth century. Although most of the cholera cases were interred in St George's churchyard, the high incidence of death in Church Street by St Giles' was linked with grisly observations of 'fluid coming through the churchyard wall'. It also came to light that the beadle and the sexton had come to an arrangement whereby the latter handed over to the former those parts of old coffins disturbed by the construction of new graves to use as fuel for the boilers for the church, ways of proceeding that the inspector thought would be considered 'crimes against the laws of nature, even amongst savages'. The grave digger witnessed to being overcome by the stench when digging one grave and contracting cholera thereafter: nevertheless he chose not to employ the boring rod or searcher, preferring to work from the rule of thumb that after seven years had elapsed a plot might be redug. So overcrowded was the place that the ground stood proud of its natural height and the local surveyor commented that if many more burials took place the congregation would 'have to go down stairs into the church'. The inspector concluded his report by recommending the closure of St Giles', the Wesleyan and the Roman Catholic burial grounds; St George's churchyard could be used for a brief interim period. He pressed upon the government 'the urgent necessity existing for a general and comprehensive legislative enactment to provide for extra-mural sepulture in country towns'.

In consequence both of disease and inquiry, interest in improving the borough's environment revived at the mid-century. About this time the the Castle Pool was improved. In 1848 a new sewer had been added in the Marsh area of the town and two years later the council eventually constituted itself a Local Board of Health and proceeded to work out a more comprehensive drainage plan. The widespread existence of springs and wells meant that the citizens of Newcastle were slow to seek other supplies: in 1727, 1795 and 1811 partial attempts were made to improve the borough's water supply to little effect, though the reservoirs of the 1795 scheme in Merrial Street were only demolished in 1935. The wretchedness of water supply is one of the clearest causes of disease diagnosed in Slaney's Report of 1845. In 1847 the Staffordshire Potteries Water Company was founded to deal with the problem in the whole area: reservoirs were established at Wall Grange, Longsdon, and in 1850 the supply reached Newcastle.

The impact of legislation and its implementation is seen in the Medical Officer of Health's Report for 1851. Piped water was already bringing down the death-rate: 'fever in a factory using one of the old polluted sources highly impregnated with noxious gas' was immediately checked once it converted to the Wall Grange supply. Similarly, the enclosure of the public wells could be expected to improve the health of a town where the mid-Victorian principle of inspection to ensure conformity with the new legislation was having its effect upon the slaughterhouses, factories and lodging houses of the area. The immediate impact was the reduction of epidemic disease: a small outbreak of Smallpox was soon controlled, Asiatic Cholera was held at bay, whilst English Cholera 'to which all towns are more or less subject during the summer and autumnal months' had less severe effects than in previous years. The report concluded rather too confidently: 'I feel convinced that when we get our drainage complete we shall be one of the healthiest little towns in her Majesty's Dominions'.

That most necessary improvement, though soon implemented, brought new difficulties for on three occasions (1861, 1875 and 1880) the Dukes of Sutherland had either to take, or threaten to take, the borough to law to prevent them from polluting the Lyme Brook and thereby jeopardising life at Trentham. James Hall, their gamekeeper, gave evidence in 1861 that his family would not leave the front door or windows of their cottage open because of the smells coming from the adjacent Trent. 'I have frequently observed' he claimed, 'fish coming into the Trent from small rivulets which run into it, as soon as they get into the river, they endeavour to get back into the clear water and, if they fail, I have seen them jump out of the water and after a short time turn over on their backs and die'.

Newcastle's first public baths were a commercial failure. There were Baths planned as part of the Municipal Hall complex but these were never built. The present baths were built in 1906 in commemoration of the coronation of King Edward VII and have four times been improved.

138

The privy at the bottom of the garden was an evil often complained of by Medical Officers of Health. Their replacement by Water Closets connected to a main drainage system has done more than anything else to improve the healthiness of the borough. These outside closets were pictured at the rear of Castle Street about 1957.

Roebuck Lane, 1926, provides a picturesque example of the housing of the old Newcastle, with its narrow cobbled streets.

Some parts of Newcastle (eg Ashfields) were however not sewered until the last decade of the century. In 1892 William Hallam, Medical Officer of Health, reported on Newcastle slums. Of the George Street district he wrote: 'There were few houses free from some nuisance injurious to health and in some 72 cases these were attributable to leaking privies and cesspools'. It was some years before the situation was to be changed: in 1894 the County Medical Officer of Health wrote 'In Newcastle there is ample field for action under the Housing of The Working Classes Act 1890 and until energetic steps are taken under that Act the town will constantly be liable to the recurrence of serious outbreaks of enteric fever and other zymotic diseases', for even at the end of the century the problem of nuisance remained in the working class parts of the town. 'Throughout the greater part of the town the system of dealing with the excrement and refuse is highly unsatisfactory. Most houses have privy middens, all of which are constructed on wrong principles, and many of which are even more unsanitary than they need to be owing to the fact that the house ashes are not applied to the excreta, so that the privy contents, in place of being kept dry, are retained on the premises in a wet and filthy condition, constantly discharging noxious putrefactive gases which render the air surrounding the houses horribly unwholesome and injurious to health.' New houses were still being built with faulty privies, though the local authority was beginning to encourage the provision of water closets and generally to take a much more active part in securing a healthy environment.

Environmental improvement in the nineteenth century meant a diagnosis of problems and the piecemeal removal of the worst abuses often with the result of making homeless those who lived in the shabbiest dwellings, the only property they could afford. Newcastle's first intervention into municipal housing was in 1915 with the building of 'Corporation Cottages'. Land had been given for building by Ralph Sneyd as early as 1900, but only four plots were bought for houses to be erected. Legislation allowing sub standard houses to be demolished

The welcoming interior of a Victorian house in Bridge Street (actually the home of Mr Wardle the barber pictured on page 22), witnesses to a changing domestic economy—from open fire, by way of gas stove to the advent of the radio.

was implemented but there was insufficient new building to compensate. Between 1909 and 1915 ninety two houses received closing orders but only sixty houses were built for all classes in the borough. An estate agent put a notice in his window, 'We have no houses to let under 7s 6d a week'.

Even the 29 'Corporation Cottages', built in 1915 replaced 65 previous buildings on the site. The enterprise, modest enough in its scope, was carried out under the 1890 Housing of the Working Classes Act; it was the fruit of the persistence of John Mayer, a bricklayer and first representative of organized Labour in the Council, over the previous ten years. Proudly the Council announced 'the absence of that working class fetish, the sitting room'. The new houses would be built without parlours; there were, of course, no bathrooms and the water closets were to be outside. The annual cost of all 29 houses to the borough was £397 against which they had an anticipated income of £376. In other words the rates were to subsidise the scheme at a rate of £20 per annum for a period of 20 years. The financial outlay was small enough, but it was a crucial new beginning, the start of municipal housing in Newcastle.

Before the outbreak of the Second World War some 2,703 housing units were built by the borough and the old Wolstanton UDC which included large estates at Knutton, Chesterton, Cross Heath and Poolfields and smaller developments elsewhere. After the war, under the wise leadership of Alderman Beattie, principal architect of Newcastle's postwar housing plans, an even more extensive programme was embarked upon and to date 6,345 housing units have been added with large estates at Clayton and Seabridge, Silverdale and Chesterton, Knutton and Bradwell.

Together with 322 miscellaneous properties this gives the council a stock of some 9,370 units in 1973. In recent years more attention has been given to the specialised needs of particular groups, especially old people, for whom both purpose built units and wardening services are provided, and physically handicapped families, where again properties specially designed to ease the problems of domesticity have, and are being, built. Unlike some councils, Newcastle has not chosen to sell council houses but instead prefers to make available 100% mortgage facilities to council tenants who have good rent records.

In addition to attention to housing, water supply and drainage, the emerging urban community of the nineteenth century required other services. Newcastle was one of the first boroughs in England to possess street lighting, 80 lamps being erected by the corporation in 1799. It was

Slum Clearance in operation: these pictures show families leaving the old Victorian terraces of Paradise Street at the lower end of the High Street and their subsequent resettlement in Beattie Avenue, Wolstanton.

The Bournville Village Trust who helped plan the development of the Westlands are architects to the borough's latest housing project: the provision of dwellings for handicapped persons in Knutton.

amongst the first boroughs, too, to possess a gas works. These were at first in Rye Croft, but in 1855 the Brook Street plant was constructed. In 1880 the borough bought out the Newcastle Gaslight Company and was able both to extend the availability of gas and reduce its cost. The works have now been demolished but even in an age of North Sea Gas, the gas holder remains as a familiar landmark. In 1899 electricity was added as a further utility with the building of electricity works in Friarswood Road.

The first public baths on the site of the present Borough Library, opened in 1852 but only operated for four years partly because of lack of demand, partly because of bad administration: it was all too easy, apparently, to get a bath without paying. Fifty years were to elapse before the King Edward VII Memorial Baths were opened in 1906, with much more certain patronage.

At the same time, Newcastle was in the vanguard of planned suburban development in the private sector with the laying out of the Westlands under the guidance of the architect of the Bourneville Trust. Attention was given to interesting road patterns, variety of building styles and the provision of amenity areas. The end result secured for Newcastle a national reputation and visits to the borough from other municipal authorities. Though initiated by Alderman Moran, a member of the Labour Group on the Council, this scheme, which increased the rateable value of the borough, was supported by all parties.

It was not until 1866 that the first municipal cemetery, suitably adorned with Gothic chapels, was opened on a site to the west of the Clayton Road. In 1872 a temporary fever hospital was built on an adjacent site. Built when the problem of fever had already passed its peak, it still served a useful function as well as standing as a monument to the gravest fears of the previous generation. Rebuilt in 1901, it survives today as the Limewood Hospital for Old People.

The contrast between the health of the borough in 1973 and the situation a hundred years ago is only too apparent. Citizens may complain about the intrusion of bureaucracy and officialdom upon their lives but it is quite clear that only by Acts of Parliament and their implementation in the locality, (through by-laws, through inspectors and through municipal initiative in building and construction and in the creation of welfare services), has that necessary improvement in environment upon which everyone depends, been effected. In consequence the 28·88 per thousand crude death rate of 1849 in Newcastle is now down to 11·7 per thousand, which is also the national average. The infant mortality rate stands at 19 per thousand, whilst the maternal

Newcastle has had a gas supply from the beginning of the nineteenth century. The corporation bought out the company in 1880 and in 1949 the gas industry was nationalised. Mr Arthur Wardle here drives the gas department's first motor cycle along Silverdale Road in 1926. The same vehicle was driven by Mr Wardle in the 1930s after it had been transferred to the fire service.

By comparison with other areas Newcastle suffered very little by way of bomb damage in the last war. The havoc caused to individual homes was still considerable as this photograph of Taylor Avenue, May Bank (1941) depicts.

mortality statistic has reached zero. The change in the quality of life for all citizens that lies behind these statistics cannot be overemphasized. As this account has been obliged to stress, the 'good old days' were not as good as memory sometimes would pretend, especially for the working people of the borough. For all its faults, the twentieth century witnesses to the co-operative efforts of national and local government to create decent living and working conditions for all, so that today the notion that any one class has a monopoly right to the same is universally rejected. Today the emphasis in public health has moved away from the establishment of basic sanitary conditions and the elimination of infectious diseases towards the more positive fostering of a healthy community in which a variety of welfare services are available, with special attention given to the old, and the young, to the school population and to pensioners.

In the late 1930s Newcastle established a place for itself in the vangard of the movement for urban development. Here, in The Westlands, private housing was provided in garden city surroundings. High standards of urban design were also adopted for the council estates of the period. Today a third of the borough's stock of housing is municipally owned.

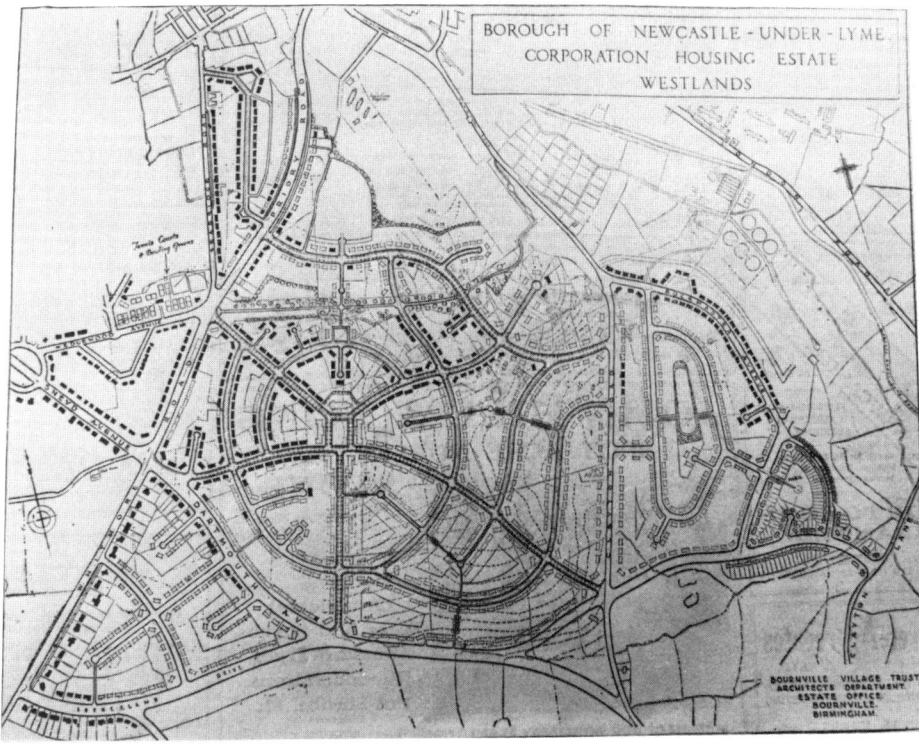

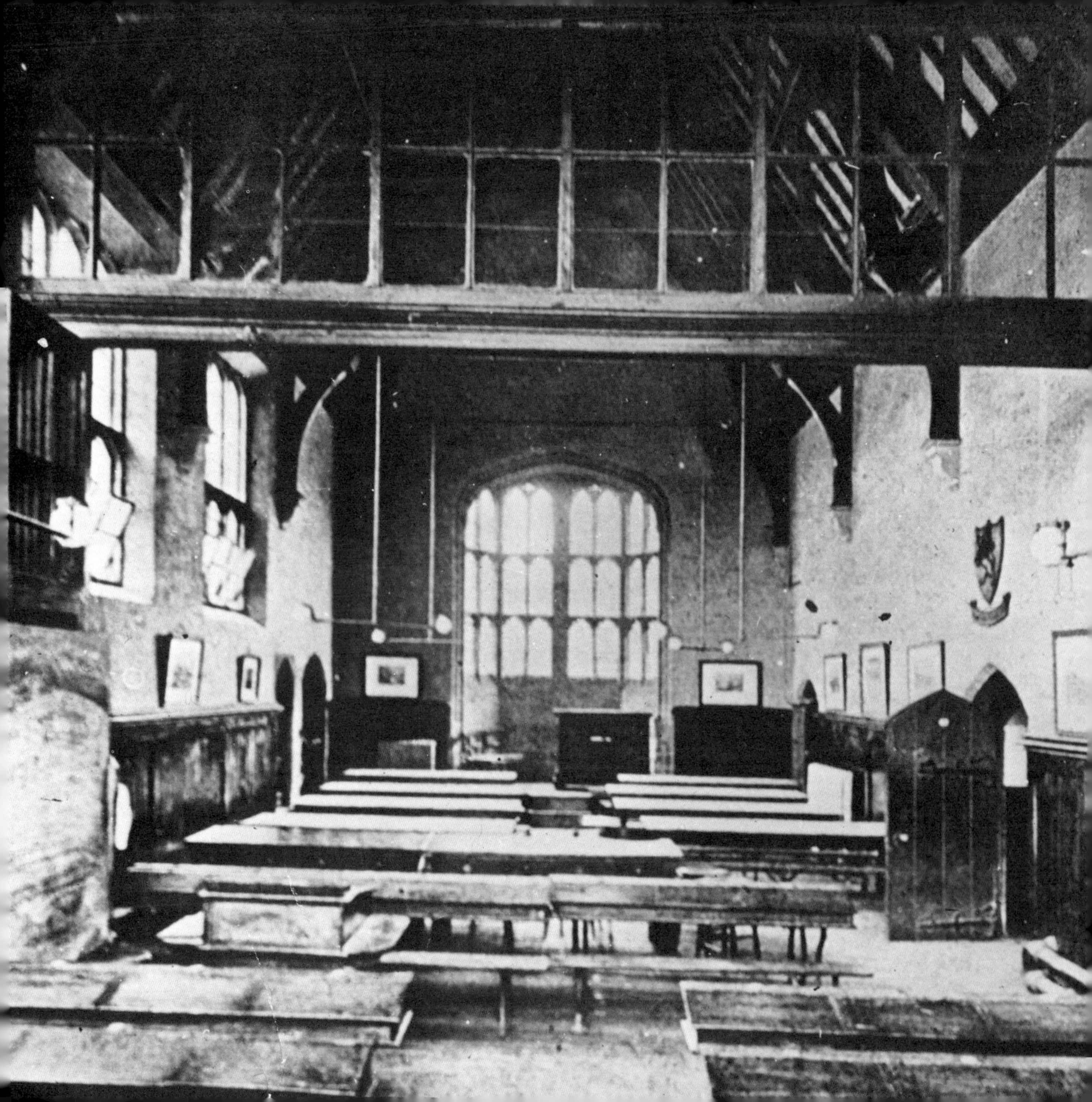

Spare the Rod

As an old established market town Newcastle was favoured with a number of educational endowments in the post-Reformation period. A free school, which may well have existed in the church yard from Elizabethan days, attracted gifts from prominent borough families, some of whom including, in particular, the Claytons and Cottons, had London connections. The first recorded bequest is that of Sir Richard Clayton, dyer of London, who in his will of 1602 remembered his birthplace and left a yearly rent of £10 from his property in the parish of St Lawrence in the Old Jewry, London, to pay a master 'which shall teach and instruct in learning thirty poor children born and to be born within the said town of Newcastle under Lyme, gratis...' A condition of the bequest in 1692 of William Cotton, former Mayor, was that the school should teach Latin and Greek freely to sons of burgesses and of poor inhabitants of the borough. In other words it was to be a grammar school and as such, closely associated with the Established Church.

The master, in addition to possessing a Bachelor of Arts of one of the Universities of Cambridge or Oxford was required to be 'of the Protestant religion, and no Papist, Romish priest, Jesuit or Schismatic...' In fact, the headmasters were all clergymen, and were licensed by the Bishops of the diocese. Their duties included the teaching of the catechism and accompanying the pupils to church on Sundays and holy days. Until the early nineteenth century the grammar school was sited within the shadow of the parish church, for even after its removal from the churchyard, when the church was rebuilt in the eighteenth century, it was housed nearby in Church Street.

It was possibly the transformation of the free school into a grammar school which prompted a former headmaster of the school, the Reverend Edward Orme, to leave the greater part of his estate to found a new 'English' school. The Orme Charity School, established at the beginning of the eighteenth century in the Presbyterian Meeting House, taught, free of charge, reading, writing and accounts to 40 poor boys. By a subsequent endowment some of the pupils were provided with free clothing. Like the grammar school, the charity school, though at first housed in dissenting premises, was closely associated with the parish church, and an applicant for the first mastership was disqualified because he was a dissenter. Special pews were provided in St Giles' for the use of 'the English master and his scholars'.

The fortunes of the Grammar School depended very much on the calibre of individual masters. An enterprising man could, for his own profit, offer extra subjects such as writing and accounts which would be useful to burgesses' sons as future tradesmen. He could also attract additional day boys as well as boarders from the neighbouring countryside. Indeed in 1825, by which time the school had moved from the centre of the town to the Marsh (by the corner of Hanover Street), the headmaster had, apart from the sons of freemen, 40 day scholars and 21 boarders. With fees of eight guineas for tuition in classics and the English subjects, the Grammar School catered for the more prosperous members of the community.

For poorer children, apart from the 40 or 50 boys at the charity school, there was meagre provision. A so-called 'petty school' or Dame's school drew on minor endowments throughout the eighteenth century until the last of the dames, feeble with old age, died in 1827. An important legacy of £2,000, which under the will of Thomas Hatrell (1794) was intended for 'putting out poor children to school at five of the poorest schools in Newcastle', became the subject of unfortunate dispute. Some seventy years after Hatrell's decease his gift had dwindled to less than a third of its original value.

The Hatrell bequest was only one of many bequests made in good faith which were eroded by changing money values or by negligent trusteeship. Some were blatantly misappropriated, others dissipated and largely wasted. The Corporation itself was not blameless. The Orme benefaction was a glowing exception to the list of charities which diminished in value. Invested in land, including an estate at Knutton which was later found to be rich in coal and ironstone, it was to appreciate dramatically

The teaching hall of the Orme School built in 1850 on the site of the former Workhouse. The partitions are a later addition: originally this hall was the only classroom, in which the master officiated with the help of pupil-teachers.

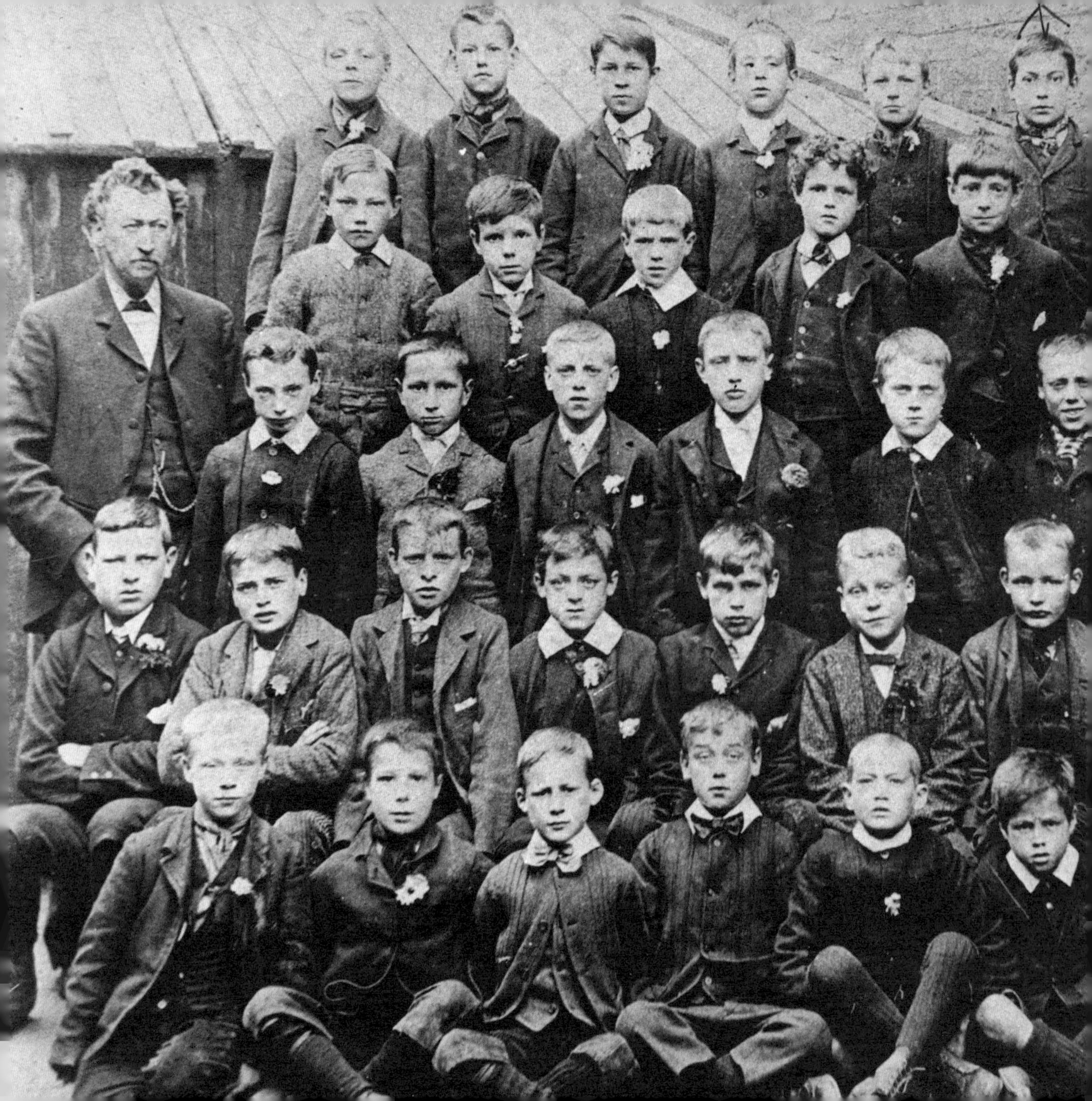

during the Victorian age. Yet in the early years of the nineteenth century this endowment was the subject of controversy and litigation. With the income in dispute and the accounts in hopeless confusion the Charity School itself was closed for twenty years.

By 1800 Newcastle had a population of almost 5,000. New industries were attracting immigrants from the countryside. Very soon child labour was to be in demand in the textile mills as well as in the neighbouring earthenware factories and brickyards of the Potteries.

With the closure of the Charity School only private adventure schools were offering weekday instruction. However, large numbers of children attended Sunday schools attached to the dissenting chapels, to St Giles' and to St George's. The punctuality and cleanliness, which were required conditions of attendance, helped to inculcate habits of self discipline. Children were instructed in reading as well as in religion and those who persevered learnt to read the Bible for themselves.

At the national level the drive for elementary education for 'the children of the labouring poor' came from rival religious organisations, the National Society for Promoting the Education of the Children of the Poor in the Principles of the Established Church, and the British and Foreign School Society which drew support from dissenters. Both sought the salvation of souls, but whereas National schools stressed Church doctrine and catechism, British schools confined themselves to simple Bible teaching. Both provided secular instruction designed to make children industrious members of society.

A class photograph taken at the Friarswood Board School in 1897 on the occasion of the Queen's Diamond Jubilee shows the variety of social intake.

The first elementary school in Newcastle was St Giles' National School, opened in 1826 in Bagnall Street. During its early years it received almost £30 annually from the Hatrell Charity, in return for which it educated 20 boys and 20 girls free of charge. Other children aged 5 and upwards paid 2d a week. However the greatest pressure on places was for infants who were too young to be turned out to work. To meet the demand St George's Church opened an infant school (charging 1d a week) in a former malthouse in Sunday Wells Street, and St Giles' also made additional provision for the 2 to 5 year olds. In the meantime a British school, founded in 1834 in Friars Road, represented Nonconformist endeavour. Some forty years later in 1871 the Wesleyans opened their own school adjoining Hanover Street Chapel. In the meantime, ever since the foundation of the Roman Catholic Church in 1833, the priest had enclosed one of the aisles for use as a school. In 1864 a separate school, dedicated to St Patrick, was built alongside the church.

Even when state assistance became available in increasing measure during the middle years of the century the schools had to struggle to make ends meet. Subscriptions were hard to come by. Parents were reluctant, indeed often unable, to pay school pence. In consequence, children left early and even when they were still on roll they attended irregularly. Frequently the master or mistress sent the child-monitors, and later the adolescent pupil teachers, to search out absentees. At St Patrick's the priests themselves visited negligent parents.

Schools offered little attraction for the children who sat on backless benches, their feet often barely touching the ground, in the long schoolrooms or in galleried classrooms. Their daily programme was based on rote learning of religion and the '3 Rs'. Their punishments were severe, for conditions of mass education required absolute obedience. Pleasures were few, and it was hardly surprising that they were tempted to play truant when the circus or the fair came to town.

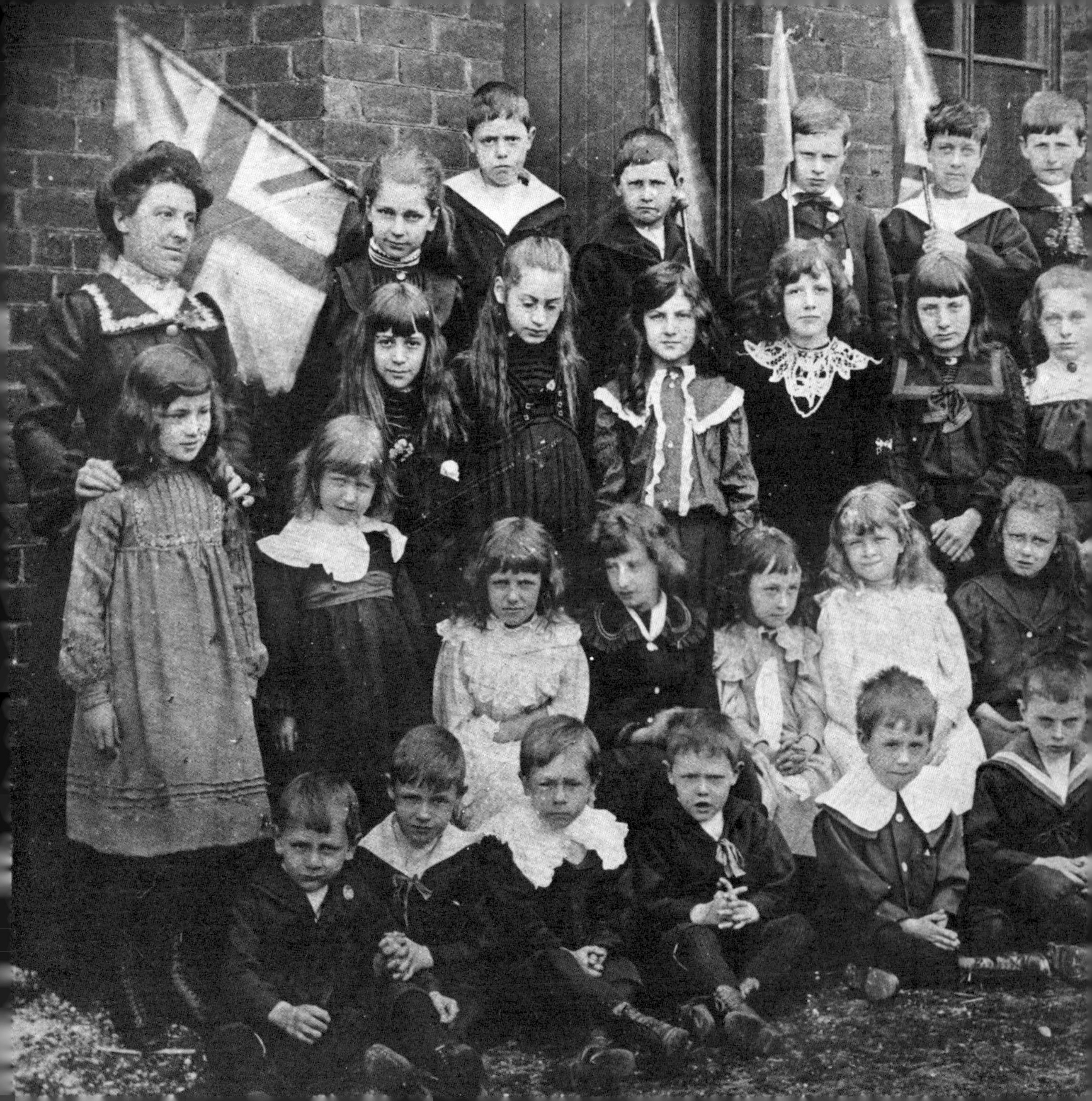

Teachers themselves were under constant supervision. In the church schools the clergy in their capacity as managers visited regularly. Their paternalism extended to promoting Clothing Clubs which teachers were required to administer. No detail of school routine escaped them and teachers who failed to give satisfaction were summarily dismissed. The British school was also visited by managers and members of the Ladies' Committee, but their superintendence was less meticulous than that of the resident clergy over the neighbouring church schools. Here everything depended on the personal qualities of the individual teacher in attracting children and earning government grants.

It was the successful master of the British School, Emmanuel Earl, a product of the British training school at Borough Road, London, who in 1851 at the age of 26 was selected to be head of the revived Orme Charity School. Housed in new buildings on the site of the old workhouse in the Higherland, the school now took on a new lease of life. Scholars were no longer necessarily poor boys, though they were required to be 'the children of the most deserving industrious persons'. In fact, they were often former pupils of the National and British schools, who were attracted by Earl's efficient teaching in 'the acquisition of the power of audible and clear reading, good plain writing from dictation and a ready and rapid use of the ruler and practices of arithmetic'. Clerks were sought from the school by attorneys and officials of the railway. By the age of 20, former pupils could earn as much as a guinea a week. Many in their spare time attended the Literary and Scientific Institute in Brunswick Street where they could borrow books and hear lectures on poetry, literature, and popular science.

Miss Beardmore's School at Wolstanton was one of many private schools which flourished in the early twentieth century. This picture was taken at the time of the peace celebrations at the end of the Boer War, for which best clothes were donned.

The Orme school was financed from its endowments which were sufficient to provide Earl with two assistant teachers for the 150 children on roll by the mid-sixties. By contrast, the neighbouring elementary schools were dependent on the Government's scheme of Payment by Results. They were overcrowded (St Giles' alone had some 500 in regular attendance), and the need to provide for half-timers in the textile mills and the potteries put them under further strain. Even after the opening of the Wesleyan school in 1871 there were insufficient school places. The superior working class families, clerks, tradesmen and shopkeepers, often sent their children to private schools. A Mr Lloyd, for example, ran a very efficient school in Marsh Street and a Mr Bridgman had a flourishing Commercial School in Bow Street. For the very poor there was in Upper Green, a Ragged School which, founded in 1862, was supported by charitable subscriptions.

By the later years of the century it had become clear that the task of educating the great mass of children, the offspring of the labouring and manufacturing poor, was beyond voluntary resources. Under the terms of the 1870 Education Act the way was open for public provision by means of elected school boards.

In Newcastle a school board, elected in 1871, surveyed the area to assess the need for elementary school places. The cost of the first board school to be built, Ryecroft (1874), was largely met from existing charities which also provided money to aid necessitous children and to sponsor exhibitions at the new endowed schools. But even before the building of Ryecroft a board school had been opened in premises rented from the Methodist New Connexion in Marsh Street. In 1876 it took over the British School, renamed Friarswood. A year later the Methodist school, was united with the existing school in Marsh Street to form the Marsh Board School, rebuilt in 1881 in Hassall Street. With the closure of St George's school, located since 1859 on the Liverpool Road, the only remaining voluntary schools were those of St Giles' (replaced by a new school in Nelson

Inspector's Report

This Department is in excellent order and has passed a good examination in the elementary subjects, the style of the work being very creditable. More intelligence should be shewn in the Arithmetic of the Third & Fourth Standards, only 5 girls out of 28 in the Third Standard and 3 out of 19 in the Fourth Standard getting the problem right. Grammar is weak in the Fifth & Sixth Standards, good in the other Standards. Needlework is on the whole very fair, but darning and tucking should improve, & the button-holes are clumsy. Singing is pretty fair. M. E. Walker & Ada Plunkett have passed fairly.

Teaching Staff for 1886.

Teacher   E. Handley.
P. Teachers   M. E. Walker & A. Plunkett
               M. Maguire.

Place in 1895 by the combined efforts of St Giles' and St George's) and St Patrick's.

The School Board era brought additions to the curriculum. Military drill, history, geography, grammar and singing had come in by the seventies and by the end of the century there were 'object lessons' for younger children, drawing and sometimes botany for older ones. The School Board even introduced cookery for girls. However, physical conditions, even in the new board schools were drab and often unhealthy. There were complaints of suffocating fumes from the stoves, and the cold and dampness affected both teachers and children. Sometimes schools were closed for several weeks on account of infectious diseases – measles, smallpox and scarlet fever.

An early attempt by the board to establish 13 as the school leaving age had met with protests from the Silverdale silk mill which would stand to lose a third of its labour force. By the early nineties, however, the tradition of regular attendance through to the sixth standard (usually attained at the age of 12) had been established by a policy of threats and rewards. By now education had become free, but there were many children who were too hungry to learn. There were many more also who lived on the verge of poverty and who had to be relieved by free soup or charity dinners in times of distress. Always there were occasional children whose names were removed from the school registers because they had gone to the workhouse.

Primary sources for the history of education are the Log Books still kept at the schools. The inspector's report on the girls' department (aged 6 to 11 or 12) at St Patrick's is shown here: on the opposite page it is stated that several children had been sent back to the infants' department because they 'did not know their letters'.

The first building to be erected by the Newcastle School Board was this school in Ryecroft. It accommodated 800 children at a cost of £3,868. Now closed as a school, it serves along with the old Orme Boys' School, as one of the town's Youth Centres.

The Grammar School moved to Church Street in 1722 when the parish church was rebuilt. A hundred years later the building was in a very bad condition, on account of seepage from the churchyard, and the school moved to the Marsh.

The Old Orme Schoolhouse built in 1715 when the school had to evacuate the Old Meeting House on its being burnt down by rioters. This building was sold when the new school was built in 1850.

Newcastle High School as it is today: the headmaster's house, seen on the left, was modelled on that of Wellington College.

Simultaneously with the expansion of elementary provision for the poorer classes, new schools were established for the offspring of prosperous citizens. The old Grammar School had fallen on bad times. The building itself was cramped and unwholesome; the teaching had become slack and inefficient. Yet, according to the visiting Commissioner, Newcastle, if only it had a good school, would be well placed to become 'the genteel suburb of the Potteries and neighbouring iron district'.

Under a scheme of the Endowed Schools' Commissioners, educational charities in the borough were to be concentrated in support of three schools which were to fill the gaps in middle-class education. A new 'first grade school', the High School, was to cater for the well-to-do who could afford tuition fees of up to £25 a year, with an additional £50 for those who chose to board. Built at a cost of £12,000 in 1876, the High School (founded 1874) drew on the whole of the Potteries as well as taking a substantial number of boarders from further afield. Various Rugby men influenced its foundation and early years. There was T H Green, the philosopher, who as Assistant Commissioner had recommended its establishment, F E Kitchener, the first headmaster, who had been assistant master at Rugby and Frederick Temple, Bishop of Exeter and former head of Rugby, who as Commissioner helped to launch the new venture and who laid the foundation stone. It was perhaps not surprising that the High School was expected to become 'the "Rugby" of North Staffordshire'.

Rugby was the model: the assembly hall, for example, was Big School, games were played in the Close and prefects were praeposters. Organised games included Fives, the Fives Court being largely paid for by the first headmaster. From the beginning academic standards were high. Boys sat for the London Matriculation examination and a steady stream went to universities and to the new 'Redbrick' institutions. Of Kitchener's staff two became professors of Chemistry and nine headmasters. Science was particularly strong and there were outstanding successes in the Natural Science Tripos at Cambridge. The leading families of the area, however, tended to use the school as a preparatory establishment before sending their sons to public school.

The second school under the Endowed Schools' Trust was the former Charity School, to be reorganised now as a Middle School for boys up to 16. With fees of £4 to £5 a year it was within the means of superior artisan and tradesman families and appealed to parents who wanted their sons to have a useful education including languages and science. The registers of the school in the seventies and eighties show the great range of parental occupations. A high proportion were self employed including shopkeepers, innkeepers, farmers, blacksmiths and saddlers. Others were professional men or works' managers.

The third school, with fees similar to those of the Middle School, was planned in response to the general movement for female education. Founded in 1876, the Orme Girls' School was a pioneer venture in North Staffordshire. Very soon, however, it was attracting not only local girls but others who came daily by train or who boarded in the town. Within a decade the original building, designed for 100 girls, had to be extended. Under its first headmistress, Miss Mary Martin, who herself had served in the famous Cheltenham Ladies' College, girls had the opportunity of sitting for public examinations. Before the end of the century there was a well established tradition of talented girls entering university.

The end of the nineteenth century saw the coming of compulsory and free elementary education. It had also seen the establishment of a range of efficient middle class schools, accessible on merit to exceptional children from elementary schools. The twentieth century was to generate new objectives, an extension of educational opportunity, a concern for children's physical welfare and a reform of curricula which was to foster a spontaneity and joy in learning.

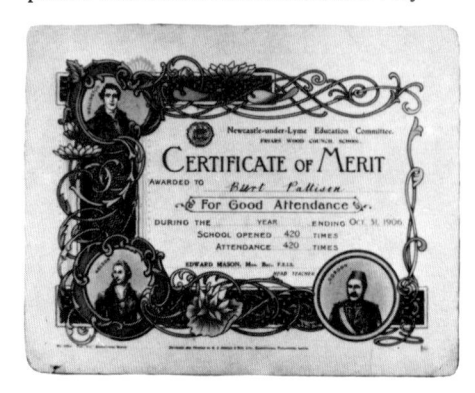

A certificate of Merit for attendance without absence in 1906 issued by the Borough Education Committee puts before the young the ideal of military service: the three cameos which decorate the certificate are of Wellington, Nelson and General Gordon.

An Employment Badge was worn by those children who, having passed the proficiency examination of the Board, were in consequence allowed to go out to work under age.

Boys from the Broadmeadow Senior Boys' School, Chesterton, off to camp at Newbold Astbury in a borough gas lorry in 1934. Such activities demonstrated the widening concept of education in the 1930s.

Attendance records at Chesterton Board School in 1895. Socks held up by string indicates something of the poverty of those years. The record attendance of five years is attained by the headmaster's son.

National legislation brought administrative change. In 1903 Newcastle became a local education authority (a Part III authority responsible for elementary education only). Following the extension of the borough boundaries to include Wolstanton, Silverdale, Knutton and Chesterton in the inter-war years, it became after the 1944 Act an excepted area under the Staffordshire authority, and had responsibility for primary and secondary education.

With the increase of places in the three endowed schools from the early years of the century, the educational ladder became broader. The High School retained independent status until after the 1944 Act. The Middle School and the Orme Girls' became grant-earning public secondary (grammar) schools from the first decade. However, under the famous Dr Rutter the Middle School so outgrew its buildings that in 1928 the entire personnel moved to new premises at Wolstanton and became a grammar school under the Staffordshire authority. Meanwhile the elementary school curriculum became more varied. For example, many girls attended housewifery centres, though, as a former pupil of the World War I period recalled, the premises (at Ryecroft) were old and dark and the instruction unimaginative. 'The tables were wooden ones which we were shown how to scrub the way of the grain. We had to clean the grate with black lead and brush'.

In consequence of the Hadow Report (1926) provision of separate buildings for the 11 plus age group had become official policy. However, shortage of money in Newcastle as elsewhere hindered reorganisation. The new schools at Knutton and the Westlands with their sports facilities and practical rooms made the most up-to-date provision for senior children to the age of 14. New primary schools which were provided at Priory Road and at St Mary's, Stanier Street, released other buildings for the use of senior pupils. Elsewhere, reorganisation was accomplished mainly by use of existing buildings, but St Giles' and St George's remained an all-age school until 1966. Additional amenities brought a new realism to education and a closer contact with the community. Open days were held and there were group excursions both in the locality and further afield.

By means of regular school medical inspections (started after 1907), the worst cases of debility and malnutrition were quickly discovered. Yet disease and poverty were persistent problems. Outbreaks of infection, especially diphtheria, occurred throughout the twenties and thirties when particular schools had to be sprayed and stoved. The extent of poverty was revealed by the numbers of children requiring free footwear and free dinners, almost a third of the numbers on roll in some schools in the borough. Thus a Mayoral Christmas visit to an infant school and the gift to each child of 'an orange, a chocolate and a new penny' was a joyful event.

In the post-war period the pace of change quickened. The requirement of secondary education for all under the 1944 Act, and successive increases in the school leaving age have necessitated large scale building programmes. In 1948 a second Girls' Grammar School was opened at Clayton Hall, whilst the Orme Girls' School like the High School became a voluntary aided school under the local authority. In the fifties and sixties new secondary schools were

How does the world look upside down? – this youngster looks quite content with his inverted position. The well equipped gymnasium is typical of the provision now generally made not only for the nourishment of children's minds but also for their physical development.

built at Bradwell, Chesterton, Seabridge and Gallows-tree Lane (the latter school, the Edward Orme School, had formerly occupied the old Orme School in the Higherland). New voluntary secondary schools, a Roman Catholic (aided) school, the Blessed Thomas Maxfield School, and a Church of England (controlled) school were built on adjoining sites in 1966. Primary schools have been erected in new housing areas and to replace those in outmoded buildings. Altogether almost half the school population is in post war buildings.

Today children and young people in schools or in institutions of further or higher education number about 17,000, almost a quarter of the total population of the borough. Each year some 200 students from Newcastle go to university or to other institutions of higher education. Within the borough a College of Further Education, built in 1966, offers the opportunity of full time and part time vocational courses for school leavers. In the field of Adult Education, in addition to a range of courses provided by the local authority, the University of Keele, founded in 1950, has close association with its immediate locality.

In the welfare state poverty no longer exists on the scale known in the past. Medical advances have conquered the old killer diseases which formerly scourged the schools. Separate provision is made for children suffering from different physical handicaps and for educationally sub-normal children. Within the borough itself there are three special schools.

Imbued by piety, the early donors of schools provided for the poor of Newcastle. In the nineteenth century the wealth of the past helped to support a new graded system of education designed to meet the changing needs of the community. With expanding provision, education in our own century has become, in very large part, a public responsibility. Today rising individual aspirations and national requirements herald further changes in local administration and organisation, changes which may sound prosaic but which will have a profound effect upon the future citizens of Newcastle.

By contrast with the rote-teaching and drill, thought to be the only form of effective discipline in the old Board Schools, these contemporary youngsters at the Westlands County Primary School enjoy every opportunity for learning through creative play.

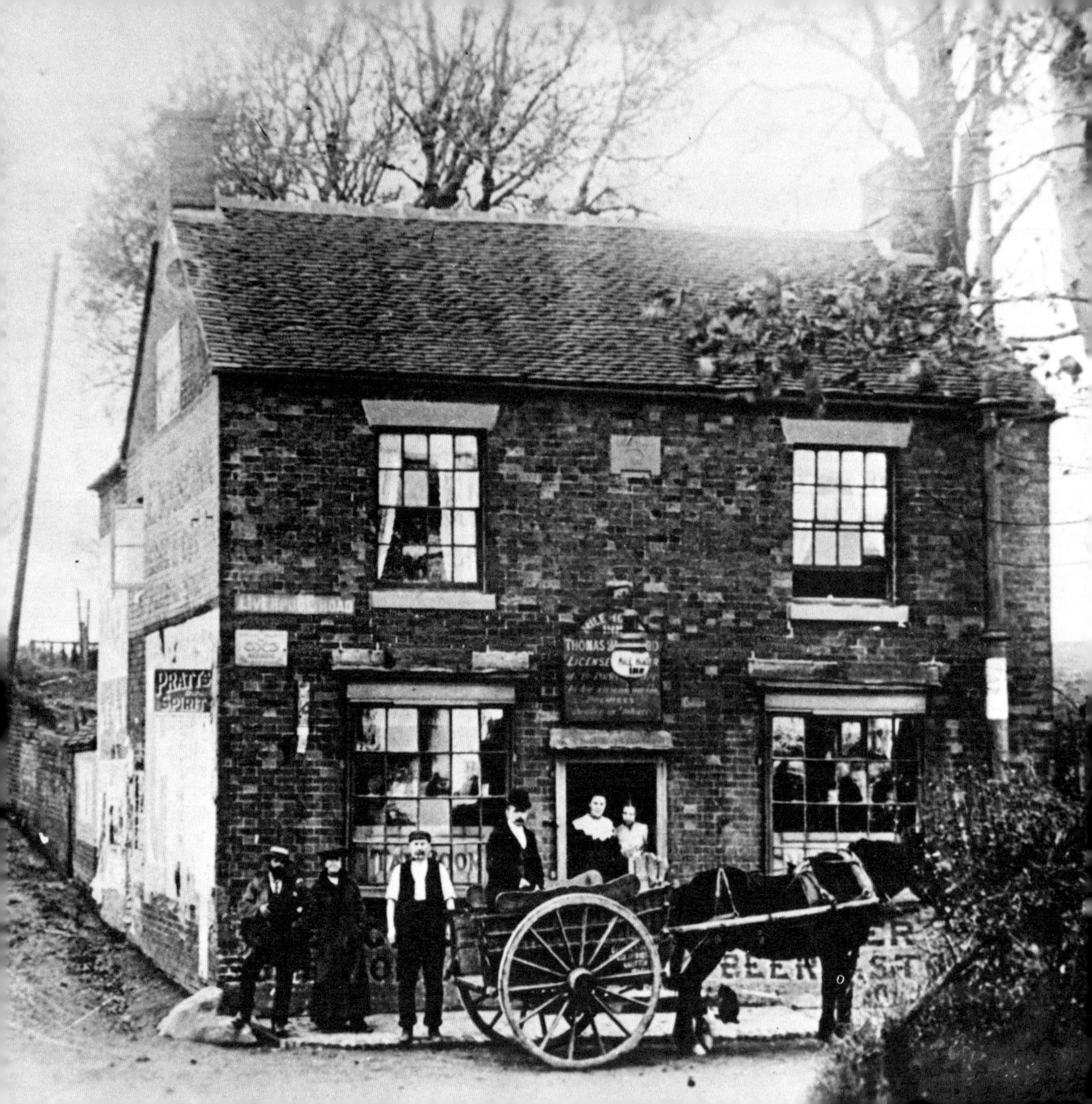
LIVERPOOL ROAD
PRATT'S
SPIRIT

All Work and No Play

Newcastle, situated where the Lyme and Ashfield Brooks meet before flowing on to join the Trent at Trent Vale, was in days gone by a much more watery place than it is now. A great lake surrounded the castle in the west, and in the east there was Colleswayne's Lake, forerunner of the Marsh. Both of these, the records suggest, offered opportunity for angling in the middle ages, although, increasingly stagnant, in later years they became health hazards. The other physical features of early days which provided for the townsmen's recreation were the woodlands of the area, especially the old Lyme forest to the north west. The New Forest, which from the first half of the twelfth century stretched south-east from Newcastle was a royal forest for the king's sport alone and the townsmen would hunt there at their peril. Also in the area were a number of deer corrals notably the great park at Madeley: these were reserved for the sport of the great lords, but still provided opportunities for poaching.

Because Newcastle was a market town, where from 1281 fairs and wakes were held, it was inevitably also a place of entertainment. Though little is known of the sports and pastimes enjoyed by the populace in medieval times, there is evidence of bear baiting. In 1372, John of Gaunt in a letter to his steward, Godfrey Foljambe, confirmed the right of William de Brompton and Margery, his wife, to levy 4d on each minstrel coming to the town at the feast of St Giles', and the same sum in respect of each bear appearing. Permission given to Thomas Hemings to extract limestone from the Bear Pits may indicate where the sport took place, but local tradition suggests that the bear ring was near the Butchery Pump in the Ironmarket, and a bull ring near Nelson Place. Cock fighting was taking place in the borough as late as 1839. Other entertainment would include a visit to the gallows beyond Thistleberry, and jeering at those currently occupying the pillory or the stocks. Nor should the market memories of more recent years be forgotten: the cries of the street hawkers of 50 or 60 years ago included the salt hawker, the stepstone man, the dolly peg and line prop man, the watercress man, and more recently the news vendor and the ice cream man with his bugle. There were also the street singer, the hurdy gurdy man with his monkey, and the German Band, all earning an honest penny, and making life more colourful as they did so.

In the early eighteenth century, horse racing became popular in Newcastle, the meeting of 1728 lasting five days. The races, discontinued in the 1740s, were revived in 1773 when a three day event was held at the Brampton. In 1788 it moved to a purposely laid out course at Knutton Heath (Silverdale), paid for by 'the gentlemen of the town and neighbourhood and the Pottery'. In 1816 the racecourse consisted of six acres of ground, a grandstand, and two buildings used as starting and distance chairs. The course was rented by the council from the lord of the manor for thirteen guineas a year. By 1823 the Newcastle meeting, the leading event in the area, was renamed the Newcastle and Pottery Meeting. From 1824, an additional event was held at Etruria, following the Newcastle meeting, but this was discontinued in 1842. Newcastle races came to an end in 1848, but were revived in 1862 and 1865, In 1895 a spring steeplechase was started on a course at Keele Park but only lasted ten years, failing to secure 'that measure of popularity and public patronage essential to success'. Fox hunting, however, has a continued existence from 1825: the present kennels are at Hill Chorlton.

Though medieval fairs would almost certainly have included side shows of a dramatic kind, the first specific reference to strolling players visiting Newcastle is in 1610. By the end of the eighteenth century such visits were becoming a regular feature of the borough's life, and in 1775 the council agreed to allow the actors to use 'the hall', presumably the Guildhall. This was not really suitable for drama, and in consequence the Theatre Royal was built in 1787–8 in Nelson Place. The large medallion of William Shakespeare, inset over the entrance, long signified the purpose of the building. From 1804 to at least 1829 a comedian called Stanton was licensed to give performances at the theatre. In 1824 the performance was billed to start at 7.30 pm 'or as soon as the race is over': prices for admission were box 3s, pit 2s, gallery 1s. Was

The Milehouse Inn, built about 1813, was noted for its long hours: 5 30 am to 11 pm. The first customers in the morning were carters, travelling to Sandbach for packing straw for the potters.

Horse racing had taken place in the early eighteenth century in the Brampton. In 1788 a special course was laid out at Knutton Heath, and for sixty years an annual event was held there. Attempts to revive racing in the second half of the nineteenth century proved unsuccessful, though the Racecourse continued first as the name of one of Silverdale's pits and it is still a street name today.

Stanton a true son of the Regency, one wonders, with perhaps an over enterprising taste for the more progressive kind of performance? For in 1829 the borough restricted his choice of play to such as might be lawfully acted in the theatres of the city of Westminster. The rigours of such censorship may, however, be doubted.

The rise of the Theatre Royal in Hanley is the supposed cause of the downfall of Newcastle's theatre, which went into disuse, except for the occasional music hall, after 1880. In 1910 it became the town's first Cinema. There were three other cinemas in Newcastle – the Savoy, which has since become a bingo hall, and the Rio-Rex. This complex was a forerunner of the modern fashion of congregating several cinemas on one site, a novelty not always appreciated when patrons went through the wrong door and saw a different film from the one they had expected.

The Municipal Hall in the Ironmarket was built as a Golden Jubilee memorial in 1888–90, to satisfy a long standing demand for a large public hall now that the expanding borough had outgrown the Guildhall. After 1862 this was, in any case, more and more filled with municipal business. The new hall was built on the site of Arlington House, which the borough's MP, W S Allen, had sold to the corporation in 1887. Sugden and Sons of Leek, J Blood of Newcastle, and Snape and Chapman of Newcastle designed a lofty red brick structure with stone dressings. With its adjacent clock tower, and Ironmarket facade, adorned with life size figures emblematic of architecture, painting, music and literature, it served as a status symbol for the borough's late Victorian sense of self importance. As the Guildhall gave focus to the High Street, so the new municipal palace, in heavier and more solid form presided over the Ironmarket. The ground floor contained a 'council chamber' and from 1891 to 1958, the Public Library. In the large hall on the first floor were hung eighteen shields of arms of families associated with the borough, including those of Lord Cadman and Lord Wedgwood. Since the Municipal Hall's demolition in 1967, Newcastle no longer possesses a sizeable public hall: from that time the council chamber has been located in the Municipal Offices in Merrial Street.

Throughout the nineteenth century there was a tradition of intellectual activity. A subscription library was started in 1812 which was absorbed by the Newcastle Literary and Scientific Institute. In 1836 this established itself in the old Shakespeare Hotel in Brunswick Street, next to the theatre. In addition to the library and assembly room, a small collection of museum items was put on display. The enthusiasm of the thirties got the project off to a good start, and large audiences attended the soirées held to mark the Great Exhibition in 1851. By the end of 1867, however, the institution had closed, though a Literary Society existed in the borough in the 1880s. It is tempting to see the local Workers' Educational Association continuing the same tradition today.

The Newcastle intellectuals had to wait until 1876 for the first establishment of a public library in the borough, when a reading room and museum were set up in Lad Lane. About 1878 study and thrift were united when the library moved to the Savings Bank premises in Penkhull Street. The first borough-financed library, which absorbed the books from the earlier collection, was that established in the Municipal Hall in 1891: in 1958 it moved to the old Wesleyan Schools in School Street. The School Street buildings give little scope for the extension of the central library, but its work today is supplemented by five branch libraries. Since 1941, a borough museum has been in existence, first in rooms in Lancaster Buildings, and since 1956 at the Firs in Brampton Park (and the octoyear will see further extensions of the facilities it has to offer.) Among other collections the museum has on display a collection of ware from the Pomona site, the borough muniments, and a collection of prints of old Newcastle. Also administered by the museum is Pitfield House, the borough's Arts Centre, which again carries on the traditions of the old Literary and Scientific Institution.

An intelligent appreciation of what was happening in the borough was also encouraged by the town's own newspress. On 6th April 1813 the first issue of the *Staffordshire Gazette* was published from Lower Street. Finding the right name proved difficult; in 1814 it became the *Staffordshire Gazette and Newcastle and Pottery Advertiser*. Five years later it was the *Newcastle and Pottery Gazette and Staffordshire Advertiser*: it had ceased to exist by 1834.

Another cluster of name changing papers appeared for the first time in the 1850's: the *Newcastle Journal* of 1855 after three changes of name finished as the *Staffordshire Times* from 1874–82. From 1881–1909 the *Newcastle Guardian,* at first Liberal but later self-styled independent, put Newcastle's news in the context of what was happening in the Potteries. Over roughly the same period there also existed the *Newcastle under Lyme Free Press,* distributed free every Saturday by its proprietor, A P Bayley. The only daily paper published in Newcastle was the short lived *Staffordshire Daily Times* which managed ten issues only in 1875. More significant than any of these as a vehicle of local communication were the two regional newspapers, the *Staffordshire Advertiser* which carried news of Newcastle from its foundation in 1795 until the 1920s and the *Sentinel* which dates back to 1854 as a weekly and from 1873 has carried daily comment on the life of the borough. From 1963 to 1972 the social life of Newcastle was noted in the *Six Towns Magazine* which continues from 1972 as the *Staffordshire Magazine*. The foundation of the *Newcastle Times* in 1935 brought the borough once more a newspaper published within its own boundaries.

George Brunt, pictured here, was appointed conductor of the Newcastle Borough Band in 1879. Known as the 'Beer and Baccy Band' they played at the very popular summer concerts at the Band Stand in Stubbs Walk after its erection in 1887.

Was this the 'Beer and Baccy Band'? This photograph from the Museum Collection exists without a title.

The Theatre Royal, built in 1787–8, seems to have thrived on light comedy and melodrama until challenged by the theatres of the potteries in the 1880s. In 1910–11 it became the town's first electric cinema, ending its life as the Roxy Cinema.

Fifty years ago there was a saying popular in the borough; 'You can stand on the Central pavement, playing with a Golden Ball, eating Cheshire Cheese, and having a sip of Old Vine, and watch the Rising Sun, setting on the Globe, which weighed Three Tuns.' No account of leisure in Newcastle would be complete without a description of its public houses. 65 inns and taverns were listed in 1839, whilst the total today is 93. The battle as to which is the oldest now rages between the Star (renamed The Superstar) in the Ironmarket and the Bull's Head in Lad Lane. Certainly most of the pre-1700 buildings, which survive in the borough are, or have been, inns. Recently demolished old inns include what had been the Market Inn (on the site of the present Woolworths), the Three Tuns (opposite 'Bookland') and Hind's Vaults (Lad Lane). Still surviving are the much-restored Wine Vaults and the former Golden Ball at the north end of the High Street, which is now a butcher's shop.

Vying with the public houses are the thirteen working men's clubs and four community centres, whose liveliness gives the lie to the accusation that television has killed social life in the suburbs. Beer and skittles, darts and bingo bring old and young, neighbours and strangers into social contact in the most cheerful of surroundings. This programme of entertainment makes both economic and social sense, though some regret the passing of the educational activities of the clubs in years gone by.

August 29th 1838 saw a triple bill at the Newcastle and Pottery Theatre – 'Valsha; or, the Slave Queen', 'Is He Jealous' and finally an 'Eastern Tale of Enchantment' called 'The Gnome Fly'. Because of the expense of the production it was announced 'no half price can be taken'.

It is difficult to over emphasize the influence of the coming of the railways on the leisure of working people: travel became a possibility for the first time, no longer were they tied to the parish pump. There were excursions now to Trentham and the Churnet Valley, to Liverpool and Derby, to Wales and to Blackpool. Whole streets were transported to a sandy paradise. Trams and buses also captured the fascination of the young. Some routes were run by private operators, Garbett's 'Little Gem' to Silverdale, Meredith's 'Quest and Pilot' to Ashley, and Poole's, then as now, to Halmerend. The touring charabancs had even more exotic names 'Maid of the Mountains', 'Purple and Lilac Domino', and many others. Older folks in 1973 can recall being taken by 'chara' to Trentham for a treat given by The Mayor and Mrs Whitfield to five local schools, and being paraded at the end of the day on the Rectory Field (Queen's Gardens) to thank The Mayor for his generosity. Queen's Gardens today house the borough band stand. Much of yesterday's entertainment was self made: it was full of the sheer enjoyment of looking at things, usual and unusual. The

A selection of the local Newspapers which were set in the foundations of the Municipal Hall and recovered on its demolition. They can still be seen in mint condition at the museum.

165

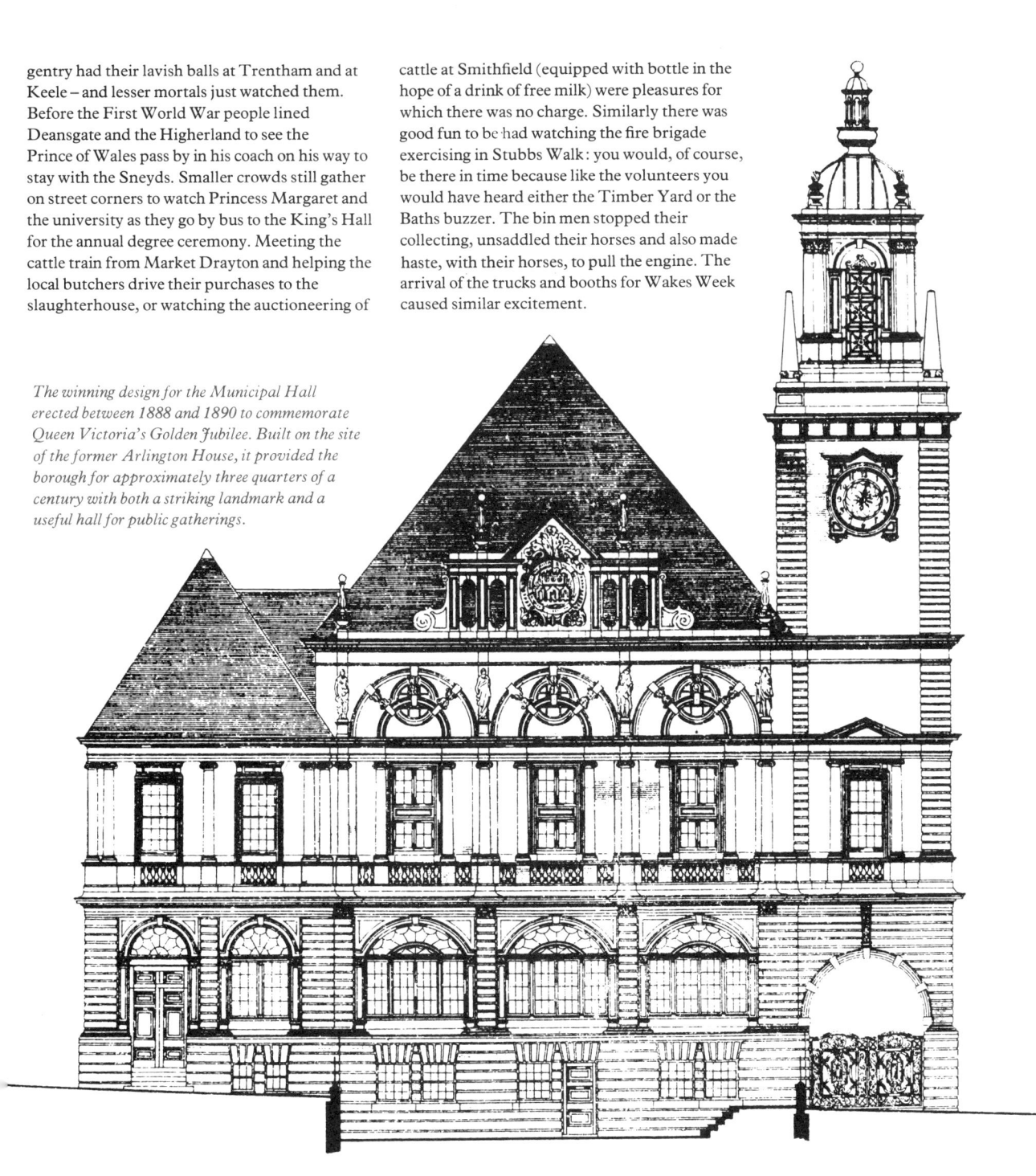

gentry had their lavish balls at Trentham and at Keele – and lesser mortals just watched them. Before the First World War people lined Deansgate and the Higherland to see the Prince of Wales pass by in his coach on his way to stay with the Sneyds. Smaller crowds still gather on street corners to watch Princess Margaret and the university as they go by bus to the King's Hall for the annual degree ceremony. Meeting the cattle train from Market Drayton and helping the local butchers drive their purchases to the slaughterhouse, or watching the auctioneering of cattle at Smithfield (equipped with bottle in the hope of a drink of free milk) were pleasures for which there was no charge. Similarly there was good fun to be had watching the fire brigade exercising in Stubbs Walk: you would, of course, be there in time because like the volunteers you would have heard either the Timber Yard or the Baths buzzer. The bin men stopped their collecting, unsaddled their horses and also made haste, with their horses, to pull the engine. The arrival of the trucks and booths for Wakes Week caused similar excitement.

The winning design for the Municipal Hall erected between 1888 and 1890 to commemorate Queen Victoria's Golden Jubilee. Built on the site of the former Arlington House, it provided the borough for approximately three quarters of a century with both a striking landmark and a useful hall for public gatherings.

H J Lawson introduced the so-called safety bicycle to Britain in 1876. By the 1890s cycling had become almost a craze; here is the Newcastle Cycling Club of that period.

Soccer and Cricket cannot easily be dislodged as England's major team sports. Here Chesterton Cricket Club at the turn of the century sports a wealth of moustaches.

Another pastime was watching the unloading of huge trees at the timber yard in School Street: teams of four shire horses would haul the drays from the country area up Penkhull Street into School Street where the unloading by the overhead crane began. 'Believe me', says one who enjoyed the scene, 'their work was intensely interesting and when the timber was stacked it was fun exploring amongst the caverns of trees before being chased away.'

All this took place in the borough itself: further enjoyment lay in the country that hemmed the town so closely on all sides until recent years. There were walks up to the Cloughs, or down to Rotterdam, across the fields to Seabridge and Clayton. Even within the borough there were Stubbs Walks and the Station Walks. Then there was the canal: one writer tells of his brother falling in at Cross Heath when on an illegitimate expedition, playing truant from Sunday School, and of his being taken to the Old Milehouse Inn to dry out. In winter, there was skating on both the Upper and the Lower Canals, or on a field specially flooded for that purpose where Sidmouth Avenue now is. Trentham Lake was specially floodlit for evening skating.

Some centred their social life in the chapel, some on the pub, and some in both. Some spent their leisure exercising their minds, others their bodies. For a majority the hours of work were too long for them to have much time to stand and stare. Because money was short, pleasures were simple. We must avoid the romanticism that paints the past genially in Pickwickian terms, and forgets the hardship that most ordinary men endured whilst the few pursued their leisure. Perhaps we for our part have become too used to having entertainment provided for us, and there is no reason why we should not learn from the past a truth or two about how to manufacture pleasure, and how to enjoy ourselves.

The former 'Golden Ball' now a butcher's shop is the sole surviving building to retain something approaching its original timbered front. It is currently being renovated once more.

'The Three Tuns' at the top of Church Street took its name in 1793 although the building is much older. A minor coaching inn it subsequently became a chemist shop. It was demolished at the end of the fifties.

A Working Men's Club in Silverdale is one of a number of clubs which have recently rebuilt their premises in a modern and attractive style.

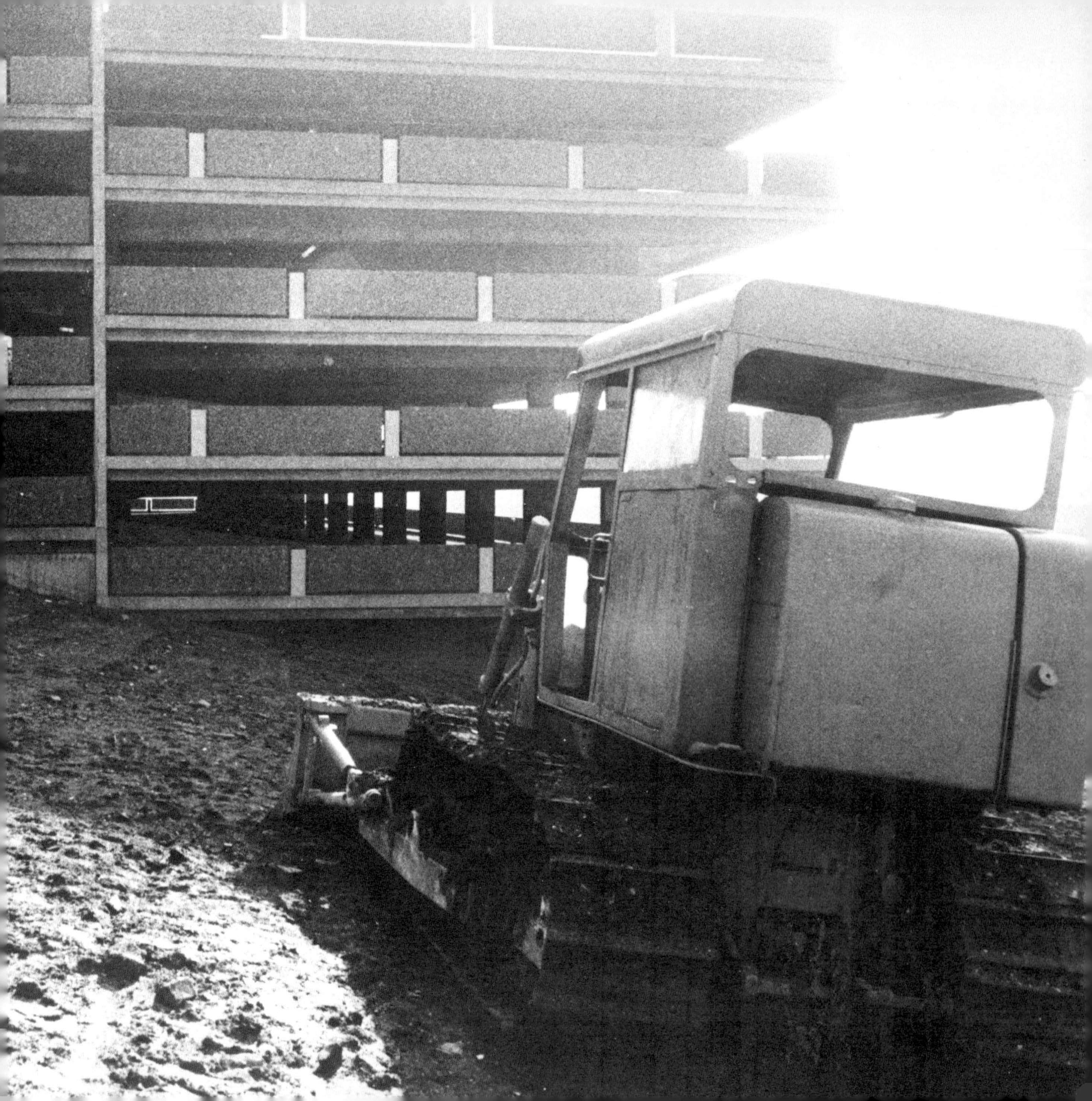

The Old Order Changeth

The citizens of Newcastle under Lyme in 1973 enter into a municipal heritage which is rich with eight hundred years of historical development. Although few buildings more than two hundred and fifty years old survive, the alert observer can still see the impact of its history in the life and appearance of the borough today. Indeed this account of the borough's history has been concerned to foster just that kind of awareness of the richness and diversity of the tradition which we inherit. While concern for the past must never be made an argument for resisting progress, it must be nurtured as an essential ingredient in our municipal development. Within an improved borough, it will be crucial to allow the healthy dimension of memory its proper scope.

Eight hundred years of development therefore gives scope not only for indulging in nostalgia – the fifty or so year span of memory of our own respected senior citizens and the much longer period of research and story telling of the historian – but also for celebration. An octocentenary is no mean achievement: even in supposedly austere times of inflation (which look like a perpetual Christmas in comparison with the destitution of yesteryear) a note of festivity may be allowed. And perhaps as we look at the ways in which people enjoyed themselves in Newcastle past, the citizens of Newcastle present may rediscover ways of personal and community enjoyment.

The story of the past, and the festivity of the present lead on to the prospects for the future concerning which all of us, most of all the historian, are loathe to speculate. Parents are concerned to know what the schools of tomorrow will be like, householders and motorists have competing interests in the shape of tomorrow's roads, conservationists and commercial pressure groups argue about the face of tomorrow's borough.

1973 as well as marking the octocentenary of the borough, will with the implementation of the Local Government Act (1972) also see a watershed in the town's evolution as an administrative centre. Just as in earlier years the town expanded to include the parishes of Wolstanton, Chesterton, Silverdale and Knutton, so from 1st April 1974, the new District Council of Newcastle under Lyme will become operative, embracing not only the area of the present borough but also the present Newcastle RDC and Kidsgrove UDC.

Under the leadership of successive Councils the borough has in recent years made substantial progress in developing the town; roads and houses have been built, slums cleared and derelict land reclaimed. The future holds possibilities of planning on a larger scale. The next few years should see the completion of a new library in the Ironmarket as well as a large hall and social centre at Clayton. More exciting perhaps is the probability that the derelict land to the north of the town off the A34 will be cleared and redeveloped. There is no doubt that the Civic Offices in Merrial Street will remain for many years the place where most decisions governing the quality of community life are taken.

In a history such as this there can be no end to the story. 1973 is the year in which the Borough of Newcastle reaches its 800th anniversary. Those 800 years have been years of continuous evolution, each change developing out of what has gone before. The tradition and spirit of a vibrant community such as Newcastle cannot be lost nor cast aside, and hence the new District Council of Newcastle under Lyme will have a sound basis on which to begin the responsible task of planning the Newcastle of tomorrow.

The motor-car that all too easily comes to govern our lives has to be provided for in a modern borough. The multi-storey car park in the Midway, already a familiar landmark, provides on its top floor an excellent observation platform for surveying the life of the town.

The International Computers Limited building in Nelson Place, on the site of the former theatre, may be allowed to represent the role of modern technology in the borough.

The cattle market together with the Christmas poultry markets, continues to link Newcastle with the surrounding rural area.

The market continues to enliven the High Street in 1973 just as it has done for over seven hundred years.

The new ring road revives the old medieval route from Stubbs Gate along Lower Street to Upper Green. Blackfriars Bakery, the Smithfield Market and the gasholder (but no longer the gasworks) all recall former days but also serve the needs of today. The traffic, both public and private, oblivious of tradition, hastens to its destination at the close ot another day's work.

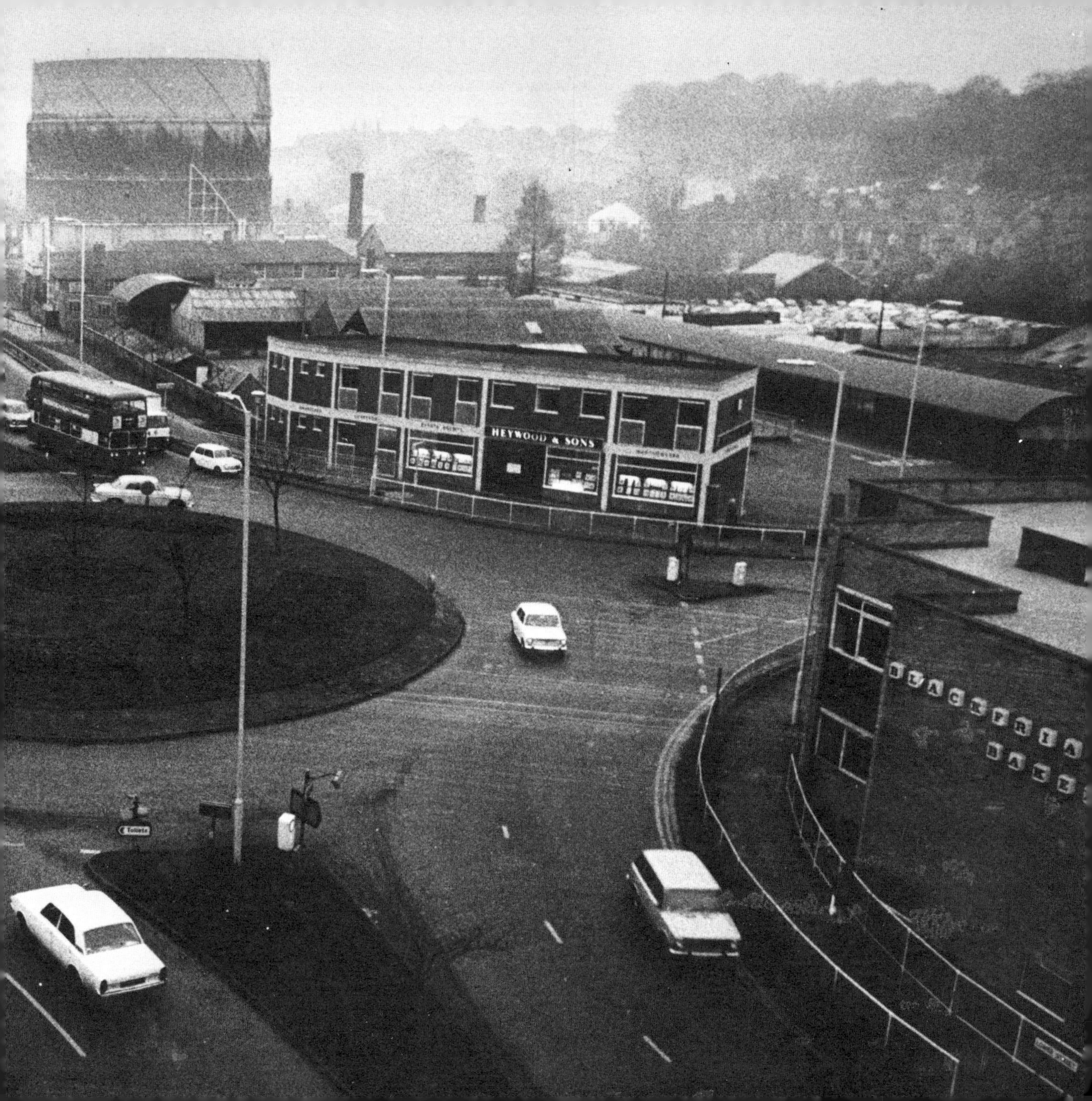
HEYWOOD & SONS
Toilets

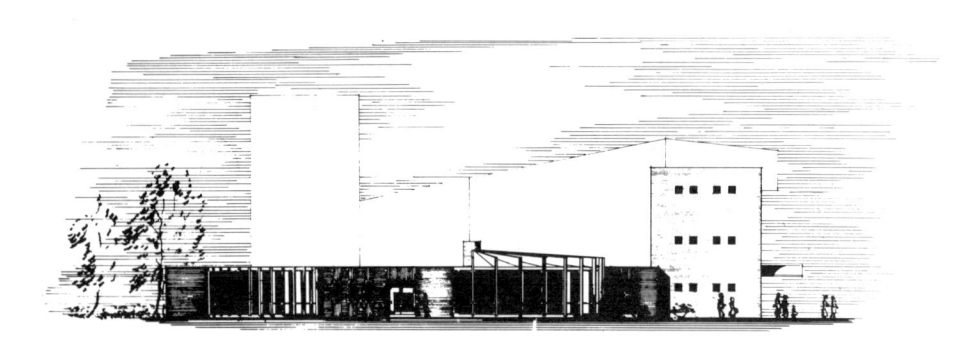

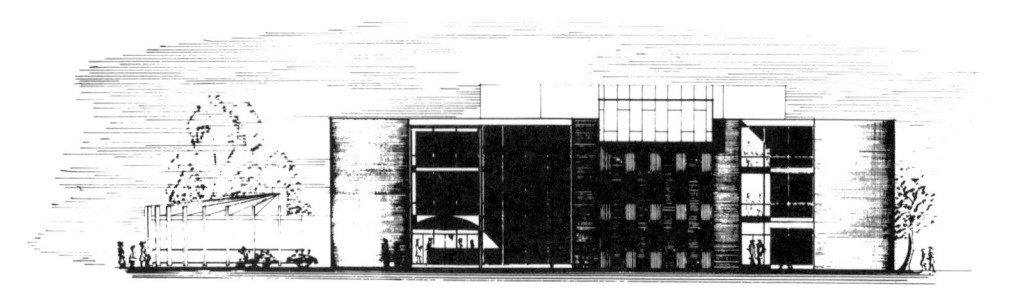

Looking to the future, an architect's drawing of the proposed Clayton Community Centre indicates something of the Newcastle of tomorrow, the Newcastle which is yet to be.

It is unlikely that Council Houses will again be built in large estates: in 1973 the tendency is to integrate private and municipal housing as in this contemporary development in Seabridge.

Modern Schools such as the Edward Orme School pictured here give the citizens of tomorrow the very best possible opportunity to prepare themselves for adult responsibilities.

The shaft at Wolstanton Pit, the deepest in England, is sunk to a depth of 1045 yards. This pit was extensively redeveloped in 1957 and now produces thirteen thousand tons of coal a week.

Finding Out More

It is hoped that this octocentenary history will not have saturated your interest in Newcastle's past, but rather whetted your appetite to find out more. There follow some suggestions of where to begin and how to go about this. An essential tool for this task is the bibliography on Newcastle currently being prepared by Mr D W Adams. Since this will be comprehensive in scope, only a select list of works needs to be cited here.

The classic histories of the county are by R Plot (1686) and W Pitt (1817) but the basic tool today is the *Victoria County History of Staffordshire*. Newcastle features as the first part of Volume VIII. Volume II has useful information on industry and leisure and Volume III on religion. Look not only at the text but at the footnotes which give useful clues as to where further information may be rooted out. Many of the sources referred to are available in the Reference Library and the records at the Museum. Also worthy of a place of honour is Thomas Pape who remains Newcastle's most substantial historian: reference to his work will be made under the appropriate sections. Journals in which to look for information about Newcastle include *Collections for a History of Staffordshire* (S C H), the *Transactions of the North Staffordshire Field Club* (TNSFC), and its successor the *North Staffordshire Journal of Field Studies* (NSJFS).

T Pape's *Medieval Newcastle under Lyme* (1928) is the crucial work for the **Middle Ages.** Like other early town histories however it concentrates heavily on political and constitutional history and has very little on social and economic history. It is more reliable than J T Coulam, *History of Newcastle under Lyme* (1908) or J P Conway *Newcastle under Lyme in the County of Stafford* (1903), though both of these are useful in part. Pape also wrote a number of articles of which the library has a collection. J Ingamells, *Directory of Newcastle under Lyme with Historical Records of the Ancient Borough* (1871 and 1881) has a lot of material in it, but all needs carefully checking. Those charters which survive may be seen at the Museum. P W L Adams, *Wolstanton* (1908) gives an account of the growth of a parish with a more ancient history (as a parish) than Newcastle's. Pape published two works on **the period 1500 to 1760,** *Newcastle under Lyme in Tudor and early Stuart Times* (1938), which again prints the sources, and a more limited work on *Restoration Government and the Corporation of Newcastle under Lyme* (1940). A further volume which takes the story down to 1760 was left in manuscript and it is hoped that this will be published as part of the octocentenary celebrations. The published Parish Registers which run from 1563–1770 are invaluable for looking at population and tracing family histories.

For **Poverty** the vital sources are the Corporation Order Books available at the Museum; the Minutes and Ledgers of the Poor Law Union are available at the Staffordshire Record Office and much work needs to be done on these. The library has on microfilm the Minute Books of St Giles' Vestry which throw much light on the social history of the early nineteenth century.

For **Religion** all the books mentioned in the medieval section can be usefully consulted. Pape also wrote a brief history of St Giles'. Annual Reports for St Giles' and St George's provide useful raw material. The incumbent of Holy Trinity Church has in his possession a manuscript history of that church. Denominational histories are available for the Unitarians (by G Pegler), the Congregationalists (by A G Matthews), the Baptists (by J H Y Briggs) and the Ebenezer Church (150th Anniversary Pamphlet). A useful source of information is the Religious Census of 1851 of which a microfilm for Newcastle is available at Keele. George Sudlow's *Sammy Brindley and His Friends* (1905) gives an interesting picture of a local preacher's recollections.

A study of **Transport** should properly start with the maps of which the Museum and Library both have collections. Some of these have been reproduced in R A Lewis' *Newcastle Maps*. He also edits *Staffordshire Waterways, Staffordshire Roads* and *Staffordshire Railways. The North Staffordshire Railway* was studied by 'Manifold' in 1952 and R Christiansen and R W Miller in 1971. J Wentworth Day's *Wheels of Service*

(1958) tells the story of the PMT on which there is also an Omnibus Society volume (1968). But for trains, trams and buses old timetables and route-maps repay study. C Hadfield's *Canals of the West Midlands* (1966) and S A H Burne's 'The Coaching Age in Staffordshire' (TNSFC) 1921–2, recall earlier periods whilst *East-West Town Centre Traffic Strategy Report* by the Borough Engineer (1971) considers the future strategies then proposed.

The **economic life** of the borough has received little attention to date though there are documentary sources for this available in the local museums (Newcastle and Stoke) and Libraries (Newcastle and Hanley). Much information can be obtained from the Blue Books of nineteenth century governments which where not available in local libraries may be consulted on microcard in the University. Local directories, a list of which is available at the local library are useful here. P J Bemrose has covered the borough's clay-working industries in a thesis available at the Museum. The Library possesses a typescript copy of W B Nixon's '*The Iron Industry of the Apedale and Silverdale Valleys of North Staffordshire, 1768–1901*', which has been found useful.

The rough and tumble of eighteenth century **Politics** is fully told by S M Hardy and R C Baily in 'The Downfall of the Gower Interest in the Staffordshire Boroughs', SHC (1950–51). Documents relating to the 1790 Election are reproduced in R A Lewis, *Staffordshire Elections 1790–1832*. An M A thesis by J S Sutton on Robert Wilmot-Horton is available at Keele. F Bealey, J Blondel and W P McCann analyse the texture of Newcastle's political life in their *Constituency Politics* (1965). In this, as in other areas, however, there is ample scope for grass-roots research, using minutes, pamphlets, poll-books and above all the local press.

The Library has a number of off-prints relating to **Health,** the most important of which is the *Preliminary Inquiry to the Board of Health on the Sanitary Condition of the Borough of Newcastle under Lyme* (1850). How the situation changed in subsequent years can be traced through the reports of successive County and Borough Medical Officers of Health. The records of the Improvement Commissioners at the Museum are also important. *Pure and Wholesome Water* (1949) tells the story of the Staffordshire Potteries Water Board. Mr Lewis has edited *The State of Large Towns in North Staffordshire*. On **Law and Order** there is a helpful manuscript essay by Mrs P M Gabriel at the Borough Museum to which Chapter XI is indebted.

On **Education,** T Pape puts us in his debt once more through his *Educational Endowments of Newcastle*. A major source of information remains the school log books (study of these by Mrs M Dash, Mrs A Roberts, Messrs P M Bradshaw, G F Edwards, J E O'Rourke and A J Wood has helped to produce the account in Chapter XIII). The log books of existing schools are held on the premises; the Education Offices have those of schools now closed.

The way in which **people enjoyed themselves** in the past can be obtained in part from the general books, but, here a particularly useful source are the tapes of reminiscences held by Radio Stoke and by the Library.

Finding out about the past cannot be confined to books and documents: something of Newcastle's history can be discovered from what remains from yesterday in the borough's townscape, road lines, buildings, graveyards, and street names, not to mention the castle mound and the remnants of the old Upper Canal enshrined in the Walks. Looking around you is certainly one way of finding out how the borough has developed and changed. Finally, for the present century there remains the invaluable record of decisions to be found in the Borough Minutes available at the Library. Active citizens will want not only to read these but to attend Council meetings for themselves to see the processes whereby decisions are taken.

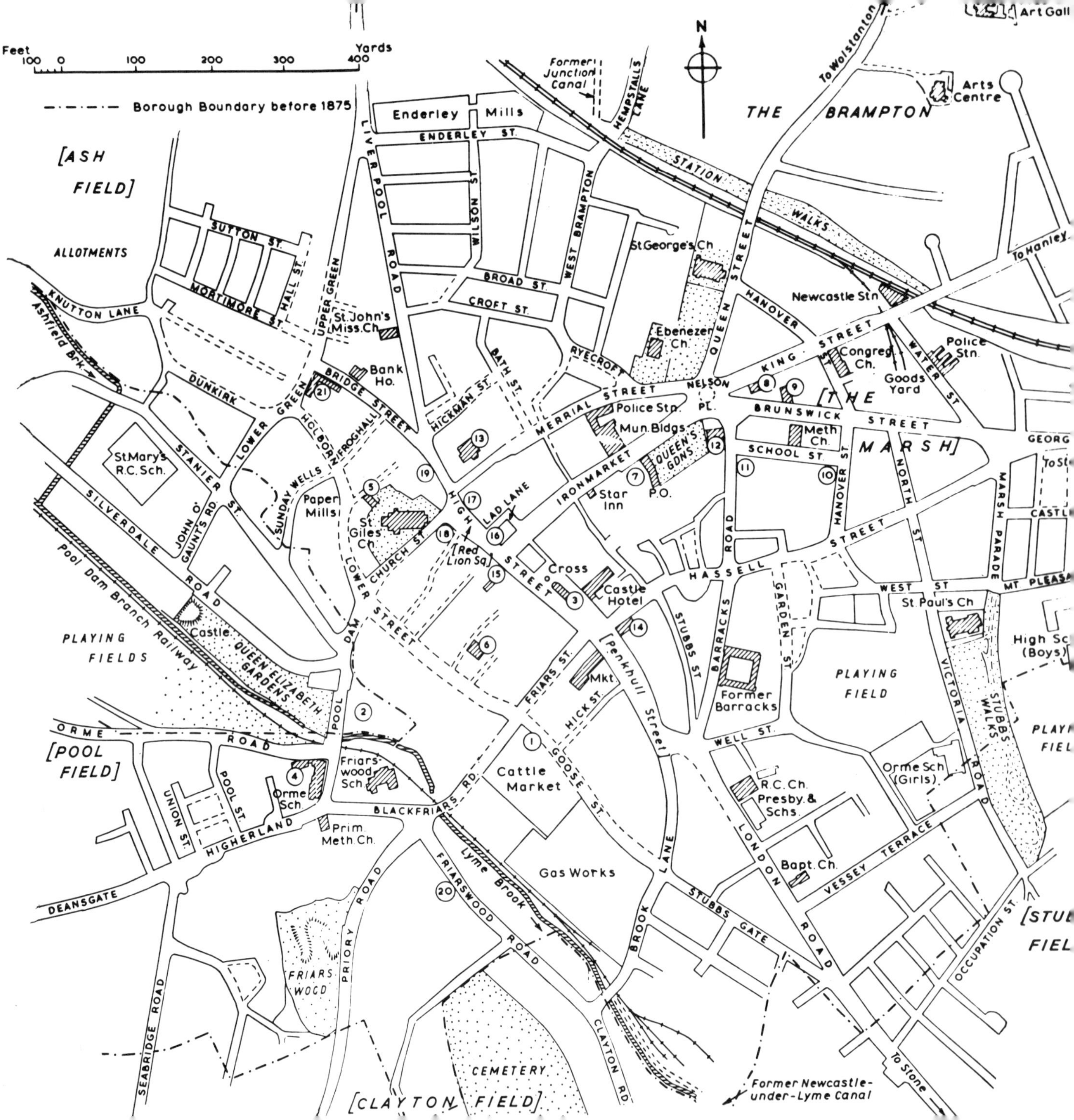
Feet
100 0 100 200 300 400
Yards
Borough Boundary before 1875
N
[ASH FIELD]
ALLOTMENTS
Enderley Mills
ENDERLEY ST.
LIVERPOOL ROAD
WILSON ST.
WEST BRAMPTON
Former Junction Canal
HEMPSTALLS LANE
To Wolstanton
Art Gall
Arts Centre
THE BRAMPTON
STATION WALKS
SUTTON ST.
MORTIMORE ST.
HALL ST.
KNUTTON LANE
Ashfield Brk.
UPPER GREEN
St. John's Miss. Ch.
BROAD ST.
CROFT ST.
St. George's Ch.
QUEEN STREET
HANOVER
Newcastle Stn.
To Hanley
Ebenezer Ch.
RYECROFT
BATH ST.
DUNKIRK
BRIDGE STREET
Bank Ho.
HICKMAN ST.
MERRIAL STREET
NELSON PL.
KING STREET
Congreg. Ch.
WATER ST.
Goods Yard
Police Stn.
[THE MARSH]
BRUNSWICK STREET
Meth. Ch.
SCHOOL ST.
GEORG
To St
Police Stn.
Mun. Bldgs.
QUEEN'S GDNS
HOLBORN
FROGHALL
LOWER GREEN
STANIER ST.
St. Mary's R.C. Sch.
SILVERDALE
JOHN O' GAUNT'S RD.
SUNDAY WELLS
Paper Mills
St. Giles Ch.
CHURCH ST.
HIGH STREET
LAD LANE
IRONMARKET
Star Inn
P.O.
HANOVER ST.
NORTH ST.
MARSH PARADE
CASTL
[Red Lion Sq.]
Cross
Castle Hotel
HASSELL STREET
ROAD
WEST ST.
MT PLEASA
St. Paul's Ch.
Pool Dam Branch Railway
ROAD
Castle
QUEEN ELIZABETH GARDENS
LOWER STREET
DAM
Penkhull Street
STUBBS ST.
BARRACKS
GARDEN ST.
High Sch. (Boys)
PLAYING FIELDS
PLAYING FIELD
Former Barracks
FRIARS ST.
Mkt.
HICK ST.
VICTORIA ROAD
STUBBS WALKS
PLAY FIEL
ORME ROAD
[POOL FIELD]
POOL
Friarswood Sch.
Cattle Market
GOOSE ST.
WELL ST.
R.C. Ch.
Presby. & Schs.
Orme Sch. (Girls)
UNION ST.
POOL ST.
Orme Sch.
BLACKFRIARS RD.
Prim. Meth. Ch.
HIGHERLAND
LONDON ROAD
Bapt. Ch.
VESSEY TERRACE
Gas Works
Lyme Brook
BROOK LANE
STUBBS GATE
DEANSGATE
PRIORY ROAD
FRIARSWOOD ROAD
OCCUPATION ST.
[STU FIEL
SEABRIDGE ROAD
FRIARS WOOD
CEMETERY
CLAYTON RD.
[CLAYTON FIELD]
Former Newcastle-under-Lyme Canal
To Stone
1 2 3 4 5 6 7 8 9 10 11 12 13 14 15 16 17 18 19 20 21

Town centre c.1960

1. Approximate site of Dominican Friary
2. Probable site of Castle Mills
3. Guildhall
4. Site of Workhouse and Prison
5. Unitarian Meeting House
6. Former Wesleyan Methodist Chapel
7. Site of parsonage
8. Former Theatre Royal
9. Former Literary and Scientific Institute
10. Site of Grammar School (1821)
11. Site of National School (1825)
12. Borough Treasurer's Office
13. Conservative Club
14. National Provincial Bank, formerly 'Steps'
15. Former Roebuck Hotel
16. Site of Woolpack Inn
18. Site of Three Tuns Inn
19. Former Golden Ball Inn
20. Site of Silk Mill
21. Albemarle Almshouses

A Map of the Borough Centre as it was about 1960, with some indication of the location of former streets.

The two principal sources of further information are the Museum and the Reference Library.

Printed in England by
Wood Mitchell & Co. Ltd.,
Stoke-on-Trent.

Filmset in 8 on 10pt Plantin